COMMUNITY COUNSELING

A HUMAN SERVICES APPROACH

COMMUNITY COUNSELING

A HUMAN SERVICES APPROACH

SECOND EDITION

Judith A. Lewis

P.A.C.E., Professional Assistance for Corporations and Employees
Chicago, Illinois

Michael D. Lewis

Governors State University

JOHN WILEY & SONS

NEW YORK   CHICHESTER   BRISBANE   TORONTO   SINGAPORE

Library of Congress Cataloging in Publication Data:

Lewis, Judith A., 1939–
  Community counseling.

  Includes indexes.
  1. Community psychology.   2. Community mental health
services.   3. Counseling.   I. Lewis, Michael D.,
1937–   II. Title.
RA790.5.L48   1983   361.3'23   83-10277
ISBN 0-471-89603-9

Printed in the United States of America

10 9 8 7 6 5 4 3 2 1

PREFACE

People involved in the work of helping others have begun to sense a need for change. Since the first edition of this book was published, there has been tremendous growth in the awareness of what services to human beings can and should be. Helpers with varying job titles, working in a multitude of settings, have worked to develop responsive and responsible human service delivery systems.

These helpers realize that they have a role to play, not just in changing individuals, but in affecting whole communities. They know that the kinds of services offered must be provided in accordance with the needs of consumers—not just in terms of traditional and comfortable professional roles. They are aware of the need to find preventive approaches. They have come to understand that the best kind of help is self-help, based on the strengths inherent in each individual and in each community.

When we first coined the term "community counseling" to describe the work of this new brand of helper, we attempted to create, for the first time, a set of guidelines to help "community counselors" plan and implement effective programs. Now, we are also able to present living examples of excellence in community counseling approaches. Special recognition should go to community counselors at the "cutting edge," including Gary Leofanti and Kathy Miner, of Aunt Martha's Youth Service Center; Bree Hayes, of the Peoria Human Service Center; Dorothy Jeffries, of Project C.A.N.; Stephen Schain, of the Washington Developmental Disabilities Planning Council; and the many leaders and participants in the efforts of The Woodlawn Organization and the Community Congress of San Diego. Thousands of other community counselors who have yet to see their names in print provide effective services to their clients and communities every day.

Leo Goldman, Lawrence Brammer, and Ursula Delworth provided encouragement and constructive suggestions that meant a great deal to us in the initial development of the community counseling concept. Allen Ivey and Michael Bailis provided valuable feedback and help as we worked on the second edition. They also shared their knowledge of effective training programs that are helping to make community counsel-

v

ing a reality. Keith Lewis, our 12-year-old son and a budding author in his own right, assisted with proofreading and indexing at the final stages of production.

Judith A. Lewis
Michael D. Lewis

CONTENTS

CHAPTER
1
INTRODUCTION
TO COMMUNITY
COUNSELING

A t a suburban youth counseling center, young people conduct research on community issues, study their rights and responsibilities as students, and learn to monitor and affect legislation that concerns them. This advocacy and leadership program provides training in the kinds of skills that people need for active participation in the institutions that affect their lives. Just as important, the community as a whole is gaining the immediate benefits of young people's involvement.

An urban human service center provides stress management workshops for people newly faced with the pressures of unemployment. Staff members of the consultation and Education Department maintain close ties with the community, so that such preventive workshops and seminars can be developed in immediate response to changing local needs. Economic and social problems are recognized before they result in a number of mental health casualties.

In a major metropolitan area, a network of small, community-based agencies has worked together to identify and meet common needs since the late 1960s. This coordinating effort continues to enhance the ability of community members to gain a fair share of limited resources for human services and to increase the rationality of budget allocations.

A mental health center in Atlanta provides outreach to children and families affected by that city's crisis of missing and murdered children. Project C.A.N. (Community Action Network) recognizes that the arrest and conviction of one man cannot erase the long-lasting effects of a crisis of fear. Programs have been developed to overcome isolation, build support systems, and enhance community competence.

In Washington, a number of statewide organizations have joined together to provide advocacy in behalf of developmentally disabled citizens. Working together, these organizations have been able to affect the attitudes and values underlying service delivery systems and to build consensus based on citizen and consumer input.

These programs vary widely in thrust, in setting, and in clientele served. Yet each helps to exemplify the assumptions and values on which the community counseling model is based.

Community counseling, far from being just another new job title or specializaton, represents an innovative set of approaches for delivering helping services to human beings. Community counselors may be volunteers, paraprofessionals, or helping professionals. They may call the people they help counselees, clients, or consumers. They may work in any of a number of settings, including the following.

Educational institutions.

Mental health centers.

Specialized community agencies.

Vocational or rehabilitation programs.

Correctional settings.

Health care settings.

Social services.

Business and industry.

Community counselors, however, have much in common. They share an orientation toward working with the client as a whole person, with many needs and just as many strengths. Counselors share an awareness of the effects of the social environment on every community member. They share the knowledge that individuals and total communities can be helped most effectively when people gain the skills and resources needed to help themselves.

BASIC ASSUMPTIONS

Although community counselors provide a variety of services in various settings, they share a set of clearly defined assumptions that guide their work.

1 Clients' Interactions with the Environment Can Have Negative or Positive Effects

Community counselors recognize that individuals constantly interact with their surroundings. This interaction can be helpful or harmful. As individuals grow and develop, they use the environment as a source of learning and support. Their personal and physical needs are met through their interactions with others. But the environment can also serve as a negative force, stunting growth and limiting development.

Because this interaction exists, community counselors know that it is ineffective to try to help people without dealing with the community at the same time. They know that there must be a constant interplay between services offered directly to individuals and those offered indirectly, through attempts to change the community.

Environmental factors are clearly at work in the development of almost any kind of problem faced by counselees. Sometimes the connection is overt and definable: the adult denied vocational options through racism or sexism, the young person victimized by destructive family or school environments, the ex-offender, ex-addict, or ex-mental patient denied free entry into the mainstream community. Just as often, however, problems that have been brought about through environmental factors become so much a part of the individual that causality cannot be clearly attributed. The individual arrives on the scene with characteristics such as feelings of powerlessness or aimlessness, inability to recognize alternatives and make decisions, failure to see beyond a highly restrictive role definition, unrewarding interpersonal relationships, unclear personal values, or a feeling that the community is hostile to his or her development. In fact, our modern environment may *be* hostile. One clue is provided by the fact that the characteristics described above are reaching epidemic proportions. We all share some of these uncomfortable feelings.

Yet if negative forces within the environment can work against an individual's growth, it is just as true that positive forces within the community can aid personal development. People vary in their ability to cope with the demands placed on them by stressful events or situations, and at least some of this variation is brought about by differences in the degree of social support that is available (Gottlieb, 1981; Holahan & Moos, 1982; Wilcox, 1981). An individual's social network can provide psychological support, access to resources, and concrete help. Recognizing this, the community counselor tries to move the community itself toward becoming a psychologically safe and growth-producing environment.

The resources needed for this kind of effort need not be created from scratch; they are already present in any community. The key to effective practice is to create opportunities for positive factors to rise to the surface.

2 A Multifaceted Approach Is More Efficient than a Single Service Approach

A multifaceted approach to helping is one that has many sides. The community counselor uses different methods to deliver services to people, never relying on just one type of approach.

Traditionally, many helpers have depended on direct, one-to-one relationships as their sole method for helping individuals. More and more, this model is being called into question.

Logic tells us that clients for one-to-one counseling come for assistance because of some immediate need. Some kind of discomfort probably precedes the request for services. The counselor may be able to help individuals having these experiences, but, if one-to-one services are the only ones offered, there is no way to reach people before the onset of problems.

Limitation to one brand of service delivery involves a poor use of human resources, with a small number of helpers being called on to present the same kinds of services repeatedly to a large number of individuals. As the population that needs services grows, so does the need to consider programs that can reach large numbers of people, increase the pool of helping resources, share effective skills as widely as possible, and bring about changes in the environments that affect human beings.

All of this involves the *human service concept,* which defines appropriate action in terms of individual and community needs, rather than in terms of the helping methods with which professionals are already familiar and comfortable. The specific job titles of helpers are not important. What is important is the ability of helpers to provide the services needed to meet individual and community goals.

Depending on one kind of service means dealing with only one aspect of each person. Using a multifaceted, human services approach means providing for the whole individual and the whole community, regardless of what special needs may be involved.

3 Prevention Is More Efficient than Remediation

Prevention aims to eliminate specific problems, or at least to keep difficulties from becoming prevalent among members of the population being served. Mental health professionals have borrowed from public health terminology to differentiate among several types of prevention, as seen in the following quote.

> Primary prevention . . . focuses on lowering the incidence of emotional problems and on promoting positive mental health among people not identified as having any special difficulty. It can be distinguished from secondary prevention, which aims toward early identification and prompt treatment of problems, and from tertiary prevention, which attempts to decrease the long-term effects of disabilities. In essence, primary prevention involves activities designed to reduce environmental stresses or to build people's competencies and life skills (Lewis & Lewis, 1981, p. 173).

Primary prevention provides the most important underpinning to the work of the community counselor. The preventive focus in mental health shares with the community counseling concept a concern for developing proactive approaches that reach healthy persons and their communities.

(1) Most fundamentally, primary prevention is proactive in that it seeks to build adaptive strengths, coping resources, and health in people; not to reduce or contain already manifest deficit.

(2) Primary prevention is concerned about total populations, especially including groups at high risk; it is less oriented to individuals and to the provision of services on a case-by-case basis.

(3) Primary prevention's main tools and models are those of education and social engineering, not therapy or rehabilitation, although some insights for its models and programs grow out of the wisdom derived from clinical experience.

(4) Primary prevention assumes that equipping people with personal and environmental resources for coping is the best of all ways to ward off mal-adaptive problems, not trying to deal (however skillfully) with problems that have already germinated and flowered (President's Commission on Mental Health, 1978, p. 1833).

If one examines human service planning in long-range terms, it becomes obvious that preventing problems allows helpers to reallocate available resources along the lines of logical priorities. Instead of deciding on objectives based on current crises, community counselors and their communities can outline goals and then develop the resources and techniques that would be most appropriate for accomplishing them. If programs are to be developmental or preventive, instead of remedial, they must (1) be aimed toward a large number of people, not just those who are experiencing some problem and (2) be provided early, before some severe difficulty has already been identified.

Programs may involve *direct* services, meaning that individuals have the opportunity to participate in new competency-building experiences. Services may be *indirect*, that is, they are meant to change the social surroundings that affect people's lives. No matter which approach is used, it is preventive, rather than remedial, if it is meant to serve a large population that has not been identified specifically as in need of special services. Direct and indirect programs can be combined to meet the needs of a particular community, and the community counselor is concerned with those total needs, regardless of the particular setting in which he or she is employed.

4 The Community Counseling Approach Is Applicable to Any Helping Setting

Any person offering psychological, social, educational, or vocational services to individuals or groups has a responsibility to some community. This fact is obvious to a worker in a community mental health center, who deals with a geographically defined "catchment area" and who has a clear mandate to identify community needs. It is less obvious in situations where "community involvement" is not a required aspect of the job, or where the nature of the community is not well defined. Counselors in educational settings, for instance, become "community counselors" if their orientation is toward recognizing the interplay between the individual and the environment. In fact, they have a responsibility to two communities: the institution itself and the outlying neighborhood in which the school or college is based.

In a complex and highly mobile society, it might not be relevant to think of "community" just in geographical terms. For the purpose of this book, we define *"community"* as *a system of interdependent persons, groups, and organizations that:*

1 *Meets the individual's primary needs*
2 *Affects the individual's daily life.*
3 *Acts as intermediary between the individual and the society as a whole.*

The fact that the individuals, groups, and organizations making up a community are *interdependent* means that they depend on one another to meet their needs. The fact that the community is a *system* means that it has unity, or wholeness, and that it has continuity. Members can learn how the community works, and they can have their expectations met regularly.

Just as the community links individuals and groups together, it also links individuals with the society as a whole. Individuals can affect the community, which can affect the world outside. The society as a whole delivers its norms, or behavioral expectations, to the individual by way of the community.

On the basis of this working definition, it becomes clear that an individual may be a member of more than one community at the same time. It also becomes clear that, while a neighborhood can be a community, so can a school, a university, a hospital, or a corporation.

No matter where we work, dealing with individuals must bring us, at some point, to dealing with their communities. People do not live in vacuums and, regardless of the thrust of a particular counseling strategy, there comes a time when we must examine both the restrictions that society places on the individual's behavior and the counselee's chances for having an impact in return. The community is the connecting link that delivers social norms to the individual and that permits the individual's responses to be implemented. No institution, no agency, no counselor can remain untouched.

NEW CONCEPTS, NEW ROLES

The assumptions guiding the community counseling concept make it impossible for the practitioner to find comfort in traditional ways of operating. Each assumption carries with it vast implications for the counselor's attitudes and behaviors. Each requires the development of new ways of organizing. Each calls for the creation of a role that may grow far beyond what professional helpers have traditionally been trained to do.

Individual in Community

Community counselors see the community as an environment that affects every individual. In this environment, there are forces that can serve either to enhance or to stunt the individual's personal-social development. That fact has implications for counselors' activities and impact on their view of themselves as workers.

A new dimension is added, for instance, in the interaction between the counselor and the individual client, since the counselor now concentrates on assessing the relationship between the client and his or her social system. In a traditional, one-to-one counseling relationship, emphasis is placed on helping the client to examine his or her own behaviors, to take responsibility for his or her actions, to change that which can most easily be changed (i.e., the self).

These activities are also valued in community counseling, but another step is taken. The environment is not seen as a stationary, unmoving reality to which adjustment must be made. The environment—not just the client—can be changed. The counselor and the counselee participate in a mutual exploration, asking the following questions.

1 *To what extent is the individual capable of resolving the issue through personal change?*
2 *What resources in the environment are available to help the individual grow?*

3 *To what extent does the solution really rest in changing the environment, rather than just changing the individual?*

4 *How can the counselor and/or the counselee act to bring about the necessary changes in the environment?*

The community counselor also examines these issues in collective terms, considering the interaction between the community and all of its members. The counselor can learn to be alert to the forces that are limiting the growth of a number of clients or potential clients. It is easy to become aware of these forces when one sees a parade of individuals all having problems as a result of the same shortcoming in the community environment. What is more difficult—and more important—is to sense the existence of those shortcomings before the fact, to be so attuned to what is going on within a community that action can be taken before casualties begin to appear.

Trying to bring about positive change in the community becomes a major aspect of the community counseling role. Action can also be applied to ferreting out and capitalizing on the positive forces in the environment. If the counselor has the strength and the skill to confront that which is harmful, he or she must also have the sensitivity to recognize and reach out to that which holds the promise of health.

Again, the professional's role is deeply affected. Community counselors see themselves as one helping resource among many. They know that there are many people in any community who have the skills needed to help others. To see oneself as one resource among many is to stop seeing oneself as an expert with the answers. Bloom (1971, p. 8), looking back at early mental health objectives, remembers:

> First, it was assumed that community residents could be sorted into those who were disadvantaged and those who were not. Second, it was assumed that some members of the community were caretakers and others were clients of caretakers. Third, it was assumed that the repository of wisdom regarding community health needs was the mental health professional and his colleagues in other social agencies. . . . This set of assumptions regarding the community and the assessment of its mental health needs has become increasingly untenable.

We now know that there is no one group of people with all of the answers, no one group that can identify all of a community's needs. The "expert" is now being replaced by the facilitator, who sets priorities in concert with the community of which he or she is an integral part.

Innovation and Risk

If a community orientation robs the community counselor of the ease in which the counselor performs his or her accustomed tasks, so does the notion of a multifaceted approach. The community counselor must learn to deal with large groups as well as individuals, to become an educator as well as a counselor, and to deal with the environment as well as the person being affected by the environment.

> (There is) a tendency for human service deliverers to concentrate more on the nature of the services being delivered than on the ultimate purposes of these services. Familiar methods are often used long after changes in community needs or agency mission should have dictated changes in professional services (Lewis & Lewis, 1983, p. 21).

In fact, as Carver points out, "it certainly is not an overstatement to observe that clinicians are primadonnas who . . . fervently believe that their method of training and legitimacy are their products, not the degree to which they are effective in producing results" (Carver, 1979, p. 3).

Community counselors, in contrast, know that it is more efficient and more effective to have a variety of resources and techniques available to them. That means, of course, that they are forced to develop expertise in areas that go beyond their formal training. It means that they are forced to become perpetual learners, developing new skills in social action, consultation, large-group processes, and planning.

A taste for innovation and risk taking is part of an approach that rises above dependence on a single service. It would be a comfortable situation if that which we know best how to do—bringing about change in individual clients—could be counted on to meet the real needs of the community. Since that is not the case, counselors need to involve themselves in continual regeneration and change, with that growth being joined by an awareness of individual limitations. If community counselors can expand their skills into new areas, they can also recognize the existence of expertise in other people—professional or nonprofessional. Instead of counting on themselves to be superpersons, they can develop and participate in interdependent teams, leading when it is necessary, following when it is not.

Action and Change

Placing emphasis on healthy development and on the prevention of problems also calls for a constant process of renewal, especially in the way problems and potential solutions are perceived.

Community counselors deal with the factors that contribute to problems, instead of just attacking the problems themselves. They work to improve the environment, as well as to help the victims of the community's shortcomings. While a more traditional approach might emphasize problems as belonging to individuals, a preventive model forces evaluation of difficulties belonging to the larger system. Prevention implies bringing about changes in the community, rather than concentrating on the victims of the system when it is too late to do anything but try another remedy.

This orientation brings with it—almost automatically—a sense of the community counseling approach as being highly active. There can be no passive waiting for the next task, the next problem, the next crisis to appear. Instead, practitioners search out the situation in which they can most effectively help, and then avidly plan and initiate new programs.

Seeking out new needs and developing new programs before problems appear means being constantly active. It also means that the counselor must be comfortable with a job that is always in the midst of change.

New Priorities

Community counselors assume that, regardless of the setting in which they work, they do have responsibility to a total community. They recognize that the tasks they perform must be affected by that fact. Being realistic, however, they know that they are sometimes alone in their assumptions.

In many agencies and institutions, the prevailing expectation is that services are limited to those directly applied to troubled individuals. Community counselors' skills are put to the test when their ideas about the breadth of the job to be done go beyond what has been expected of them.

In those situations, community counselors are forced to rewrite their own job descriptions and to work toward gaining support for a new set of priorities, a process requiring the following.

- Strong conviction that a community-based approach is right and that they are competent to carry it out.

- Understanding other points of view.
- Willingness to be accountable, to prove that a community-oriented approach is both effective and efficient.
- Ability to build a base of support from whatever resources—expected or unexpected—might be available.
- Power to discriminate between those occasions when leadership should be assumed and those in which the community counselor should act as part of the support base for another individual or group.

In the final analysis, the effectiveness of community counselors might be measured in terms of their ability to implement an innovative model without being forced to use all of their energy protecting it. That kind of model cannot be developed or implemented in isolation. The community counselor must work as part of a team, developing appropriate goals along with community members and co-workers. If the community counselor has a responsibility to the community, that responsibility includes creating every opportunity for broad-based, active involvement in all aspects of the program.

FROM CONCEPTS TO ACTION

On the basis of what we know about the community counselor's assumptions and attitudes, we can begin to define the guiding concept in more specific and concrete terms.

Community counseling is a multifaceted, human services approach. This approach combines direct and indirect programs in order to:

1 *Help community members to live more effectively.*
2 *Prevent the problems most frequently faced by consumers of our services.*

Implementing this approach seems to require some rather special personal characteristics, including (1) an orientation toward being active instead of passive, (2) a sharp awareness of the social forces affecting individuals, (3) a willingness to take the risk of developing new techniques and skills, (4) an awareness that the counselor is only one positive resource among many, and (5) an ability to build new bases of support for a truly flexible approach.

To be flexible, however, does not mean to lack guidelines for action.

The activities in which the community counselor engages can be divided into distinct categories.

First, a distinction is made between *direct* and *indirect* services. Direct services are provided to community members and give them the opportunity to learn new skills or develop fresh understandings that can help them to live more effectively and more independently. Indirect programs deal with the community setting. The community counselor intervenes, or enters into the situation, in order to bring about some change. The purpose of these interventions is to make the environment more suitable for individual growth.

Second, a distinction is made between *community* services and *client* services. Community services are available to every member of the community. They are meant to reach large numbers of people in a positive way, and not to intervene very deeply into their lives. Client services are more concentrated. They are meant to make greater changes in the lives of people who have identified themselves as clients, needing more active assistance.

Implementing the community counseling approach thus involves four distinct facets.

1 *Direct community services.* Community education programs that provide direct experiences, available to the population as a whole.
2 *Indirect community services.* Community organizing efforts that attempt to make the entire community more responsive to the needs of its members.
3 *Direct client services.* Client counseling programs that provide special experiences to individuals or groups needing assistance.
4 *Indirect client services.* Client advocacy programs that intervene actively in the environments of specific individuals or groups, allowing their special needs to be met.

These facets, along with the types of activities involved in each, are presented in Table 1.1.

Direct Community Services (Community Education) Counselors providing direct community service act as community educators, dealing with the population at large. The thrust of their interventions is educative. Their purpose is to share whatever human knowledge and skills are available, and thus to lessen the need for professional helpers. Ideally, through participating in these new experiences, community members can gain the skills needed to help themselves.

Table 1.1
Four Facets of Community Counseling

	Community Services	Client Services
Direct	*Community Education* Developing preventive educational programs. Designing models for educational interventions.	*Client Counseling* Proactive counseling. Accessible counseling. Intervening in "at-risk situations."
Indirect	*Community Organization* Community-based planning. Community action for change.	*Client Advocacy* Strengthening socially devalued populations. Maintaining responsive helping networks.

Voluntary educational programs provide the occasion for individuals and groups to develop the increased awareness and skills that can help them to live more effectively and deal with their problems more competently. These programs may run the gamut from value clarification seminars to assertiveness training, from lessons in self-modification techniques to interpersonal relations laboratories, from courses in decision making and life planning to workshops in cross-cultural understanding, and from programmed curricula in consumerism to the formation of groups dealing with the problems of parenting.

The possibilities are endless. For each of the foregoing suggestions, and for numerous others, the techniques, the concepts, and even the course outlines already exist. The need lies in generalizing their availability, in bringing them within reach of a broad range of people.

Binding all of these community education programs together is the drive to help individuals and groups feel a sense of their own effectiveness. These programs are developmental; they aim to provide positive growth experiences for any community members desiring them. In fact, community education programs aim to develop so much competence within a community that professional helpers will no longer be needed.

Indirect Community Services (Community Organization)   In addition to providing helping experiences to individuals, the community counselor is often faced with the need to intervene in the environment. This happens when conditions in the community are seen as limiting instead of facilitating the growth and effectiveness of community members. Intervention also happens when there is a need to plan for more effective ways of meeting the human service needs of all community members. Community organization efforts can take the form of community-based planning or of participation in community action for change.

At one time, it might have been assumed that social planning could be carried out by a small group of individuals having the power and the resources to implement programs. Now it is becoming more and more apparent that, if programs of any type are to meet the real needs of the community, many people must be involved both in planning and in implementation. Goals must be set and programs developed and evaluated, not just by governmental authorities or social scientists, but by the people who deliver and use services and facilities. Community counselors, as human service practitioners, have a role to play in developing broadly based planning efforts. It is possible to involve coalitions of human service agencies, professional and paraprofessional workers, volunteers, and community members in developing programs and securing the financial resources needed to carry them out.

Sometimes, helping the community as a whole to be more responsive to the needs of all of its members can involve conflict. In some situations, the values of one group may not coincide with those of another, and no clear "common good" can be identified. When the needs and values of the powerful and the powerless diverge, the community counselor may become an advocate and defender of the "have-nots." A portion of the community is now being asked to share its power and its resources. The skills needed in that case are really political: organizing a base of support and developing and implementing strategies for bringing about real change.

Direct Client Services (Client Counseling) An effective counseling approach recognizes that it is impossible to help a counselee without, at the same time, dealing with his or her environment. That may mean changing what is damaging in the environment. It may also mean discovering and utilizing what might be helpful and supportive. When community counselors provide direct services to clients, they attempt to work in an environmental context, identifying positive sources of help in the client's support system and confronting negative or destructive environmental pressures. Throughout the counseling process, attempts are made to discriminate between problems that can be resolved through individual change and issues that can only be settled through change in the environment.

Such counseling services should be available to all individuals who decide that they wish to participate in relationships with counselors. An important aspect of this service is that it must be "accessible," or very easily available to any member of the community.

The attempt to make counseling accessible may involve physical movement, away from institutional structures that may be imposing, and out into the places where life is lived. Accessibility is also increased when counseling services are offered by a number of persons with different orientations. A combined service of professional, paraprofessional, and volunteer counseling allows the growth of resources to meet a need. "Professionals" are normally characterized as persons with graduate level training. Usually, their training emphasizes theory and research, as well as supervised experience in counseling or therapy. "Paraprofessionals" may also work full time as counselors. Usually, their academic work has been of shorter duration, with greater emphasis on practical experiences and on-the-job training. "Volunteers" generally have some career identity outside of their role as helpers. Whether they are students, retirees, or persons who hold other jobs, volunteers contribute their time to participate in training and implement their skills in helping relationships.

When professionals, paraprofessionals, and volunteers are all available, counseling becomes more accessible to the community. This avoids the disastrous effects of long waiting lists for formal appointments with specialists who are already stretched too thin. At the same time, this approach brings counseling closer to the individual's grasp by making it clear that this is a community service offered by community members.

Only if counseling is really accessible can it be developmental or preventive. If the service is distant or threatening, people will not use it in time. This is particularly true of crisis situations.

In crises, immediate action is of primary importance. The counselor intervenes with the hope that the individual in crisis can grow from the experience and develop more effective ways of dealing with the world. Just as important, however, is the prevention of crises. Programs can be offered, on a voluntary basis, to people whose lives are reaching the point of sudden change. Depending on the needs of a particular community, that might involve such widely diverse groups as youths about to enter the work world, adults about to retire, couples anticipating parenthood, recent widows, or recent immigrants.

Individuals are always free to accept or reject the services offered and to decide on the nature of their own involvement. However, counselors should be aware of stressful situations that place people at risk for the development of problems. The opportunity to make contact with others having some of the same needs should always be available.

Indirect Client Services (Client Advocacy)   The need for bringing about change in the environment also becomes clear when the counselor works with individuals and groups who have special needs. Client advocacy involves intervening very actively in the surroundings of specific individuals or groups, so that these special needs can be met.

One way this is accomplished is through identifying groups of people who might benefit by increasing their own strength. A good example of this is provided by "socially devalued populations," or people who, because of some disability or past behavior, are downgraded by the community at large. Their worth as people is not fully appreciated by others, and they have become separated from the mainstream community.

The community counselor attempts to prevent further difficulty by helping to enhance the strength of such groups or individuals. Attempts are made to encourage self-help groups and to develop programs using volunteers, who can help to provide bridges between devalued populations and the community as a whole. No matter what kind of group may be involved, the community counselor's goal is always one of increasing independence and effectiveness, and the resources of the community itself are never overlooked.

One important resource is the "helping network," which is made up of all the persons and agencies available to provide personal assistance when it is needed. The community counselor can provide links between the individual and potential helping resources. He or she may also act as a consultant, assisting other workers to increase their effectiveness. There are also times when individual or group needs have gone unmet and more active support is needed. When inequities exist, when rigid rules or attitudes impinge on the individual's right to grow, or when someone's rights are being violated, the community counselor may step in to act as an advocate. One example, among many, might be provided by a teen-aged single parent who is denied free access to public education. A traditional approach might be to help her find private tutoring or plan a career in a field requiring few academic qualifications. The community counselor would battle the policy of exclusion, both for the sake of this individual and for the sake of others to come.

There are, in fact, countless situations in which client advocacy can make a difference to large segments of the population. When a group having potential difficulties is identified, services to that group can be complemented by attempts to make the community a help instead of a hindrance. Whether the community counselor is building favorable attitudes toward hiring ex-offenders or striving to bring the handicapped into the mainstream of community life, indirect client services are being enacted.

The Unified Approach   The four facets of community counseling combine in practice into a unified whole that can be implemented in virtually any human service or educational setting. There is no need for a community counselor to choose between being a helper of individuals and being an agent of social change.

Lerner (1972, p. 11) brings perspective to the issue of psychotherapy versus social action in the following statement.

> The conflict over individual versus group methods in community mental health rests on a false dichotomy because the essential nature of constructive psychotherapy and social action is the same. So too are the goals of both: to promote effective action in one's own behalf, in the former case by removing internal psychological obstacles to such action and, in the latter, by removing external social obstacles to it . . . the only real dichotomy is between those who work on and those who work for their clients.

Community counseling, too, is concerned with ultimate goals. It has attained its goal when human beings live effectively in a community that encourages them to define themselves and the nature of their own effectiveness. Community counseling has achieved success when a democratic and egalitarian community is populated by persons who sense and act on their opportunity to mold their own future.

Community counselors cannot, of course, attain these goals alone. They cannot even enact a multifaceted counseling program alone. Community counselors can, however, make sure that they are part of a team or a network of agencies that provides all of the needed services. They can actively seek an understanding of the real needs of their own communities and ensure that someone, somewhere, is striving to meet them.

COMMUNITY COUNSELING IN ACTION: "AUNT MARTHA'S"

The community counseling approach may seem idealistic. Yet more and more agencies and institutions are finding that it is possible to provide preventive, multifaceted programs meeting the needs of their client populations. "Aunt Martha's" is one of them.[1]

"You've Got a Friend" is the theme of Aunt Martha's Youth Service Center, Inc., a community-based youth-serving organization which offers comprehensive programs to meet the needs of young people and families residing in a fifteen-township region of metropolitan Chicago. Established in 1972, Aunt Martha's offers a range of services for young people and their families who are in need of assistance and has created innovative programs which enable young people to participate as positive contributing members of their communities. The initial community commission which led to the creation of Aunt Martha's was composed of both young people and adults.

The name *Aunt Martha's* was chosen to reflect the quality of warmth and concern one would find in the home of a close relative and which the community hoped young people would find at Aunt Martha's Youth Service Center. Since its beginning, Aunt Martha's has grown from a simple counseling center to a complex, highly-structured agency serving a wide geographic area through a dozen programs, a staff of 40 and over 250 community volunteers. Aunt Martha's serves a richly varied population, including both suburban and rural residents, as well as ethnic, racial, and economic groups. The service area also encompasses industrial areas with many of the characteristics of an urban setting. . . .

Aunt Martha's founding principles strongly advocated community participation at all levels, particularly with regard to the involvement of young people in the planning and operations of programs. Additionally, every effort was made to ensure that services were accessible to all young people in the community and that the bulk of service delivery was to be accomplished by community volunteers. These principles have been followed in the development of Aunt Martha's programs. Youth and adult volunteers are the heart of Aunt Martha's service delivery system. . . . Thus Aunt Martha's offers the community, especially youth, the opportunity to give as well as to receive help and to advocate on their own behalf.

Community and youth participation assure programs which are responsive to young people and to the community. Volunteers are involved at all levels of the agency's operations—service delivery, program planning and policy-making. Most of the staff are long-time residents of the communities they serve; many were previously volunteers. Volunteer training and supervision are crucial aspects of Aunt Martha's programs . . .

Aunt Martha's Youth Service's commitment to youth participation both within the organization and throughout the community is based on the belief that the majority of youth problems which communities experience are

[1]The description of Aunt Martha's Youth Service Center comes from E. Mazer, and C. G. Leofanti, *You've got a friend*, published by Aunt Martha's in 1980, and other materials disseminated by the agency. It is reprinted with permission.

caused by alienation and the perceived lack of access to meaningful social roles on the part of young people. Thus, Aunt Martha's comprehensive approach not only offers assistance to those who are experiencing problems but also seeks to provide vehicles through which young people may experience the senses of competence, usefulness, belonging, and potency needed to develop as healthy, productive adults who are integrated members of the community.

In the years since its development began, Aunt Martha's has offered a wide variety of innovative direct services, including the following:

1 Walk-In Counseling Center

Trained youth and adult volunteer counselors provide individual, family, and crisis counseling 24 hours a day.

2 Alternative Shelter Care

Alternative living shelters are offered through a licensed community network of short and long-term foster homes . . . Long term placement services are available to state wards in Aunt Martha's Group Home, which houses ten young women between the ages of 12 and 18.

3 Teen Health Clinic

Counseling, information, and medical services concerning human sexuality are provided several times a week for young women and men. Sessions include contraception counseling, VD diagnosis and treatment, pregnancy testing, and pre-natal care. A "parachute group" is held for young women carrying their babies to term, covering pre-natal care and parenting skills.

4 Outreach Projects

Individual and family counseling and shelter care are offered to eleven south suburban townships . . . Staff and volunteers offer services in people's homes or other nearby locations. The Eastern Will County Project also runs a drop-in center several nights a week.

5 Specialized Group Services

Groups are offered as a separate program and to enhance the effectiveness of existing Aunt Martha's programs . . . Types of groups include parent support groups, peer support groups, after school activity groups, outdoor adventure groups, family groups, and non-competitive game programs.

6 Drug Emergency Response Program

Drug emergency assistance is available 24 hours a day through contact with Aunt Martha's specially trained professionals and volunteers. Licensed by the Illinois Dangerous Drugs Commission, the Drug Emergency Response

Program works closely with hospital emergency rooms to aid young people who are experiencing serious reactions to drugs and alcohol. Preventive drug counseling and educational talks are held at area elementary and secondary schools.

7 Youth Employment Program

The Youth Employment Program provides a number of services focused on out-of-school youth, including:

a E.D.G.E. (Employment Direction and Growth Experience), a training program to enhance job seeking skills.
b Job Club, a structured support group to diminish discouragement.
c G.E.D. classes.
d Public Service Work Experiences, involving on-the-job training in local organizations.
e Private Sector Job Development, including components of job identification, recruitment, training, placement, and consultation.

8 LISTEN: A Youth Participation Project

Youths involved with LISTEN perform in a play /discussion which highlights the importance of youth involvement in the decision making process. Specially trained youths then act as consultants to community groups to create new opportunities for youth within these organizations and in the community at large.

9 Speakers' Bureau

Aunt Martha's Speakers' Bureau provides speakers and slide presentations to community organizations on topics ranging from foster care, volunteerism, health education, and Aunt Martha's Services.

10 Connections

Connections, published four times a year, is a newspaper written for youth by youth. It offers a journalistic forum for all young writers in the community.

11 Youth Legal Services

In this program, practicing attorneys volunteer confidential advice and counseling to young people on legal problems such as contracts, school-related concerns, family problems, and criminal law.

12 "Who Needs It?"

This innovative alcoholism prevention program hired and trained teenagers to counsel elementary school aged youth, helping them clarify values and strengthen decision making skills. This counseling was designed to help young people better cope with peer pressure to use alcohol. The program traveled to local elementary schools to conduct sessions.

In addition to offering direct, innovative services, Aunt Martha's interacts with other youth-serving systems, increasing access of youth to those systems, and dramatizing the right of youth to exercise legitimate involvement in community affairs. The Center for Student Citizenship, Rights, and Responsibilities (CSCRR), supported by the Chicago Community Trust and the Woods Charitable Fund, is a youth leadership, involvement and advocacy program which seeks to promote the development of leadership skills among youth and the active, informed involvement of youth in the decision making processes which affect their lives. "The underlying belief is that the active participation of young people in the institutions of which they are a part produces benefits for all: young people experience a more healthy development; institutions become more effective as better decisions are made; the community gains members who are better informed, more skilled and better prepared for democratic participation in community affairs" (Aunt Martha's Youth Service Center, 1982, p. 1). Some of the activities involved in the CSCRR effort include:

1 Youth Day: An event organized by young people to educate the community about the value of youth and to promote a positive self image among youth.
2 Publication of a Book: A book designed to raise consciousness about issues affecting youth, including racism, drug and alcohol abuse, the draft, and other major concerns.
3 Seminars: Educational seminars on law-related education and "alternatives to suspension" offered in local schools.
4 Newsletter: Updates to increase awareness of the advocacy effort and recruit new participants.
5 Educational Forums: Meetings on specific issues selected by CSCRR participants.
6 Study Groups: School-based study groups dealing with such issues as student rights and responsibilities, school attendance policies, student representation on school boards, and gang activities. Research completed by study groups is disseminated through community education efforts such as Youth Day, forums, and newsletters.
7 Legislative Committee: A committee to identify issues of concern to young people and learn how to monitor related legislation and act on issues of concern. Committee members might assist in organizing young people to write to legislators, testify at hearings, visit legislators, or draft legislation.
8 Training: Intensive training programs directed at the needs of young people participating in Center activities and including such topics as negotiation, conflict resolution, public speaking, coping with stress, and time management.
9 Internships: Placements for young people with elected officials at the local and state levels and with Behavioral Research Institute, a political consulting firm.

The Center was responsible for a survey of high school dropouts, resulting in a report and recommendations to help school districts prevent dropouts and better meet the needs of young people experiencing problems. Aunt Martha's has also been instrumental in bringing about changes in state legislation to encourage the use and development of community based youth services and to decrease the involvement of the court in non-criminal situations.

These approaches exemplify the basic community counseling concept that direct and indirect services, as well as programs for those with special needs and for the community at large, complement one another. As the director of Aunt Martha's points out,

> Services must be guaranteed to the most seriously troubled youth residing within the jurisdiction of the youth agency. Youth agencies must develop the resources needed to reach the most troubled and reduce the number of young people who become subject to large non-community based institutional programs. Services to this group provide the youth agency with first hand information regarding the failings of community institutions and a base to propose community change (Leofanti, 1981, p. 25).

Help is always given to the victims of the community's shortcomings, but the staff and volunteers who provide services never lose sight of the fact that problems must be prevented through efforts to build problem-solving competencies among young people and through active advocacy on their behalf.

SUMMARY

Community counselors work in a variety of roles in many different settings. They have in common a set of assumptions, including the following.

1 *Clients' interactions with the environment can have negative or positive effects.*

2 *A multifaceted approach is more efficient than a single service approach.*

3 *Prevention is more efficient than remediation.*

4 *The community counseling approach is applicable to any helping setting.*

These assumptions affect the community counselor's attitudes and behaviors and require the development of new ways of organizing and new definitions of helping roles. The community counselor is (1) active, not passive, (2) aware of the social forces affecting individuals, (3) willing to take risks and develop new skills, (4) aware of the many positive helping resources in the community, and (5) able to build new bases of support.

In practice, the community counseling approach includes four facets.

1   Direct community services (community education).
2   Indirect community services (community organization).
3   Direct client services (client counseling).
4   Indirect client services (client advocacy).

These four facets complement one another, so that a unified program is created. One agency that exemplies this approach is Aunt Martha's Youth Service Center, a youth-serving organization in metropolitan Chicago.

ACTIVITIES TO ENHANCE UNDERSTANDING OF CHAPTER 1

1   Visit a community agency or counseling program in your locality, using the community counseling model as a tool to help you understand the program's thrust. Think about the agency or institution in these terms.

   a. What kinds of direct, communitywide services are offered?

   b. To what degree is the agency involved in community change efforts?

   c. What direct client services are offered? Do these services seem to take environmental factors into account?

   d. Is the agency involved in indirect client services? Are there active advocacy efforts in behalf of consumers of the agency's services?

   In many instances, you will find that one or more facets are missing from an agency's program. If that is the case, can you generate some ideas about services that might enhance the agency's effectiveness in meeting its goals?

2   Think about a specific group or population (e.g., physically disabled adults, victims of child abuse, unemployed professionals, women,

seniors, high school students). Consider what aspects of the social environment might affect the well-being of this group. Are there social, economic, political, or psychological pressures that might affect members of this population? Taking these factors into account, develop some ideas concerning appropriate services for the population you have selected. You will probably notice that direct counseling services alone are unlikely to meet the group's needs. Beginning with a clear statement of your goals, develop a hypothetical community counseling effort involving all four facets of the model described in Chapter 1. At this point, concentrate on the general thrust of each facet, rather than dwelling on the details of each service. Give your agency a name and begin to think of it as your own. As you become even more familiar with community counseling concepts, you will be able to think about your agency's services in more concrete terms.

CHAPTER
2
COMMUNITY
EDUCATION

Many clients having similar concerns are likely to be found in any agency or institution. Traditionally, some counselors, psychologists, or social workers might have found this phenomenon comforting. Encountering a particular problem or issue frequently, they knew exactly how to deal with it.

While familiarity might have bred competence, it also bred repetition. A professional, counseling on a one-to-one basis, spent countless hours assisting in the solution of individual problems that might have been avoided.

Now, there is increasing recognition that *counselors are educators and trainers* (Matthes & Dustin, 1980). Community counselors attempt to recognize the needs that are common to many community members and to develop large-scale programs that confront significant issues head on. By attempting to reach large numbers of people before their problems become critical, community counselors work more efficiently. At the same time, they help to prevent crises and dysfunctions by training people in the life skills and competencies that can be used to withstand stress and maintain good mental health.

> Mental health education attempts to develop important competencies within normal and at-risk groups. Such efforts, often referred to as competence training, are designed to improve the capacity of normal and at-risk populations to cope with predictable life transitions and to more effectively manage stressful situations. The premise underlying this approach is that disorders can be avoided by strengthening an individual's or group's capacity to handle environmental stress or life crises (Ketterer, Bader, & Levy, 1980, p. 271).

The purpose of "community education" programs is, in fact, to build life competencies for community members who have not been identified as having specific problems. The elements of competency include (Adler, 1982, pp. 36–37) the following.

1 Performance of major social roles.
2 Self-concept.
3 Interactional functioning.
4 Management of affect.
5 Navigation of developmental transitions.
6 Management of stressful events.
7 Access to available resources.
8 Cognitive functioning.

If participants develop these kinds of abilities, they are less likely to need more intensive interventions.

Community counselors, when involved in this kind of competency training, are actually educators, rather than clinicians. Their purpose is not to solve problems, but to prevent them; not to cure ills, but to enhance wellness.

> This approach uses the school as its model and instruction as the means for enhancement. The intervenor becomes a teacher, rather than a therapist. Adopting such a model allows the intervenor to be a skill trainer who teaches the client . . . life skills . . . and facilitates the retention of the skills through the lifespan (Danish, 1977, p. 150).

Community education programs are appropriate strategies for dealing with general mental health concerns, but they are also used to help clients deal with the kinds of issues most frequently faced in a particular setting. Thus, a university counseling center presents workshops on test anxiety and educational decision making; a career counseling agency offers life work planning groups; a family service agency teaches parenting skills; a women's center provides courses in assertiveness and self-defense.

What these efforts have in common is their attempt to provide people with knowledge and personal skills that they can use to help themselves. What these efforts have in common is the part they are playing in the movement to make professional helpers, someday, obsolete.

That "someday" is still a distant dream. But the fulfillment of dreams, as strange as it may seem, requires nothing more than practicality. In this context, the most practical of programs are those that hold the promise of far-reaching, lasting effectiveness. Several rules of thumb emerge.

COMMUNITY EDUCATION GUIDELINES

1 Programs are Effective When Participants Develop Skills that They Can Utilize in an Unforeseen Future

To be most effective in the long run, educative programs concentrate, not just on the solution of immediate problems, but on building resources to be used in the solution of problems yet to occur. As individuals are trained in specific techniques for examining and dealing with their own behavior, they develop control over their actions. That control can be exerted whenever necessary, through a reapplication of the learned techniques.

Self-Modification

A particularly interesting innovation is the notion of teaching the techniques of behavior modification to individuals so that they can use their knowledge of human behavior to bring about changes in specific aspects of their own lives.

This process works under the assumption that behaviors are learned through the interaction between an individual and his or her environment. Behaviors that are attempted can be strengthened or weakened, depending on their consequences. Some behaviors are continued because they are positive, or "reinforcing," in and of themselves. Some are continued because they are positively reinforced by other events that follow them. A *positive reinforcement* is a consequence that rewards a behavior and therefore makes it more likely that the behavior will be repeated. A positive reinforcer can be recognized for these reasons (Foster, 1974).

1 *The positive reinforcer follows the response.*
2 *The positive reinforcer increases the rate of that response.*

If, on the other hand, a particular behavior were followed by an unpleasant response, or punishment, the rate of that behavior would *decrease*. Thus, specific responses become stronger—more frequent—if they are followed by *positive reinforcement*. When a behavior is not reinforced at all, it is, in time, *extinguished*.

> Responses which have previously been established or maintained by reinforcement will decrease in rate when that reinforcement is withheld (Foster, 1974).

When a behavior is positively reinforced only some of the time, extinction takes longer.

Sometimes an individual engages in behaviors for which the reinforcement is not obvious or apparent. The behavior may have begun originally to gain a positive reinforcement or to avoid a negative consequence. The person has learned to interpret a particular stimulus from the environment as a signal that reward or punishment will follow a given behavior. In time, that cue itself evokes behavior—even when its original purpose has been forgotten.

Individuals are aware of their own behaviors and of the kinds of situations that are likely to trigger their actions. They also have unique knowledge of what rewards are most reinforcing to them. Thus, people without advanced psychological training are in a good position to modify their own behavior in accordance with their personal goals, once they have learned the basic theory involved.

When self-modification techniques are taught, individuals develop plans that are specifically suited to their own lives. They identify specific, measurable behaviors that they would like to develop or to increase in frequency, and then decide on the reinforcements that are most likely to strengthen the desired behavior. They then make the reinforcement *contingent* on the performance of the behavior. In other words, they give themselves positive reinforcement *only when the action has been performed with the desired frequency*.

Watson and Tharp (1972), working with college-age adults, have developed a step-by-step guidebook that can be followed independently by persons desiring to make particular changes in their own behaviors.

The reader begins by examining the dissatisfactions in his or her own life, finally selecting one problem area that can be described in terms of *concrete behavior* in *specific situations*. Ideally, a goal is stated in positive terms: that is, an increase in the occurrence of a behavior that is desired in itself or that is incompatible with some undesirable behavior. (For example, increasing the occurrence of speaking up in groups instead of decreasing the occurrence of withdrawal.)

The individual then begins to gather *baseline data*. He or she develops a convenient record-keeping system and keeps accurate count of every instance of the desired "target behavior." It is important that record keeping be maintained, so that small, steady behavioral changes are readily noted. The responses being recorded must be obvious and measurable.

Since positive reinforcement is needed to increase the desired behavior, potential reinforcers are then analyzed. Each person is unique, so each must select a reinforcer that is strong and accessible in his or her own life and that can be readily controlled.

All of this paves the way for a highly personalized contract with the self. The individual develops an *intervention plan* that schedules specific reinforcements for the performance of the desired behavior, preferably in small steps, with the criterion for reinforcement very gradually becoming more stringent. The plan also takes into account, and attempts to control, the *antecedents*, or cues, that relate to the target behavior.

Finally, the plan is implemented, with record keeping used to show changes in comparison with the baseline data. It is terminated when the individual no longer needs it. Watson and Tharp (1972, p. 208) point out to their readers that:

> We do not advocate formal self-modification as a life-style. Rather, we urge the contrary; we see formal reinforcement contracts as a temporary expedient, a device to use when you are trapped in a behavioral-environmental bind that requires particular planning to break. Therefore, the fact that self-controlled reinforcement is no longer necessary means that you have really succeeded—succeeded in achieving an adjustment so that you and the environment are mutually supporting a pattern that you endorse.

Foster (1974) developed another self-teaching guidebook, arranged according to behavioral principles, with the reader answering specific questions after each section of the text and gaining immediate feedback by comparing answers with those of the author. The text discusses the methods for changing behavior, for measuring behavior change, and for maintaining behavior change, with each section being followed by a self-test. As Foster points out (p. 129), "Through self-control one can truly achieve freedom."

Natural reinforcers eventually replace intervention plans, so that charts and graphs are no longer needed or desirable. The behavioral knowledge involved, however, is now part of the individual's repertoire, giving him or her the more permanent feeling that life is, indeed, controllable.

That sense of power over the self and the immediate environment can be accessible to all. Although much work has been done with college students (Menke, 1973; Watson & Tharp, 1972), academic sophistication does not seem to be a necessary factor. Ivey (1973) has developed methods for helping hospitalized psychiatric patients to change self-selected, observable behaviors. Goshko (1973) helped elementary school children to develop strategies for changing, improving, or adding new behaviors and used videotape to help in the selection of target behaviors and the evaluation of success.

Self-modification, then, is a tool to be considered, regardless of the population with which the community counselor works. Workshops and self-directed learning programs can aim toward the development of behaviors that are desired by a number of individuals or can allow for complete individualization, with each participant working on a different set of behaviors.

Stress Management

Preventive stress management programs also work to develop skills that participants can use throughout their lives. Stress is, of course, a part of life. Either external or internal pressures can place demands on people, causing their bodies to respond. Stress management education teaches people how to adapt appropriately to stressful situations, or even how to control the degree of stress in their lives.

The content of stress management information usually focuses on two major factors: techniques for minimizing life stressors and methods of coping with stress when it does occur.

In workshop situations, participants may be taught to examine their life-styles for examples of continuing stressors that could be avoided, including these issues.

- How to cut down on activities that they tend to find stressful.
- How to reduce noise in their environments.
- How to plan their time to allow for relaxation.
- How to build recreational activities into their lives.
- How to develop assertiveness in resisting pressures from other people.
- How to reduce the pressures they unnecessarily place on themselves.
- How to give priorities to the issues and activities that are important to them.
- How to recognize the signs that they are becoming overstressed.

The concept of stress management also recognizes that the environment is not always controllable. When individuals cannot cut down on stressors affecting them, they can learn to handle their own physiological stress through such methods as biofeedback, relaxation training, self-hypnosis, or meditation. Training is sometimes included in educational sessions devoted to the whole concept of stress management. Just as often, agencies offer training sessions devoted specifically to just one of the relaxation-oriented skills.

Biofeedback training teaches individuals to control various aspects of their physiological functioning through interaction with instruments that provide immediate information, or feedback, about functions that are not as involuntary as expected. Clients learn to bring stress-related physical symptoms under control and also to reach states of calm through their own efforts.

> EMG feedback, which can teach a person to relax muscle tension; GSR feedback, which can teach a person to relax autonomic nervous system arousal; temperature feedback, which can teach a person to relax vascular tension; and EEG feedback, which can teach a person to produce alpha waves associated with mental relaxation—all lead towards physiological states which are incompatible with anxiety (Sarnoff, 1982, p. 358).

As Romano (1982) points out, biofeedback can demonstrate the close connection between mind and body, expand physiological awareness, facilitate self-regulation and self-control, and encourage self-responsibility.

Similarly, *relaxation training* can also assist the individual's efforts to maintain control over physical tension. Clients can learn to use directed mental imagery, though which they develop the ability to relax by picturing scenes or states that are associated with a lack of tension. Just as useful are muscle relaxation methods, which help people to take note of the differences between tense and relaxed muscles. "By systematically moving through major muscle groups of the body, individuals become proficient at recognizing tension and then allowing the tension to drain out of the muscles" (Murphy, 1982, p. 24). Once this skill has been learned, an individual can use it independently as a method of controlling stress levels. Although there are literally hundreds of techniques available for use in relaxation, "all have the same basic objectives of teaching the individuals to relax the muscles at will. . . . If one is able to distinguish between tension and relaxation, control over tension follows almost effortlessly" (Girdano & Everly, 1979, p. 202).

Achieving a relaxed state can be a first step in the utilization of *self-hypnosis*. The major factor that distinguishes between relaxation and hypnosis is the use of suggestions, with the subject imagining that what is being "suggested" is actually happening.

Doing hypnosis successfully requires the subject to shift into a literally extraordinary frame of mind. While ordinarily we direct our mental processes toward coping with the outer world as we reconstruct or define it within our self-interactions, in hypnosis you shift your attention away from the objective universe, to focus instead upon the imaginary universes you construct internally. You literally forget about the "real world" and concentrate upon the ever-shifting inner reality you are creating for yourself as you think, feel, and imagine along with the suggestions (Straus, 1982, p. 51).

The suggestions utilized can deal with changing behaviors, with adjusting attitudes and perceptions, or with managing stress. "A very important set of self-suggestions are those for absolute calmness and total mental-physical relaxation. These kinds of deep-relaxation suggestions, which are typically given subvocally to oneself while alone, with eyes closed, are especially helpful for relieving stress and tension and for alleviating psychosomatic ailments" (Barber, 1982, p. v). While counselors are, of course, familiar with the idea of using hypnosis to help clients bring about changes in their lives, they should consider the extra benefits to be derived through training in self-hypnosis. Individuals can learn both to deal with specific problems in their lives and to perceive the degree to which they alone can control their own well-being.

Individuals can also deal effectively with stress through *meditation*, which produces a state of consciousness that can best be described as peaceful.

According to the teachings of Buddha, the source of man's problems is his extreme attachment to his senses, his thoughts, and his imagination. Peace can be attained only when he frees himself from these attachments, directing his awareness inward, transcending the incessant bombardment of the consciousness so as to experience a quiet body, a subtle mind, and a unified spirit (Girdano & Everly, 1979, p. 168).

Individuals can learn to free the mind and body of turmoil by using any one of several measures that aid concentration. Some techniques use visual imagery or attention to breathing. A number of approaches, including the popular "transcendental meditation," use verbal or mental repetition of a word or sound to induce the desired state of consciousness. Benson's "relaxation response" (1975), also a form of meditation, uses the word *one* as a sound to be repeated while entering a tension-free state. Regardless of the method used, clients can control their abilities to withstand stress by attaining purposeful control over their physical and psychological responses.

Life Planning and Decision Making

Counselors in all settings are likely to deal with a number of individuals grappling with the need to make decisions concerning their personal or vocational plans. Although these kinds of issues can be resolved effectively through individual counseling, they also lend themselves to community education formats such as workshops or simulations.

Workshops   A number of workshop approaches to career decision making and life planning have been developed over the years. Hansen and Borow (1973, p. 216) cite the Vocational Exploration Group, developed by Daane, who piloted the approach with participants drawn from public employment service applicants and other governmental agencies. The group focuses on job functions, job demands, and job satisfactions, and helps individuals to examine the world of work, to share occupational information, and to focus on specific plans.

The Life Planning Workshop, as described by Drum and Figler (1973, p. 157), also takes a group approach. Participants perform a structured series of activities, all aimed to clarify the individual's general life goals, values, and desires. Exercises include the identification of real and ideal roles; the creation of one's own future, through descriptions of typical and special days as yet unexperienced; the completion of life inventories to focus on strengths and on areas in which change is sought; and goal setting, when each individual identifies behaviors to be adopted in the immediate future.

A similarly structured workshop is Life Work Planning (Kirn & Kirn, 1979), which can be used with or without a leader for any number of small groups working simultaneously. Groups use a number of exercises, all described in detail in their workbooks, to examine their current life work situations, their insights about past experiences, their values, their preferences, and their personalities. Participants are encouraged to fantasize about ideal futures, as well as to make practical assessments about the constraints that are significant in their lives. On the basis of the self-awareness brought about by the exercises, individuals attempt to make specific plans while developing skills in program planning, decision making, force field analysis, and idea building. Ideally, each participant emerges from the experience with some kind of concrete plan for immediate action. More important, however, is the fact that life planning skills that can be used when needed become part of each individual's repertoire.

In each of the models discussed above, individuals deal directly with the problems or decisions that they, themselves, are facing. Other techniques offer the opportunity to practice problem solving in simulated situations.

Simulations In simulations, individuals try out and evaluate new behaviors in response to hypothetical situations. The "Life Career Game," for instance, provides an example of the chance to obtain practice in making decisions and examining their consequences.

> Students who play the game are able to span eight to ten years in the future as the decision-maker of a fictitious person presented to them in the form of a profile, that is, a written case history. Students play in teams, working with the same profile person, attempting to plan the most satisfying life for that person over the eight-year period. Teams plan this life by making decisions as to how the person will allocate a certain amount of time (84 hours) to doing different activities during a typical week for each of the eight years. Players are then fed back the consequences of these decisions in the form of scores or game points which are indications of the relative satisfaction of the life being planned (Varenhorst, 1973, p. 308).

Through this procedure, individuals become involved in decision making and receive the kind of immediate reinforcement that enhances the learning of a complex skill. At the same time, questions of their own values and life goals rise to the surface to be examined.

Another type of simulation, described by Krumboltz and Sheppard (1969), allows young people to become familiar with the kinds of problems normally faced by workers in particular occupations. The individual can choose from a number of self-contained kits. Each kit briefly describes the activities performed by members of a given occupation, provides necessary background information, and then presents a problem to be solved. People completing a kit receive immediate feedback concerning the solutions they have selected, and they often are stimulated to seek more information and to examine their own reactions in greater depth.

Although each of these models differs in approach, each attempts to provide a means for attaining skills. When they are internalized, those skills become lasting resources, always on hand for individuals who are learning to live their lives independently.

2 Programs Are Effective When Learning Spreads from Person to Person in the Community

In any attempt to have real impact on the community, it is important to devise programs that have long-lasting, developmental effects on participants. It is just as important to develop strategies that have a "radiating effect," with learning being transferred from the initial participants to their families, friends, and neighbors. Programs that allow for this kind of learning can reach larger numbers of people than could ever be reached by professionals alone. At the same time, community members have the chance to take responsibility for their own learning and growth and that, in itself, is beneficial. A community counselor can touch the lives of many individuals by training a small number of people who can in turn act as leaders in the attempt to spread their new learning to others within the community. This kind of program can be most effective in helping people to deal with practical problems of everyday living. A small number of community members, armed with some basic, practical information and with minimal training in leadership skills, can make a great difference in their own locality.

An example of this kind of process is provided by the growth of "parent study groups." As early as 1959, a number of parent study groups had been established in conjunction with Child Guidance Centers in Chicago, Iowa, New York, Los Angeles, and Oregon (Reed, 1959). Since that time, groups of parents sharing their knowledge and ideas about child rearing have sprung up in virtually every state, with "experts" providing only the initial impetus, materials, and study guides. Often, a professional leads one parent study group, training that group of parents as leaders who can then convene new groups and conduct them with a minimum of supervision.

Some groups use the text *Raising a Responsible Child: Practical Steps to Successful Family Relationships* (Dinkmeyer & McKay, 1973), with each parent reading the material as an adjunct to the group experience. A study guide, usable by laypersons, outlines suggested procedures and presents topics to be covered in each of ten sessions. Parents use these sessions to examine a number of concepts, including the goals of behavior and misbehavior, the purposes of emotions, the processes of communication and encouragement, the role of natural and logical consequences for given behaviors, the family meeting, and effective problem solving in the family.

For some years, many groups have used another book, *Children the Challenge* (Dreikurs & Soltz, 1964). The accompanying leader's guide for this text (Soltz, 1967) also provides step-by-step procedures and study outlines, and additionally presents a fund of information concerning effective leadership techniques.

The structured parent study group is a growing phenomenon but, like other models, is subject to adaptation. The notion of parent-led groups can be adapted to fit the needs of parents who prefer an experiential group without accompanying written material.

The spreading effect, which is exemplified by parent study groups, is present whenever a group of community members learns something worth sharing with neighbors and friends and evolves a method for sharing it. This method is appropriate for the development of "parenting" skills because the subject matter involves basic psychological knowledge, which can be easily taught, along with an emphasis on the knowledge that parents, themselves, can gain through experience. Discussion groups include room for the sharing of both kinds of information. Other subject matter areas, which lend themselves to this kind of programming, include those that are:

1 *Intrinsically important and interesting to people, having practical significance for everyday life.*
2 *Capable of being discussed in terms of practical, concrete facts.*
3 *Capable of being discussed in terms of people's own experiences, so that all participants have something to share.*

Some examples of the kinds of subject areas that meet these criteria might include consumer issues, basic nutrition, information concerning legal rights, or preventive health care. All of these meet everyday concerns of community members, allow for the transfer of concrete knowledge, and lend themselves to discussion based on practical experience. It would be possible, for instance, for a small group of community members to learn a set of basic facts concerning family nutritional needs through a combination of programmed instruction and consultation with experts representing several areas of knowledge. This group could then share their information with other community members, who could learn the basic facts and add to them on the basis of their own experiences. People who had been group members could go on to become leaders of new groups in their own neighborhoods. This approach is much more efficient than a traditional approach, which would require "experts" to spend many hours presenting the same material to a number of groups. At the same time, the radiating approach allows community members to take responsibility for their own learning and to help and encourage one another.

3 Programs Are Effective When They Are Responsive to Needs Expressed by the Community

The community counselor can often provide leadership by developing innovative programs, publicizing them effectively, and then relying on the dynamics of supply and demand to determine the staying power and growth of services that meet real community needs. In these instances, the development of programs *precedes* community awareness that specific services are needed.

Just as frequently, however, the need for particular services is firmly and consciously felt by community members. Those feelings can be translated into action when formal surveys aimed at assessing community needs are conducted, and also when community members are actively involved in all aspects of program planning. They can be translated into action when the voice of the community is clearly heard and heeded. Programs can only be effective when they are used, and they are most likely to be used when they respond to community expressions of need and desire.

One dynamic example of responsiveness can be found in the rapid growth of services directed specifically toward women. Women of all ages have greeted these programs enthusiastically and used them in great numbers, primarily because they, themselves, demanded them.

Women's Centers

Thousands of community-based women's centers have appeared within the last 10 years. Some of these centers are aimed specifically toward helping mature women to focus on their own identity and values, some on initiating specific vocational planning, and some on a combination of the two. Options for Women (1972), for instance, was created in Philadelphia to help a heterogeneous group of women take the following actions.

1 Define and clarify their personal goals.

2 *Explore the options available, including employment, education, volunteer work, and independent undertakings.*

3 *Confront the issues involved in choosing an option.*

4 *Discover new directions.*

5 *Plan to utilize their talents.*

6 *Find and create new and flexible opportunities, particularly in the job market.*

Most such centers, whether private or connected with educational institutions, combine individual and group work. Some emphasize the vocational aspects of women's development, and some the personal aspects. Some are professionally run, and some are organized strictly by volunteers. Some have sliding scales for payment of fees, and some are free. Regardless of their differences, most have in common the fact that they are being used to their capacity.

Growing just as quickly are self-help centers that concentrate on increasing women's knowledge and awareness of their bodies and related issues. Self-Help Clinic One, for instance, was among the first of many to embark on a physical and psychological consciousness-raising effort, providing a setting for women to talk about birth control, abortion, sexuality, women's unique physical health problems, and psychological myths. Although this self-help clinic originated in California, such clinics now exist in most major cities.

Another innovation that has made it possible to reach thousands is the self-teaching course, *Our Bodies, Our Selves*, created by the Boston Women's Health Course Collective (1971). Used independently or as background material for groups, the book combines solid information with the sharing of thoughts and feelings by women for other women.

The unique needs of women are also being met through the widespread adaptation of assertiveness training to be used with groups of women. This kind of training is used to help people learn to stand up for their own rights in interpersonal relationships and to express their feelings directly and appropriately without impinging on the rights of others. Training can include discussion of the issues involved in assertive responses, observing models of assertion, and rehearsing assertive behavior that can then be implemented in the individual's own life. Assertion training is being utilized extensively with women, simply because so many women have problems in this area. Sometimes assertion training is combined with peer counseling so that women learn not only to behave more assertively when they wish to, but to help others work through the same kinds of issues.

In many ways, the services that women are providing for other women illustrate a human services viewpoint. Professionals and nonprofessionals are equally involved. Stress is placed not on the perceived role distinctions among service givers, but on the needs and demands of the community. The result has been the beginning steps toward integrated, holistic services that could well be duplicated with other populations.

Many women's centers have been created by women who saw the need for more responsive services and who did not feel that they could be provided by traditional agencies or institutions. Other groups have also seen the need to develop new, alternative human service agencies.

Alternative Agencies

In more and more localities, community members have begun to create human service agencies in accordance with their own values and goals. These alternative agencies are actually owned by community members and are characterized by democratic decision-making processes, by flexible approaches to service giving, and by active participation of many people in all aspects of planning and implementation. Often such agencies are developed by specific populations wishing to meet their own needs. Just as women have created their own agencies, so have homosexuals, young people, senior citizens, minority groups, and other populations. These alternative agencies often come into being because of a perception that traditional social services are too distant from the people or lack full understanding of the group being served. They are created for the purpose of making programs totally responsive to the people being served.

These agencies, which have responsiveness as their reason for being, seldom make the error of limiting their services to the remediation of individual problems. A central purpose of alternative agencies is to help people gain control over their own lives, and this requires the development of knowledge, awareness, and practical skills. When community members plan their own programs, they tend to include educational experiences that are available to all. When they create their own alternatives, they find the resources needed to teach them what they need to know in order to maintain their independence.

Alternative agencies, which by definition respond to the needs identified by the people being served, provide programs that can help consumers to develop the skills they need, whether those skills include forming helping relationships with one another, solving practical problems of everyday living, or learning to appreciate the strengths of themselves and their group.

4 Programs Are Effective When They Use a Holistic Approach to the Enhancement of Wellness

A holistic approach to helping means that community counselors take into account physiological, environmental, and psychological factors affecting clients' well-being.

The advantages of a holistic program are numerous for both clients and counselors. Some of these advantages include the following:

1 It teaches clients a total sense of personal responsibility.
2 Its effects are immediate and create a better sense of well-being.
3 Wellness rather than the absence of symptoms is the main goal of therapy.
4 All modalities of healing are used.
5 The client's inner capacity for change has a distinct and clear direction to better health and well-being.
6 Clients can continue patterns that are healthy and significantly decrease problem reoccurence.
7 Self-discipline is learned and appreciated.
8 Disease prevention is enhanced for clients.
9 Counselors can benefit from all these aspects and be a significant model for clients (Martin & Martin, 1982, p. 22).

In a holistic approach to wellness, clients are encouraged to take personal responsibility for their physical and mental health, with the ideal outcome being "high-level wellness" (Ardell, 1977), rather than just the absence of negative symptoms. The key element in this conceptualizaton is the need for the individual to take control over his or her well-being. Individual behaviors affect the development of physical and mental health, and the term "behavioral health" is also descriptive of the approach.

Behavioral health is an interdisciplinary field dedicated to promoting a philosophy of health that stresses *individual responsibility* in the application of behavioral and biomedical science knowledge and techniques to the *maintenance* of health and the *prevention* of illness and dysfunction by a variety of self-initiated individual or shared activities (Matarazzo, 1980, p. 813).

Thus, community education programs related to wellness teach individuals to deal with a number of components of their well-being, including (Carlson, 1979) *physical fitness, nutritional awareness, environmental awareness, stress recognition and management,* and *social skill.* Educational interventions are designed both to help raise the consciousness of community members about health issues and to train them in the specific knowledge and skills needed to enhance wellness.

An example of such an approach is provided by the "Strategies for Wellness" program offered by The Wellness Center of Olympia Fields Osteopathic Medical Center, in Olympia Fields, Illinois. The introductory lecture series, "Welcome to Wellness," introduces participants to the nutritional, emotional, and physical components of health, and includes the following topics.

1   *"What is Wellness, and How Well are You?"*
2   *"Fitness I: Physical Fitness & Exercise–Awareness of Your Current State of Fitness"*
3   *"Nutrition I: The Prudent Diet and Personal Goals for Nutrition"*
4   *"Lifestyle I: Stress—Its Causes and Effects"*
5   *"Fitness II: Awareness of Tension & Relaxation"*
6   *"Nutrition II: Weight Control and Rating Your Diet"*
7   *"Lifestyle II: The Importance of Leisure"*

In addition to this general introduction, the Wellness Center offers "Working on Wellness," for individuals attempting to make health-related changes in their life-styles. Courses include aerobic dance, fitness series, weight reduction clinics, and "I Quit" smoking class.

Depending on the particular setting in which services are being provided, wellness programs may be full-scale offerings or enhancements to other educational interventions. As a concept, wellness relates closely to the community counseling approach because of its emphasis on self-responsibility, interdisciplinary efforts, and holistic thinking.

5 Programs Are Effective When They Are Designed to Reach Large Numbers of Community Members

Each of the programs discussed here has the potential to reach a significant number of people within a given community. That goal can be achieved by identifying subject matter that is relevant to developing personal resources and by organizing material so that it is accessible to many community members. Whether individuals want to learn about vocational decision making, parenting, body awareness, or assertiveness, effectiveness depends on the way the material is presented. The methods that seem to hold the most promise for efficiency include use of structured groups, training programs for individuals who can then train others, self-directed learning programs, and the media. Each of the examples we have included in these pages uses at least one of those techniques, and some combine two or more. What is important is that much of what has traditionally been handled in one-to-one professional settings could be adapted to reach large populations that have never before been touched. Community counselors can spend a small amount of time reaching a large number of people if they adapt their programs so that the most sensible method of providing information or building skills is used.

If a particular skill can be learned independently, and if many people would be likely to have an interest in it, the development of a self-instructional package or use of a computerized program makes sense. If group interaction is likely to be helpful, programming for large-group sessions or radiating groups would be most effective. If the desire is to reach a communitywide population, advertising media can be useful.

Effective programs stress *independence* (as in the use of self-instructional methods) or *interdependence* (when learning groups allow participants to use one another's resources—to depend on one another, instead of depending solely on the help of one specified leader). In each instance, the community or one of its members is freed from the bondage of *dependence* and is allowed to use the human potential that has always been there, waiting to be tapped.

6 Programs Are Effective When They Provide Skill Training for Natural Caregivers in the Community

Just as community counselors can provide experiences to enrich the personal resources of *individuals*, they can also create programs that release the helping elements present within the *community*. Educative experiences help to increase people's independence by allowing them to develop knowledge and skills that can serve them in their own lives. The community as a whole also needs knowledge and skills, as well as new methods for bringing to the surface the powerful reserves already in existence.

If community counselors can develop programs that encourage their communities to draw on their own resources for helping, the end result can mean that the personal needs of individuals are met through their natural, everyday associations, without reliance on the leadership of mental health professionals. It can also mean that the community, viewed collectively, develops an independent, self-directed life of its own.

Programs that help individuals to develop their *personal* resources can be paralleled by programs that encourage whole communities to develop their *helping* resources. The major thrust of such programs must be in the direction of ensuring that human needs are met within the community by community members. When that happens, dependence on professional assistance becomes less and less necessary.

Brammer (1979, p. vi) points out that:

> Our basic problem is how to bring the existing vast resources for helping to bear on the equally vast human problems plaguing our society. We cannot depend solely upon helping specialists and human relations experts to close this large gap. A helping commitment must be encouraged and helping skills be widely dispersed in the population until human satisfactions and better social organization make formal helping, as we know it, unnecessary.

It is possible for helping skills to be "widely dispersed in the population." Through workshops and brief training programs, community counselors can share the attitudes, the techniques, and the competencies that form the basis of one-to-one helping processes. If many community members obtain the needed skills, "helping" can become a part of community life. When individuals need personal assistance, they know that it can be forthcoming without formal application or needless waiting.

Training community members in the development of helping skills must be seen as a high-priority task, since it can make a real difference in the life of the community. Those who receive help are affected, of course, but so are those who never have the need to request aid from their neighbors. The community itself can become a different kind of place.

Help Can Be Easily Accessible   There have never been enough professionals to go around. Because helping resources have always been severely limited, people have assumed that participation in a counseling process should be limited to those experiencing severe discomfort in their lives. In fact, many people can benefit from the opportunity to enter into a "counseling"-type relationship through which they can examine their own thoughts and feelings and make decisions concerning immediate issues and problems in everyday living. Through such relationships, people can learn to set goals in accordance with their own values and to plan for the development of behaviors that can help them to meet those goals.

If helping resources are immediately available, more people are likely to enter into such relationships and gain the benefits that they can offer. This is likely to occur when many community members become trained helpers, both because the actual number of available helpers is increased and because the gap between the person giving help and the one receiving it is narrowed. Instead of going to a professional and specialized "expert," a community member can request assistance from a trusted associate. Through all of this, scarce helping resources become plentiful.

The Community Can Become More Independent   Historically, the helping process has always been a part of community life, with neighbors turning to neighbors in times of stress. In the twentieth century, urbanization has brought with it increased specialization, so that "counseling" came to be seen as the realm of professional experts. As more community members receive skill training, the helping function can return to the community, where it has, in fact, always belonged. If this trend becomes widespread, communities can become more independent, with citizens recognizing that they can take responsibility for themselves and for one another. The skills needed for the development of helping relationships are not totally different than those needed for effective interpersonal living. There is nothing so mystical about the helping process that makes it necessary to remove this function from the hands of the people.

Those Who Learn to Be Helpers Benefit from the Experience   It is important that people who desire personal help be able to find it within their community. It is just as important that community members know that they have it within their power to help others. Receiving help is beneficial; giving help may be even more growth producing.

Skovholt (1974), describing the "helper therapy" principle, points out that those who have the opportunity to give assistance to others gain as many benefits as the people they seek to help.

> The benefits one receives from helping can be summarized here: (1) The effective helper often feels an increased level of interpersonal competence as a result of making an impact on another's life, (2) The effective helper often feels a sense of equality in giving and taking between himself or herself and others, (3) The effective helper is often the recipient of valuable personalized learning acquired while working with a helpee, and (4) The effective helper often receives social approval from the people he or she helps (Skovholt, 1974, p. 62).

As more people within a community gain competency, and as they develop a real sense of that competency, the helping resources of the community as a whole are strengthened. Those resources have always been there. The community counselor can bring them closer to the surface.

The greater the accessibility of training, the more chance there is to create a climate of effective personal interaction. Accessibility means getting the skills to the people so that they can begin to use them. To implement these programs, community counselors need to identify the groups of community members that are most easily reached and that might have the greatest potential for putting skills into practice.

In many communities, *open workshops or training programs* in basic helping skills can be implemented. Instead of choosing a specific population for training, the community counselor can provide training opportunities for any individuals or groups sensing a need for or an interest in developing helping skills.

There are many such people: individuals to whom others seem to be drawn when in need of personal help, figures whose jobs or places in the community give them opportunities to help or harm others, and persons who simply want to relate more effectively to others around them.

These people are often enthusiastic about the opportunity for short-term training. An open training program can reach large numbers through its repetition, with a series of short-term courses or workshops being offered for rotating groups. This sharing of skills with anyone who wants them awaits only the trainer's ability to eliminate the assumption that helping is the professional's territory. It is useful to remember that people relate to others anyway; we can only influence their effectiveness in doing it.

Although everyone may relate to others, some individuals—because of their roles or work settings—are placed in potentially helpful situations more often than others. The community counselor might wish to identify groups of those people and create programs designed specifically for their needs.

Training for role-based helping can be provided for people who come into direct contact with many people in the course of their normal workdays. Role-based helpers are required to deal with people, yet their interactions can be either facilitative or harmful. People such as police officers, members of the health professions, workers dealing with children or youth, and employees of governmental agencies come quickly to mind. There are others, however. Family practice lawyers (Doane & Cowen, 1981), hairdressers (Cowen, Gesten, Borke, Norton, Wilson, & DeStefano, 1979), community service volunteers (Frisch & Gerrard, 1981), and bartenders (Cowen, McKim, & Weissberg, 1981) might not think of themselves as helpers or counselors, but they can, with consultation and training, learn to be resources for help and care in their communities.

COMMUNITY EDUCATION IN ACTION: THE HUMAN SERVICE CENTER OF THE PEORIA AREA

The community-based approach just outlined is built on the assumption that community members can learn the skills and attitudes they need to help themselves and one another. This life competency approach is becoming a major strategy of preventive efforts in mental health. Comprehensive community mental health centers are mandated to include consultation and education as part of their service delivery system. At the Human Service Center of the Peoria Area, Inc., the consultation and education program maintains an effective prevention thrust under the directorship of Dr. Bree Hayes.

The Consultation and Education Program is oriented toward sharing mental health-related skills with the community at large. As their public relations brochure makes clear:[1]

"The mental health professionals at the Human Service Center are people who not only care for others, but care about others. A part of this caring is

---

[1]Excerpted from Consultation and Education brochure of Human Service Center of the Peoria Area, Inc. Reprinted with permission.

sharing. A willingness to share knowledge and expertise with others, and the belief that this is an effective way to reduce the incidence of life crises is why a primary prevention program has been established at the Human Service Center."

The Consultation and Education program provides direct educational programs to organizations and to the community at large. Some of the addressed topics have included:

Activity Therapy
Alcoholism and Addiction
Adolescent Adjustment within the Family
Adolescent Drug Abuse
Assertiveness Training
Biofeedback
Child Abuse
Children of Divorce
Child Psychology
Communication Skills
Crisis Intervention Training
Defining Structures within the Family
Depression
Depression and Women
Developmental Phases of Children
Divorce
Drug Abuse and the American Culture
Drug Abuse Education
Elderly: Problems After 65
Expressing Anger Constructively
Families and Family Therapy
Family Coping with Chronic Illness
Group Therapy: Reasons and Practice
Growing Old Gracefully
How's Your Family?
Jogging for Better Mental Health
Leisure Awareness
Leisure Counseling
Leisure Education
Marijuana
Marital Discord or Compatibility
Marital Therapy
On the Road to Good Mental Health
Psychodrama
Psychopathology
Resolving Family Conflicts
Self-Enhancement Training

Sex Education
Sibling Rivalry
Staff Morale
Stress Management
Suicide
Teens: Coping with Sexuality
The Art of Parenting
The Changing Role of Women
The Family
Why Children Fail in School

Perhaps one of the greatest strengths of the "C. and E." program is that these educational programs are designed to meet real community needs. Staff members are closely involved with their community. They conduct continuous needs assessments—both formal and informal—in order to determine what kinds of life skills and competencies are important to community members. They are willing to offer, at least on a trial basis, any kind of mental health-related workshop that is requested, and most of these sessions are provided in the places where people live and work.

The C. and E. program also identifies pressing issues by monitoring the kinds of problems being presented most frequently to clinicians in the Center's outpatient programs and by maintaining a sensitive awareness of community trends and events. Thus, when a rash of layoffs and plant closings forced many Peoria residents into unemployment, the program began to offer well-attended workshops on stress and joblessness. When a number of cases of child abuse or neglect appeared at the clinicians' doorsteps, a popular workshop on "parent burnout" was originated. When counselors reported dealing with a number of troubled families, programs on family conflict provided preventive outreach.

The C. and E. department does not limit itself to "one-shot" educational programs. The staff places just as much emphasis on the long-term relationships that help to enhance the effectiveness of natural care givers in the community. Ongoing consulting services include, for instance, a contract that provides for training sessions and workshops for parents of children with handicaps. Still another effort on which the Center has embarked involves a preventive approach for dealing with substance abuse in a local housing project. The program, which is targeted at adolescents, will utilize a number of change agents, including parents, young people, and community leaders, as well as consultants. While the C. and E. program can offer such services as education about drugs, workshops in alternative stress management techniques, assertiveness training, peer counseling training, and instruction in decision making—all of which might be useful in preventing substance abuse—the focus of the program is on reaching goals set by community members. In such ongoing programs, consultants begin by meeting with local leaders and help in the development of a core committee to plan and manage interventions. The focus remains on helping community members to help themselves and one another.

Finally, the Consultation and Education program provides a valuable link between the center's service components and the community. Stress is placed on educational outreach as a public relations function, and the C. and E. department likes to "let the community know what they have." Through posters on buses, the media, speeches to clubs, and other kinds of contacts, the Human Service Center sends a continuing message to the community. This information lets people know what services are available. At the same time, it serves to raise the consciousness of the community about mental health, about the quality of community life, and about the fact that problems are preventable.

SUMMARY

The purpose of community education programs is to train community members in the life skills that they can use to maintain good mental health. This approach strengthens individual and community competencies, while preventing stress-related dysfunctions.

In general, community education programs are most effective if they help participants to develop skills that they can use over the life span, allow learning to spread from person to person in the community, respond to needs expressed by consumers, use a holistic approach to the enhancement of wellness, reach large numbers of community members, and provide skill training for natural caregivers. Such programs all try to educate community members in the skills and attitudes that they need to help themselves and one another. The Human Service Center of the Peoria Area, through its Consultation and Education program, exemplifies this preventive thrust.

ACTIVITIES TO ENHANCE UNDERSTANDING OF CHAPTER 2

1 Community counselors must frequently develop and implement workshops for community members. They can do this most effectively if they use regular, step-by-step planning procedures. Think of a particular topic and audience you would like to address, and develop a workshop plan by following these steps.

   a. *State the specific objectives of the workshop. (How do you want partici-pants to be different after the workshop than they were before? What new skills, attitudes, or knowledge are you trying to create? Be as specific as possible in specifying the desired outcome.)*

   b. *Select the kinds of activities that are most likely to meet your objective. (Remember that methods can involve minilectures, panel discussions, case conferences, media, gaming, role playing, discussions, simulations, or any of a variety of other approaches. Which are most likely to bring about the desired outcome?)*

   c. *Consider the resources that would be available, including the nature of your own skills.*

   d. *Consider the audience you are addressing. What do you need to do to ensure their active involvement and interest?*

   e. *Taking into account your analysis of the foregoing factors, develop a detailed design for the workshop, including the time and materials needed for each activity.*

   f. *Design an evaluation method. How will you determine whether the workshop's objectives have been met?*

2 After reading Chapter One, you developed in broad outline a commu-nity counseling program to meet the needs of a particular type of population. Now, consider in detail the kinds of community educa-tion programs that might be appropriate for this target group. What specific outreach activities might help to build needed competencies?

CHAPTER
3
COMMUNITY
ORGANIZATION

Community counselors are aware that human beings constantly interact with their surroundings. Because of this, counselors seek to affect the community as a total environment. Their goal is the creation of a community in which all people are allowed—and, in fact, encouraged—to grow and develop in their own unique ways.

One approach that such programs can take is the development of "community-based planning." Community counselors become involved in efforts to include a wide range of community members in the planning for services or facilities that are meant to serve them. They try to ensure that all attempts to solve community problems or to improve the services offered revolve around the needs of the community as the citizens see them.

This approach assumes that there can be some commonality of purpose among all segments of the community. At times, however, counselors must move to protect the rights of those segments of the community that lack the power to govern their own lives or to obtain an equitable share in the community's resources. Community counselors, in partnership with other individuals and groups, participate fully in community action for change.

COMMUNITY-BASED PLANNING

Community counselors, in their attempt to define and deliver the services most important to consumers, become involved in the process of *social planning*. Effective planning involves assessing the needs of the community, setting priorities, identifying available resources, and developing facilities or programs to meet the needs that have been identified. Social planning is used both to solve problems that have become apparent in the community and to create services meant to improve the quality of life for community members.

Traditionally, social planning has been left in the hands of small groups of people—either governmental leaders, who have the power to control the ways in which resources are used, or social scientists, who have the technical expertise needed to collect and analyze information.

It is becoming apparent, however, that planning can be much more effective if many community members are involved in the process. Planning that is "community-based" can be more effective because:

1 *The goals that are developed represent the desires of community members* as they see them.

2 *Greater human resources are available to carry out necessary tasks because more people are really committed to the projects or programs being developed.*

3 *Programs are more flexible because planners are sensitive to the changing needs and wishes of the community.*

4 *Planning is more creative because new ideas and new leaders are constantly emerging.*

5 *Resources are used more efficiently because none are wasted on facilities that have little appeal to the community members who will be using them.*

6 *While immediate problems are being solved, the community as a whole is developing expertise that can be used to solve future problems, or even to prevent them.*

When planning is community-based, attention is paid both to the *tasks* that must be performed and to the *process* through which problems are solved.

Task goals entail the completion of a concrete task or the solution of a delimited problem pertaining to the functioning of a community social system—delivery of services, establishment of new services, passing of specific social legislation. Process goals or maintenance goals are more oriented to system maintenance and capacity, with aims such as establishing cooperative working relationships among groups in the community, creating self-maintaining community problem-solving structures, improving the power base of the community, stimulating wide interest and participation in community affairs, fostering collaborative attitudes and practices, and increasing indigenous leadership (Rothman, 1974, p. 27).

It is unrealistic to try to separate task and process, or to make distinctions between community planning and community development. Community members will only seek involvement in community affairs and attempt to maintain cooperative working relationships when they are participating in concrete tasks that might make some differences in their own lives. The tasks involved in effective planning can only be performed when community members are using their energy to work together. In community-based planning, the task and the process come together as community members attempt to create the kinds of services that they know are needed.

Characteristics of Community-based Planning

In traditional social planning processes, community members and human service workers are often given the opportunity to have input into the decision-making process. Planning that is truly community based goes beyond this. Community members and agency workers are planners and decision makers themselves. The ways in which planning is carried out are distinctive, and differ in a number of ways from traditional processes.

1 The People Who Deliver and Use Services Are Active in Planning and Evaluating Programs

In a traditional approach, services are planned and then workers are hired to perform specified roles in service delivery. In community-based planning, the creation and evaluation of new services is an ongoing process. Workers *at all levels* within agencies attempt to recognize community needs and to create or change programs to meet those needs. Planning is a fluid process, with no clear beginning and no end. Often, when workers and community members recognize the need for a particular kind of program, they create "spin-off" agencies, using existing skills and resources in new programs or new locations.

Ongoing assessment of services, with consumers very actively involved, works most effectively when agencies are small and belong to the neighborhoods in which they are placed. But small, localized agencies lack the power and the resources to have impact on communitywide planning. For this reason, other mechanisms are needed.

2 Agencies Work Together in Cooperative Helping Networks

When agencies are small, workers and community members can feel a sense of ownership, a sense that the agency belongs to them. There is ample opportunity for participation in planning the programs offered *by the specific agency*.

Yet, in every community, there must be some kind of centralized planning. Resources are limited, and they must be allocated in terms of priorities. These small, localized agencies can only play a part in the planning that affects their own futures if they join together in cooperative networks. If agencies *do not* form cooperative networks, they find themselves simply competing against one another for limited funds. When they *do* join together, they can recognize gaps in the community's services, plan joint progams when they are appropriate, and share valuable resources. Most important, agencies working together have the power to influence the decision making of governmental bodies and established social planning agencies. Only then can the people who actually *deliver* services be involved in the communitywide planning process. The planning, delivery, and utilization of services can be part of the same process, with community members involved in all of its phases.

3 There Is a Permanent Coordinating Organization That Represents Workers and Community Members in the Planning Process

If members of the helping network are to be adequately represented in the planning process, they must have some ongoing structure that they can count on. There must be an organization or a group of people willing to keep tabs on community needs and to be aware of changes in available resources. The existence of such a body means that:

a *Ongoing relationships with other segments of the community and other planners can be maintained.*

b *Planning can be continuous and developmental instead of being limited to reactions to specific situations.*

c *Support can be mobilized immediately when it is needed.*

An ongoing group can recognize problems when they arise and can also see the positive potential in legislative changes. As long as effective communication is maintained, the coordinating group can call on all member agencies when necessary and keep them informed of community changes.

4 There Is a Mechanism That Allows for Reaction to Specific Issues

In addition to making long-range plans, the network should be prepared to make quick use of opportunities when they arise and deal intensively with specific issues. One way this can occur is through the formation of alliances or coalitions with other community groups. When an issue or opportunity arises that is relevant to the needs of a number of groups, they can join together. This happens most efficiently when ongoing communication ties are maintained. If a situation requires joint planning, separate organizations can be forged quickly into effective working units.

Another mechanism that can help in dealing with specific issues is a task force or research group created to deal with a particular topic. Small groups, such as task forces, can devote time to the intensive study of community needs and resources in a particular area. They can gain in-depth knowledge, generate concrete plans, and share the results of their studies with other network members. This planning strategy is particularly efficient because the strength of large numbers (the network) is combined with the specialized involvement of small groups (a number of task forces). If social planning is to be broadly based, those who wish to participate must share the traditional planner's expertise in diagnosing community needs, assessing available resources, and evaluating all possible options. Small groups can develop this expertise with regard to their specific areas of concern.

5 Conventional Planning Agencies Are Open to Broad Participation

It is not enough that the work of community members and agency workers parallel the efforts of agencies that have traditionally been involved with central planning. There must be constant interchanges between expert planners and in-the-field workers, between social scientists and community members. This can take place most effectively when planning agencies themselves are open to participation by individuals representing a variety of community groups. Community control should exist, not just in regard to direct service agencies, but in regard to agencies in the private and public sector that have the power to allocate funds. It is, after all, in the financial decisions that are made that a community implements its real priorities.

6 There Is An Ongoing Dialog among Governmental Agencies, Social Planning Agencies, Direct Service Agencies, and Community Groups

Planning is most effective when all individuals, groups, and agencies involved in the process are interdependent. At times, the dialog may be confrontive instead of solely collaborative. In the long run, however, planners may find that they are able to resolve philosophical differences in the interest of relevant and efficient delivery of human services.

When diverse agencies and institutions are able to work together, the results of planning are efficient. It is possible to analyze community needs and to allocate resources in a realistic manner. It is possible, for instance, to determine which services should be performed by governmental agencies and which can more efficiently be delivered by funding agencies in the private sector. Competition for scarce resources is avoided, since the most is made of each available dollar, each available property, and each available worker. Throughout the community, the duplication of services from one agency to another is replaced by attempts to provide programs that complement one another. Most important, the rights of consumers are protected because there is no separation between the planners, the deliverers, and the users of each service.

7 The Rights of Consumers, As Well As the Uniqueness of Each Agency, Are Protected At All Stages of the Planning Process

Planning can only be termed "community based" when it remains sensitive to the needs of individuals and to the will of the community as a whole. Planners working in isolation can inadvertently overlook the rights of individuals. When planning proceeds from the basis of a broad coalition, it is more likely that advocacy in behalf of every segment of the community will play a part in all decisions that are made. It is also more likely that each agency can maintain the flexibility and informality necessary for maintaining its real roots in the community.

Community-based planning is surely more difficult to implement than the traditional approaches ever were. It calls for complex organization, for the building of active bases of support, and for the development of a new kind of expertise among many individuals. In the long run, however, it is worth the effort because the programs created are those that have real meaning to the community. Planning, implementation, and evaluation of services and facilities are a continuing, unified process. As the community changes, its human service network changes with it.

Community-based planning is not a dream, but a reality. The fact that it can occur has been demonstrated, and nothing can prove the point more fully than a current, active example.

Community-based Planning: An Action Illustration

The fact that a community can make rapid strides in the direction of community-based planning with the participation of a broad coalition is illustrated by the experiences of the Community Congress of San Diego. The history of the Congress began in the 1960s, with the active commitment of a small group of people who had nothing to work with but their own energy. Now, the Community Congress serves as an umbrella organization for a large number of agencies funded through revenue sharing, and is part of a "Coalition of Coalitions" joined by the Chicano

Federation, the Black Federation, and the Union of Pan Asian Communities of San Diego County. The following passages, excerpted from a training grant proposal (Community Congress of San Diego, 1975),[1] describe their progress.

The Community Congress has its origin in San Diego's first street agencies which emerged in 1967 as an organic community response to the unmet needs of alienated youth and the drug subculture. *With almost totally voluntary staffs, the new agencies developed the first no-bust drug counseling services, hotlines, draft counseling and runaway houses. The high energy level was a product of the agencies' commitment to being an alternative, which came to mean the demystification of the therapeutic relationship through a reliance on peer counseling and paraprofessional services, and the throwing out of bureaucracy and red-tape, replacing them with non-hierarchical, participatory decision-making, meaningful work roles and a sense of community. Clients found the approach as satisfying as did the volunteers (indeed, many of them eventually volunteered), and the agencies soon began to experience an unprecedented level of success in dealing with San Diego's youth communities.*

As the demand for the services increased, so did the need for full-time staff to coordinate the delivery of those services, leading to a corresponding need for funding resources. Early church sponsorship had provided seed funding, but it was clearly not able to provide the needed resources. Yet other local sources, and the United Way, City and County in particular, had difficulty relating to the street agencies. So in 1969 the then six original alternative agencies *(In-Between, Community Crisis Center, Message Information Center, Bridge, Escondido Youth Encounter and Crisis House)* organized the Drug Coalition *as a way of creating a cohesive voice in their attempts to gain understanding, recognition and funding.*

The viability of a unified approach was quickly seen as the Drug Coalition experienced two successes: the creation of the Mayor's Council on Youth Opportunities *(which provided summer employment for agency staff)*, and the First County Drug Task Force. *Through the task force the Coalition was able to convince the County to fund and administer DEFY (Drug Education for You), a hotline and outreach program, which later joined the Congress. The task force has since evolved into TACDA (Technical Advisory Committee on Drug Abuse), with the responsibility of advising the County Department of Substance Abuse. The Congress maintains representatives on TACDA, who in turn meet regularly with other agency persons as part of the Community Congress Drug Task Force, and many agencies now receive funding through Substance Abuse.*

[1]Reprinted with permission of Community Congress of San Diego, Inc.

The Drug Coalition's negotiations with the United Way weren't as productive, however. In 1970 the Coalition re-organized itself, recruited other community-based agencies, and took the name of the Community Congress. *The new coalition's* first action was to draft a proposal for an open membership system for United Way. *When discussions continued to be unproductive, the Community Congress mobilized its constituency of agency boards of directors, staff persons, volunteers, clients and community persons to attend a United Way Board of Directors meeting. With several hundred persons filling the board room and overflowing into the halls,* the United Way voted to create a small *($300,000.00 or 5% of the total fund)* Demonstration and Development Fund open to non-United Way members such as the Congress agencies. *The Community Congress celebrated its victory but did not give up the goal of an open United Way. A number of Congress representatives were able to gain appointment to planning and policy committees internal to the United Way. Working with other Congress agency staff persons as the United Way Caucus, they strategized and helped implement incremental reforms.* Finally, in September of 1974, four years after the initial Congress proposal, the United Way adopted what is thought to be the first open membership United Fund in the Country, *and Congress members and other community-based agencies began to be reviewed for membership. The next task of the United Way Caucus will likely be funding parity between traditional and alternative agencies.*

The second major task that the Community Congress addressed was advocating that some of the newly available Public Employment Program (PEP) positions be outstationed in the community-based human care system. *A Community Congress task force researched the legality of such placements, reviewed civil service rosters to produce job titles that fit with alternative human care job roles, and lobbied with City Council persons. The result was the PEP Outreach Program, again thought to be the nation's first, which placed over eighty PEP employees in community agencies. The new positions allowed many services to expand their services, others to hire their first full-time staff persons, and provided the staff necessary to create two new agencies: ECHO (Emergency Community Housing Organization) which was the direct result of a Community Congress task force dealing with San Diego's lack of short-term crash places for transient youth, and the Farm, a residential group home for adolescents with problems.*

The announcement of San Diego as the site of the 1972 Republican Convention created the third major task that the Community Congress was to address: the provision of services to the thousands of demonstrators expected to protest the re-nomination of former President Richard Nixon. *The Community Congress coordinated the efforts of hundreds of volunteers from member agencies and other parts of the dissident community who worked throughout the Spring and early Summer in what came to be known as the* August Project. *Core funding was obtained from the national churches, food was hustled, campsites obtained, emergency health and first aid services planned, and so forth. When the decision to move the Convention to Miami was made, the Congress had developed a large network community of volunteers, contacts with numerous government departments and community organizations, and a public image of a coalition dedicated to working toward social change.*

The increased community and government contacts and a great deal of the volunteer energy generated by the August Project were quickly transferred to the other major issues. California State Senate Bill 714, *which threatened to impose severe restrictions and possible elimination of many alternative drug programs, was such an issue.* The Mental Health Action Collective was formed as a Community Congress Task Force to coordinate a community response. *In July of 1972, with the passage of the bill imminent, over 70 collective members participated in formulating position papers which registered concern over such issues as the creation of a state department of narcotics and drug abuse which separated the drug problems from the social-mental health-health arena, and the open-ended state control of drug program licensing and regulation with no regard to local, community input or representation of providers and consumers of drug programs. Legislative letter writing campaigns were instituted and two representatives were flown to Sacramento to discuss community concerns with legislators. The resulting bill amendments made the legislation tolerable if not perfect.*

The Mental Health Action Collective next addressed the allocation *decision of the San Diego Director of Medical Institutions to use within county programs $830,000.00* of federal/state funds targeted for social rehabilitation services to welfare linked individuals. *The Collective challenged the total lack of community input. With the cooperation of the Mental Health Advisory Board, the decision was delayed and an open process of fund allocation was instituted. The Collective then held informational workshops for community agencies, and monitored the proposal process. Ten community agencies were recommended for funding.*

The Mental Health Action Collective next addressed the lack of community involvement in regional mental health planning. *In September, 1972, the Collective developed a proposal for regional boards composed of providers, consumers and citizens and presented it to the Mental Health Advisory Board. The proposal had significant impact on the final planning recommendations which the Advisory Board presented to the County Board of Supervisors.*

The Mental Health Action Collective next addressed a Health Care Agency decision to create a new County Drug Advisory Board to replace the three *existing but inactive boards. The Collective requested a delay in the decision in order to allow for an open, community hearing. The Collective again sponsored information/action workshops on the topic, and then developed a* proposal for both community drug boards and a drug advisory board, *all with full community representation. And again the proposal had significant impact on the final policy decision.*

Throughout the Fall and into the early part of 1973, the Mental Health Action Collective continued to meet regularly, publish their own internal newsletter and address still more issues. They pushed the County to address recommendations made by a private research firm's study of problems in the mental health delivery system; they assisted the formation of a Mental Health Consumers Coalition; and they rallied community support for a recommendation by the Comprehensive Health Planning Agency Drug Sub Committee to abolish TIP (Turn In Pushers) programs.

In the Fall of 1972, the Community Congress began to study the potential effects of the newly enacted General Revenue Sharing Plan on local community-based human services. *Intertwined in the Revenue Sharing issue was the prospect of the PEP Outreach Program losing its federal funding with no contingency funds to replace them.* A Revenue Sharing task force was created, information sharing workshops organized, a proposal to fund community agencies submitted to both the City Council and the County Board of Supervisors, and a network of persons mobilized to function effectively at public hearings and meetings. *A long series of such meetings followed, some being attended by as many as 750 persons. During them* the Community Congress was joined in full partnership by the Chicano Federation *in successfully advocating that the City and County pool their funds for human care services and that they be joined by the United Way in allocating and administering the funds. Simultaneously, the coalitions were able to gain an emergency forty-five day extension of the PEP Program.*

Next they advocated that the total funds made available be adequate to the need for services ($3.6 million was initially allocated to 84 human care service agencies) and that there be a special appeals process to insure adequate consideration of community agencies, particularly those who were losing their PEP positions (an additional $600,000.00 was given to 19 agencies). The percentage of the total Revenue Sharing sum allocated to San Diego's human care services was well over ten times the national average. *The coalitions provided technical assistance to member agencies both when writing a proposal for funding and when negotiating a final contract. During the implementation stages, the Community Congress and the Chicano Federation again joined in successfully advocating that a proposal means test be dropped, that agencies maintain full autonomy over staffing patterns and policies, and that client confidentiality be insured.*

In the 1973–74 round of Revenue Sharing, several other coalitions joined the Congress and the Chicano Federation in advocating community and agency needs. *Included were the Black Federation and the Union of Pan Asian Communities (UPAC).* When non-Revenue Sharing issues of mutual concern were identified, the coalitions began to meet regularly. *The availability of Comprehensive Employment and Training Act (CETA) funds was such an issue.* As a result of the planning done by the Coalition of Coalitions, as it came to be called, a number of community agencies have been awarded Manpower Training (CETA Title I) *contracts, including the Community Con-*

gress. In December 1974, the Congress People Power Project was begun, providing subsidized work experience jobs for ten agencies spread across the Coalition of Coalitions network and spin-off training events open to that entire network. This was the first non-advocacy project that the four Coalition of Coalitions members jointly participated in, and served as a model for distributing trainee positions which has been adapted in this proposed training program. The Coalition of Coalitions *has sponsored workshops on and* now has task forces planning community responses to newly available resources created by the Public Service Employment (CETA Title II) allocations and the Neighborhood Block grants administered by the Department of Housing and Urban Development.

The Community Congress has also continued to work on its own major advocacy goals. *The biggest victories have been won by the* County Budget Task Force, *which has* opened up that entire budget setting process *to public input, an* Ad Hoc Task Force, *that* acquired 30 VISTA Program for Local Services (PLS) volunteer placements *for Congress agencies, and the* Juvenile Justice Task Force, which has blocked the construction of a new multi-million dollar juvenile hall *until there has been adequate time to explore community-based alternatives.* During 1973–74 the Congress also initiated its first projects which were not directly related to advocacy efforts. *A fully equipped cooperative print shop was established to provide low cost printing services to member agencies. Congress accepted sponsorship of* C /O, The Journal of Alternative Human Services, *a national publication designed to provide an information, training and dialogue forum for the alternative services movement. And, in April of 1974, the Congress was awarded a contract by the County Department of Substance Abuse to coordinate a three-month training program for staff of local drug programs.*

With the initial successes of the Community Congress and the Coalition of Coalitions in the acquisition of secure (if not equal) funding from the United Way and Revenue Sharing, community-based agencies have experienced a tremendous growth in program size and capability as well as a corresponding increase in the program accountability requirements placed on them. If the agencies are to maintain their ability to adapt to the new and changing needs of their communities, they must now develop clear data upon which to plan and define structures with which to decide. And if agencies are to remain autonomous, they must become as sophisticated as their funding sources in all areas of record keeping and program evaluation. *In all cases, however, the emphasis must be on data collection, decision-making or evaluation systems which are consistent with the service and organizational goals which have characterized the alternative human service network since the initial street agencies of the late 1960's.*

A perfect example of the potential benefits of program developoment systems for the alternative human service network can be seen in the work produced by San Diego Five, *a one year data collection and staff develop-*

ment program funded with Runaway Youth Act funds administered by NIMH. As a direct result of the program, San Diego's five residential runaway houses are for the first time collecting similar client profile data in order to determine the characteristics of the runaway population that each agency seves and the specific needs of those runaways. From the new data the agencies are learning that the needs of their target populations are different from one part of the County to another and that the needs are changing rapidly. The agencies are also learning how useful the data is for internal agency planning and inter-agency cooperation.

The data collection also serves as a pro-active method for meeting funding source requirements in this area, allowing the agencies to avoid the time-consuming hassles over issues such as client confidentiality, which seem inevitable when the record keeping or evaluation system is imposed by persons outside the alternative network. Thus the agencies are able to choose a creative means of coding a client (i.e., by using astrological signs) so he/she can be traced through an agency's records, while still insuring complete confidentiality.

The data collected by the San Diego Five Project has also become essential information necessary for the factual documentation of the claims made in the various position papers, public testimony and lobbying efforts of the Juvenile Justice Task Force as it has argued proposals for a community-based alternative to a single, massive Juvenile Hall. Thus program development techniques not only provide for internal planning and a buffer from funding sources; there is also a crucial link between such techniques as data collection, information systems and program evaluation, and the continued success of community advocacy efforts.

The Community Congress and its sister coalitions have stood the test of time, providing the basis for protection of urgently needed human services in the face of severe attacks on their funding base. Over the years, the San Diego area has utilized a contract-for-service system, allowing the County Board of Supervisors to let contracts for the delivery of services by community-based agencies. Although this method has been more cost-effective than the provision of comparable services by county personnel, the early 1980s brought a funding crisis, with attempts made to slash the county human service budget in half and to revamp the entire funding mechanism.

The San Diego experience of 1980–81 simply mirrored a nationwide trend toward reduced funding and toward criticism of mandated services. Yet the community-based agencies of San Diego had a history of cooperation that helped them avoid the competitiveness that spelled the downfall of service delivery systems in other areas. Their strategy included (Takvorian & Haney, 1981, p. 12) the following.

1 Educating and informing the Board of Supervisors and county bureaucrats of the cost-effectiveness and high quality of services provided by community based agencies.
2 Obtaining information relevant to the budget process.
3 Rapidly disseminating this information to the network.
4 Developing position papers.
5 Consistently dispersing information to the media.
6 Organizing regular and frequent meetings of service providers throughout the network and in each district.
7 Mobilizing mass attendance at key Board of Supervisors' meetings.

Although the human services could not maintain their funding at previous levels, they received considerably more than had originally been allocated for the fiscal year 1981 −82, and the viability of the network as a whole was maintained. As two members of the network point out, "The bottom line is that networks who have the support of their communities can significantly influence the expenditure of public monies" (Takvorian & Haney, 1981, p. 14).

The brief history of the Community Congress illustrates the tremendous strides that can be made in a relatively short time when advantage is taken of every opportunity for movement and cooperation. With regard to each characteristic of true community-based planning, San Diego has at least made a start.

1 The People Who Deliver and Use Services Are Active in Planning and Evaluating Programs

The alternative agencies that make up the Community Congress arose from the communities of which they are a part. They were created by groups of people who felt that traditional social service agencies failed to meet their needs or to respect their unique values. Community members created those agencies for themselves or for people whose contributions they valued. Many of the agencies are, in fact, "self-help" group endeavors.

From the beginning, then, all of their programs were planned by people who would deliver or use the services developed. In fact, people who had experienced one agency often created another. For instance, volunteers who were trained at the "In-Between," one of the first street agencies for youth, created "spin-off" agencies in other neighborhoods. With the base of what they had learned at the "In-Between," they were able to develop programs that could respond to differing local needs. That group of agencies formed the original core of what would become the Community Congress.

These agencies all used democratic decision-making processes and possessed a strong sense of community that was shared by those who delivered and used the services. It was when the need arose to reach beyond their own limits that the individual agencies needed a coordinating structure.

2 Agencies Work Together in Cooperative Helping Networks

As agencies began to join together, they were able to identify common needs and to take on tasks that could not have been accomplished by separate agencies working in isolation. People working in unison were able to obtain funding that would not otherwise have been available to *any* of the agencies. They were able to fill a gap in service delivery through their influence on the creation of new units, such as those developed to deal with drug education. They were able to mobilize a broad base of support that they thought would be needed to deal with expected national convention protests. They were able to have an impact on the total community.

3 There Is a Permanent Coordinating Organization That Represents Workers and Community Members in the Planning Process

The fact that the Community Congress existed as a central, coordinating force meant that member agencies were able to react quickly to new challenges and opportunities. The Congress and its sister coalitions were able to see the potential in the Public Employment Program and to use the new positions created through that program to expand human services in their communities. They were able to mobilize the numbers of people needed to advocate on behalf of their agencies for Revenue Sharing funds, and to develop expertise needed for proposal writing and contract negotiating. They were able to communicate, as a unified force, with other planning institutions and governmental figures. At the same time, they were able to develop the resources needed for long-range, developmental planning.

4 There Is a Mechanism That Allows for Reaction to Specific Issues

The "Coalition of Coalitions" has been able to make great gains through the ability to join together around specific issues that affect a broad range of member agencies. Each coalition is able to advocate more strongly in behalf of the human care needs of the community, and planning that affects the total community can respond to the broadest possible interpretation of the public interest.

The creation of task forces to deal with specific areas of concern has also allowed for more effective responses to issues. The Mental Health Action Collective, a Community Congress task force, was able to fight for community involvement in mental health planning. The revenue sharing task force devoted the time and effort needed to study the possible effects of new methods of distributing funds. The Congress and the Chicano Federation were able to work with a strong basis of information and analysis. The County Budget Task Force has worked to increase citizen involvement in the budgeting process. The organization of the coalitions means that task forces can be set up to make intensive studies of relevant issues, and that the results of their work can quickly become part of the network's total efforts.

5 Conventional Planning Agencies Are Open to Broad Participation

The Community Congress has been successful in obtaining funds through agencies such as the United Way. In the long run, however, their influence on the decision-making process will prove to be still more important. The fact that a number of Community Congress members are also involved with United Way committees means that all aspects of planning and funding involve a broader community base than was true in the past. An open institution is surely more likely to be a responsive one, and it is that long-term responsiveness that is likely to influence the course of human services development in the area.

6 There Is an Ongoing Dialog among Governmental Agencies, Social Planning Agencies, Direct Service Agencies, and Community Groups

To some degree, human service networks must have an adversary relationship with those who have the power to enact public policy and allocate funds. The networks' function is to ensure that governmental and social agencies remain responsive to the needs of all groups within the community, and there must be times when the protection of rights involves confrontation.

It is possible, however, to maintain ongoing relationships and work toward cooperative endeavors. When coalitions are strong and based on broad community support, they can communicate more effectively than they could as a collection of separate, independent agencies. The results of the process of negotiation concerning revenue sharing funds in San Diego have been said to have created "a new era of cooperation and relationships between City/County and the alternative human care services agencies . . ." (Frederickson, 1974, p. 26). This "new era" is just beginning.

7   The Rights of Consumers, As Well As the Uniqueness of Each Agency, Are Protected At All Stages of the Planning Process

The Coalition of Coalitions has worked to increase the involvement of citizens in all aspects of planning. Member agencies have also fought to ensure that granting proposals and administrative and evaluative structures allow for the rights of consumers to service and to confidentiality. They strive to ensure that the agencies themselves maintain their uniqueness and flexibility. As Frederickson states (1974, p. 29),

> Never compromise your principles of person-oriented service delivery just to receive the buck. You can win this battle if you stick together and fight. Administrators will attempt to remold your style and structure to fit into bureaucratic regulations. Your style and structure may be the most important things you have to offer, so don't sell out!

While it is important to "stick together and fight," it is also important to be able to defend all programs and services provided on the basis of hard facts and solid data. Community counselors, including paraprofessionals and volunteers, must be able to plan as effectively and as efficiently as the mental health professionals who have traditionally seen planning as their own bailiwick. Community counselors will never replace those *specialists* who devote full time to social planning. Both practitioners and consumers of their services can, however, carve out roles for themselves in the total planning process. Only when everyone shares program development skill and expertise can community-based planning become everybody's business.

COMMUNITY ACTION FOR CHANGE

Community counselors try to help individuals. They try to assist them in their attempts to solve problems in living and to grow in the ability to live independently and creatively.

Yet, as community counselors work, they tend to become more and more aware of the many problems that individuals alone are powerless to solve. They begin to perceive the many obstacles that stand in the way of each individual's freedom to develop in unique ways. They note the vast numbers of people whose lives are stifled by poor living conditions, unemployment, inadequate education, racism and sexism in social institutions, lack of services, or undemocratic decision-making processes. They realize that individuals are often punished for being different. Most of all, however, they learn that *people in general feel powerless to affect the ways in which their own lives are lived.* People are affected by the environment, but do not know how to affect it in return.

Community counselors often react to this situation with feelings of frustration and despair. They can see the need for change in the environment, but they, too, feel powerless to do anything about it. Some react by turning away from these problems. Others try to act singlehandedly—alone—to right the wrongs that they see. Yet, even if community counselors *could* solve all of their clients' problems, they would still be failing to get at the roots of the *real* problem: powerlessness.

The only possible solution lies in organizing people into community-based coalitions through which they can act to help themselves.

> If people are organized with a dream of the future ahead of them, the actual planning that takes place in organizing and the hopes and the fears for the future give them just as much inner satisfaction as does their actual achievement. The kind of participation that comes out of a People's Organization in planning, getting together and fighting together completely changes what had previously been to John Smith, assembly-line American, a dull, gray, monotonous road of existence that stretched out interminably, into a brilliantly lit, highly exciting avenue of hope, drama, conflict, with, at the end of the street, the most brilliant ending known to the mind of man—the future of mankind.
>
> This, then, is our real job—the opportunity to work directly with our people. It is the breaking down of the feeling on the part of our people that they are social automatons with no stake in the future, rather than human beings in possession of all the responsibility, strength, and human dignity which constitute the heritage of free citizens of a democracy . . . (Alinsky, 1969, pp. 49–50).

Community counselors cannot solve the problems of their communities. They can, however, offer what skills they might have to community members attempting to redefine the nature of power and of progress. They can be equal partners with others who share their concerns and their frustrations.

People's Organizations

People's organizations are meant to provide a vehicle through which people can exert influence to change their own environment. Their purpose involves both dealing with specific issues and affecting the ways in which community decisions are made. Those who believe that such actions are necessary are, in fact, assuming that real change requires a redistribution of power within the community, so that influence is shared more widely.

> Social action presupposes a disadvantaged segment of the population that needs to be organized, perhaps in alliance with others, to make adequate demands on the larger community for increased resources or treatment more in accordance with social justice or democracy. Its practitioners aim at basic changes in major institutions or community practices. They seek redistribution of power, resources, or decision making in the community or changes in basic policies of formal organizations (Rothman, 1974, p. 5).

Community counselors who become involved with community action groups are actively aligning themselves with one side of a struggle or controversy. Instead of maintaining objectivity, they are joining forces with the powerless segments of their communities in the hope that both resources and power can be shared equitably. They are making a commitment in the direction of social change.

People's organizations may be neighborhood associations through which citizens living in a particular locality join together for the purpose of facing and solving mutual problems and improving the conditions under which they live. Often, however, organizations are formed, not around the residence of their members, but around specific issues. Examples of special interest groups of this type might include senior citizens' groups, tenants' or welfare rights organizations, consumer advocacy groups, women's political action groups, or self-help groups for handicapped individuals. In all of these instances, the groups' members are relatively powerless and must confront policies made by others. Their purpose often revolves around their need to exert a greater degree of control over their own lives and to protect their own rights and dignity.

Whether the organization in question is based on the needs of a neighborhood or of a special interest group, some basic principles still hold true. The Midwest Academy (1973, pp. 37–38) points out that organizations should:

1 *Win reforms that improve people's real conditions.* This means meeting people's needs, serving their self-interest and being seen as a winner and a realist. . . .

2 *Give people a sense of their own power and potential.* This can only be done through an organization. Only an organization can be the bearer of past successes and have force greater than the strength of its individual members. Only organizations will make it clear that problems are social, not just personal. . . .

3 *Alter existing relations of power.* This means weakening the real power of those now exercising arbitrary control. It can be done most effectively through winning new structures for popular control. . . . It is the most difficult of the three criteria for organization, but will be the most important to insure the permanence of victories.

While outsiders may participate in organizing and in sharing concrete skills, in the long run, real leadership must emerge from within the group itself. Only then can there be a guarantee that the issues being attacked are those that have the most meaning to the membership. Only then can a real, ongoing power base be developed with the assurance of some degree of permanence.

In order to follow these principles, people's organizations must be structured to allow for maximum participation and maximum opportunities for clear-cut victories. This involves both the selection of appropriate issues and targets for action and the development of the strongest possible organizational methods.

Experience seems to show that citizens' organizations work most effectively when they begin their work with actions concerning concrete issues that are amenable to change. When the group experiences success in dealing with the environment—when a necessary change has actually been accomplished—the organization is on its way as a powerful force for change.

People can be organized, initially, around a practical, concrete issue that is important to their lives. If this issue is not too unwieldy—if it is one that holds a chance for successful resolution—the group gains spirit and cohesiveness from participation in a useful endeavor. More people can be attracted to the organization and, most important, the group is then ready to take on other projects. There are always connections to be drawn between one issue and another and, in time, the work of the organization can become more broadly defined. A success experience can break through apathy, can help to eliminate the feeling of helplessness that is common among many individuals, and can, in fact, give citizens a "sense of their own power." Many successful organizations have begun in response to one problem that had to be faced and then gone on to build successful coalitions dealing with many related issues.

The concept of "coalition" is particularly important. It must be remembered that, with regard to many issues, differing interest groups may have stakes in their resolution. It is possible that many organizations can come together to lend their strength to a particular change process and then work separately on other projects.

The use of coalitions can also help to resolve the problem of citizen involvement and strength. Individuals are likely to become most actively involved in small organizations with which they have a close identification and in which they feel that they are important. The smaller the organization, the more likely it is that its members can each feel central to its success or failure. At the same time, however, citizen strength is found in *numbers*. The combination of active involvement and success experiences can be brought about when a number of small groups band together, maintaining the advantages of small, close-knit organizations *and* the advantages of a large mass of people working together for a common cause.

For a people's organization to work successfully, it appears that the most practical steps might be the following:

1 *Allowing leadership to emerge from within the group.*
2 *Attacking specific, concrete issues and then dealing with broader goals from a base of success.*
3 *Using coalitions to combine both active involvement and large numbers of people.*

The effectiveness of a group organized along these lines can best be illustrated through a living example. The Woodlawn Organization, based in Chicago, provides an illustration of the kinds of gains that can be made in a people's organization that began through the attempts of a small number of people and grew into a large, broad-based neighborhood coalition.

Community Action: The Woodlawn Organization

The Woodlawn Organization of Chicago was built in accordance with the ideals of the "people's organization" concept. An examination of its history illustrates the way this concept can become a reality.[2]

Woodlawn is a mile square neighborhood in the heart of Chicago, Illinois. It has the potential to be an exceptional place to live, since it is close to Lake Michigan, close to Chicago's thriving downtown areas, close to some of the world's finest museums, and actually adjacent to the University of Chicago.

Yet, in the milestone year of 1960—the year its citizens decided to organize themselves—Woodlawn's potential seemed grim. It was true that the University of Chicago was the immediate neighbor to the north. It was just as true that the campus was clearly separated from the community by a length of barbed wire fence!

Woodlawn is a community where one out of every ten men cannot find a job; where six out of ten high school students drop out; and where one quarter of the population is on welfare. Other statistics are equally depressing; its infant mortality rates, venereal disease rates, and premature birth rates are among the highest in the city (T.W.O., 1970, p. 43)

The people of Woodlawn were paying high rents for substandard housing, high prices for low-quality food and clothing. Health care, social services, and educational facilities were all inadequate. No one in the public or private sector took responsibility for enhancing the accessibility of either goods or services, and every day more local businesses disappeared. It was to wipe out hopelessness and to bring about community self-determination in its place that The Woodlawn Organization (T.W.O.) was created.

The Beginnings

As the decade of the 1950's drew to a close, four of Woodlawn's religious leaders realized that, unless something was done to break the cycle, the community's descent into despair would never be stopped. Doctors Leber and Blakely of the First Presbyterian Church, Father Farrell of the Catholic Church, and Reverend Profrock of the Woodlawn Emanuel Lutheran Church examined the problems they saw around them and turned to their churches for help. By 1960, Leber, Blakely, and Farrell had secured funds from the

[2]Reprinted from M.D. Lewis and J. A. Lewis, *The Woodlawn organization: Community action and mental health.* Chicago: Governors State University and T.W.O., 1978. Developed under a grant from the U.S. Dept. of Health, Education and Welfare, National Institute of Mental Health. Grant # 5T41MH-14562-02 MHST. Reprinted with permission.

Catholic Archdiocese of Chicago, the Schwarzhaupt Foundation, and the First Presbyterian Church of Chicago. Forming the Greater Woodlawn Pastors' Alliance from what had been the entirely Protestant Woodlawn Ministers' Alliance, they took the first major step toward community organization. They called in Saul Alinsky and his Industrial Areas Foundation (I.A.F.), which had been formed to provide technical assistance to communities attempting to build their own "people's organizations."

The approach that underscores all of the I.A.F.'s work presupposes that the people living in slum communities are trapped there, unable to leave and victimized by outside powers. The problems of urban decay and citizen apathy are related to the political, economic, and social forces that control the life of the ghetto and keep its population dependent. People can improve their own lives only by first seeking and maintaining power.

The I.A.F.'s strategy for change is the development of indigenous people's organizations, which provide the only possible means for obtaining broadly based power. In a community like Woodlawn, the only resources available to the residents are their own numbers. The initial organizational approach is (1) to attract people by dealing with the concrete issues about which they are really concerned, (2) to give them an avenue through which they can raise and resolve conflict, and (3) to provide an opportunity for local leadership to arise.

In January of 1961, a meeting of representatives of the Woodlawn Block Club Council, the Woodlawn Businessmen's Association, the Greater Woodlawn Pastors' Alliance, and the United Woodlawn Conference (the U.W.C. subsequently dropped out) resulted in the creation of The Temporary Woodlawn Organization, with Reverend Robert J. McGee as president, Reverend Arthur Brazier as "official spokesman," and the I.A.F. as technical advisor. It was important that the organization be deemed "temporary," since the goal of those present was to build a community-based organization that would respond to the needs and desires of a broad range of civic groups in Woodlawn. Toward this end, the Temporary Woodlawn Organization embarked on a series of activities intended to deal with the most important issues immediately facing the community, while building a support base that could have a voice in the creation of its own permanent organization.

Urban Renewal

The most difficult and immediate concern of the Woodlawn community in 1961 was an expansion plan that the University of Chicago had announced the previous summer. The University intended to have cleared a strip of land one mile long and one block wide along the southern boundary of the campus. They would build their South Campus expansion in the space. Having the area declared a blighted slum would mean that the University could expand at low cost, while the city would benefit through the availability of federal urban renewal funds.

The residents of Woodlawn were concerned, not just about that one-mile-long parcel of land, but about the South Campus plan's long-range implications for the community. T.W.O. wanted an over-all plan for urban renewal, a plan that would involve community members as full participants, that would set out objectives with the people's interests in mind, and that would prevent the University from swallowing up the whole Woodlawn community in time. The fledgling organization rallied support within the community, opposed the plan in Washington on the basis of lack of citizen participation in planning, and embarked on a long and bitter conflict with a seemingly unbeatable adversary. T.W.O. even hired independent city planners to draw up alternatives to the plans developed by the University and by the city.

Finally, in 1963, an agreement was reached. A citizen's committee, with T.W.O. providing a majority of the members, would take part in all urban renewal planning in Woodlawn. The South Campus plan would take effect, but only after the deteriorated non-residential buildings in another large piece of land were cleared and low-cost, low-rise housing erected in their place.

T.W.O. had won recognition as the organization that could speak for Woodlawn. It had won recognition of the right of Woodlawn residents to participate in all planning affecting their lives. At the same time, this struggle brought the organization into a new and long-lived stage in its own development. T.W.O., with the Kate Maremont Foundation, later developed this land under the auspices of the T.W.O.-Kate Maremont Development Association, and built, owns, and manages the 502 apartment units of Woodlawn Gardens.

Business Ethics

Just as important to many individual Woodlawn citizens was the issue of exploitation by businesses within the boundaries of their community. The primary problems involved false advertising, unfair credit practices, overcharging, and, in the case of food stores, inaccurate weighing.

Woodlawn residents had few shopping alternatives, and while they resented being cheated by unscrupulous business people, they felt powerless as individuals in dealing with the problem. At the same time, honest business owners within the community were concerned about these grievances, too.

The Temporary Woodlawn Organization created the Square Deal campaign, beginning with a large parade along one of the main shopping streets in the area. The follow-up to this very visible beginning included a check-out counter set up in the yard of a church. People who had just completed their grocery shopping could bring their purchases there, have them weighed accurately, have their cash register totals checked, and find out immediately whether they had been cheated. Stores that were identified as exploiters of Woodlawn consumers were subjected to widespread publicity and threats of boycott. Individuals who had been cheated were encouraged to share this information with their neighbors.

The result of this concerted campaign was that Woodlawn merchants agreed to sign a Code of Business Ethics that had been drawn up by a group of community leaders and representatives of the Woodlawn Businessmen's Association. A Board of Arbitration, with representatives from the Businessmen's Association and consumer groups, was set up to deal with future problems. The people of Woodlawn had an impact on business practices through these tactics. At the same time, they became increasingly aware of a new force within their community.

Tenant's Rights

One of the primary motivations for organization in Woodlawn had always been the actual physical deterioration of the buildings in which the residents lived. Many of these buildings were medium-sized structures that had been subdivided again and again and had been allowed to fall into disrepair by absentee landlords. Neglecting to maintain buildings often spilled over into refusal to take care of even emergency repair needs like broken windows, faulty plumbing, and non-existent heating. Yet, because of a lack of alternatives, tenants were paying high rents that landlords collected while patiently waiting for "slum clearance" and the sale of their buildings.

When the majority of tenants within a building found the situation intolerable and formed a tenants' committee, T.W.O. would help them in their negotiations with the landlord, sometimes turning to such tactics as going to the owner's suburban neighborhood to picket in front of his or her home. When all else failed, rent strikes were organized, with the tenants putting their rent checks into an escrow account until needed repairs were made. Ideally, landlords would complete repairs upon notification of the committee's demands, and this happened more frequently after a few hard-fought battles had been won.

Again, the tenants' organizations played a role in the strengthening of the young T.W.O., while the community organization was beginning to have a visible impact on concrete problems.

The Schools

Another emotionally-charged issue in the urban ghetto has always been the public school system. In Woodlawn, parents saw their children packed into over-crowded schools and forced to attend in double shifts, while a few miles away white children studied in half-empty classrooms. T.W.O. again turned to dramatic demonstrations of community concern.

"Truth squads" visited white schools and took pictures of vacant classrooms to point up the fact that Chicago's schools were, in fact, segregated. Hundreds of community members appeared at a city-wide public hearing. At their own hearing in the Woodlawn community, parents heard reports by masked schoolteachers, afraid of reprisals if their identities were known. Each meeting of the Board of Education was attended by the "Death Watch," groups of parents wearing black capes to symbolize the fate of their children in the Chicago public schools. A one-day boycott of an elementary school was highly effective, and placed Woodlawn in a leadership position among the protesting neighborhoods of metropolitan Chicago.

New Visibility

All of these activities, along with a major voter registration campaign that included transporting bus loads of citizens to City Hall for registration, made the Temporary Woodlawn Organization a viable force in the community. Those with political and economic power in Chicago were becoming aware of the organization. More importantly, the community members themselves were becoming aware of it. By 1962, it was time to create a permanent organization.

T.W.O. was set up, not as an association of individual members, but as an umbrella organization for member groups, including block clubs, religious institutions, business associations, and other civic action groups. Each member organization sends delegates to delegate meetings and the annual convention, with ongoing functions carried on by a steering committee and by a number of standing committees, including the housing committee, the schools committee, the community maintenance committee, the consumer practices committee, the social welfare committee, the civil rights committee, and the fund-raising committee.

On the basis of this organizational mechanism, T.W.O. had in the beginning—and continues to have—the ability to speak for masses of Woodlawn residents. By the mid-1960's, the organization's role as representative of the people had been established. Major issues had been raised. The organization could now turn its attention to building programs that could provide long-range solutions.

T.W.O. and Community Development

In 1972, T.W.O. created the Woodlawn Community Development Corporation (W.C.D.C.) to "develop long- and short-range programs in the areas of real estate development and management, commercial development, manpower training and education, neighborhood improvement and conservation and health on behalf of the Woodlawn community" (T.W.O., 1976, p. 2).

The W.C.D.C. is a non-profit agency, but it can operate profit-making businesses and funnel the profits into community services. Now, the people of Woodlawn can determine the kinds of services they need and ensure that those are the services they will receive. T.W.O./W.C.D.C., which remains, as always, a "people's organization," now creates and maintains a variety of its own programs.

Programs for Children and Youth

Early Childhood Development

T.W.O./W.C.D.C. operates both a day care center and a Head Start program, providing service to hundreds of pre-school children.

Youth Services

Programs included youth advocacy and services to status offenders and their families.

Adoption and Foster Care

Through Homes/Ltd., adoptive homes for children have been found for several years. Additionally, assistance for foster families is now being provided, with all of these programs falling under the auspices of the Woodlawn Child Care Institute.

Child Abuse

T.W.O./W.C.D.C. has moved into the area of child abuse prevention, developing family counseling services for prevention and for crisis situations.

Employment

Manpower/Training

T.W.O.'s traditional interest in training and job placement, particularly for the young, has been expanded. First through the Woodlawn Career Vocational Institute, and now through the model Multi-Service Agency, services include job development, counseling, skill training, remedial education, on-the-job training, and job placement.

Public Service Employment

T.W.O./W.C.D.C. has been able to provide jobs for many unemployed residents through Public Service Employment funding. In addition, CETA funds have been used as the basis for job slots for unemployed *seniors.*

Income Maintenance and Social Services for Special Populations

Counseling and Consumer Education

T.W.O.'s budget counseling service has been enhanced by the Food Stamp counseling program, which provides outreach services to many families.

Services to Seniors

A range of services is being provided for seniors, with emphasis on organizing senior citizens as an interest group.

Developmental Disabilities

A group home for Woodlawn citizens with developmental disabilities allows these community members, too, to receive the services they need within the boundaries of their own neighborhood.

Individual Problems

T.W.O. continues to act as advocate for individual citizens seeking assistance with unique problems.

Real Estate Development

Woodlawn Gardens

T.W.O.'s first housing accomplishment, Woodlawn Gardens, has been in existence since 1969. The residential complex also includes a small commercial section.

Jackson Park Terrace

Jackson Park Terrace apartments include townhouses, a high-rise, and a mid-rise. Subsidies for low income families allow for a heterogeneous mixture of tenants.

Woodlawn Redevelopment #2

In addition to building new structures, the organization has taken on the task of renovating existing structures and renting them. Rented sites are now scattered throughout the community.

Park Shore East

Another major development, Park Shore East includes residential and commercial units.

Home Improvement Loans

It is hoped that the Home Improvement Loan Program, providing loans to home-owners in conservation areas of the community, will expand in the coming years.

Commercial Ventures

Many profit-making ventures now help to support the services being provided to Woodlawn citizens. Companies such as the T.W.O./Hillman's Supermarket, the T.W.O./Maryland Theatre, the Observer Newspaper, and the T.W.O. Security Service have provided high-quality goods and services to the community, while remaining good financial investments as well.

Woodlawn still has problems that need to be solved and a great deal of work that needs to be done. Yet, things are different now, for everyone in Woodlawn knows that the solutions to those problems—right or wrong—will come from them, and will not be imposed by some external force.

The standard (and accurate) narrative is to refer to Woodlawn as a mile-square black ghetto on the south side of Chicago immediately to the south and adjacent to the University of Chicago. Its houses are substandard, its people poor. It has less than its share of jobs, income and vital services, and more than its share of dependence, dirt, disease and early death. . . However-er, there is an important "difference" which distinguishes Woodlawn . . . The Woodlawn Community has a voice . . . (T.W.O., 1970, p. 28).

COMMUNITY ORGANIZATION AND COUNSELING

In the past, community organizations, particularly those involved in social action, have functioned apart from individuals who identified themselves as counselors or human service professionals. Counselors can no longer turn their backs on the need for social action, however, because it is a natural continuation of the counseling process. *Helping individuals and dealing with social-political systems are two aspects of the same task.*

Beyond the fact that specific aspects of the community situation can have great effects on individual community members, it must also be remembered that the degree to which individuals feel that they can control their own environment is important in and of itself. If people within a community feel powerless to affect their environment and to control their own lives, that, in itself, is a major mental health problem. Mental health and competence in living require that the individual possess a degree of self-esteem, while self-esteem may well depend on the individual's belief that his or her own behaviors can affect the world. Those feelings cannot be developed solely through self-exploration or through attempts to modify attitudes. They can be developed only through experience.

The well-being of the community may require that feelings of power, effectiveness, and self-determination be generated both among individuals and in the atmosphere of the community as a whole. Social action, then, must be a major concern of the community counselor:

- Because negative aspects of the community environment may be detrimental to the growth and development of individuals.
- Because positive aspects of the community environment can support individual growth and development.
- Because community counselors are helpless in their attempts to serve individuals if environmental factors do not change to keep pace with individual adaptations.
- Because self-determination is not only a political goal, but a mental health goal.
- Because community counselors, working alone, and individual citizens, working alone, are both powerless to make the community responsive to the needs of community members.

Community counselors, like other citizens, have a need for involvement in organized community action. The potential role of the community counselor must, however, be defined. What unique contributions can the community counselor offer? Community counselors who participate in a social action are entering a new arena. Many have been trained primarily in one-to-one or small group counseling techniques; their concern for social change arises from their own experience. Although some social workers have been trained to specialize in community organization, this whole field is new to most human service workers. They must forge a new identity as people concerned both with individuals and with the environment. That identity must relate to the unique attributes that community counselors can bring to the tasks of social change.

1   Community Counselors Have a Unique Awareness of Common Problems Faced by Community Members

In their work with individuals, community counselors become aware of recurring themes—of large numbers of people facing the same difficulties and the same obstacles. Through these interactions, counselors become ever more aware of specific aspects of the environment that appear to be damaging to members of the community. The experience of attempting to help all of these individuals becomes an exercise in frustration, as counselors realize that new victims continually appear. This occurs when community counselors are concerned with the total mental health needs of poverty-stricken neighborhoods. It also occurs, however, when vocational counselors become aware of inequitable hiring practices; when rehabilitation counselors note the obstacles their clients face in trying to obtain their rights to equal treatment; when school counselors face inhumane educational practices; when agency counselors dealing with special populations try to offset the community's tendency to stigmatize particular groups of people. It happens whenever a counselor's attempts to help his or her clients find their own strength and power are counterbalanced by environmental forces that weaken or stifle growth.

When counselors become aware of specific difficulties within the environment, they can bring those problems to the surface. They can encourage action for change:

a   *By making the community as a whole aware of specific problems and their consequences for human beings.*
b   *By alerting existing organizations that are already working for change and that might have an interest in the issue at hand.*
c   *By joining with others in an attempt to organize citizens who can fight for change on their own behalf.*

Community counselors have a unique perspective, which allows them to recognize the seriousness of community problems and to join with others in the search for new solutions

2 Community Counselors Can Encourage the Development of New Leadership and Provide Support to New Organizations

Through the nature of their work, community counselors have intimate contacts with the most powerless segments of the population. In the past, many have used these contacts to teach the groups with which they work to adjust to the demands of the larger community. More and more, community counselors are trying, instead, to encourage and support the growth of active self-help organizations that can *make* demands on the community.

It is not unusual for human service workers to bring together groups of community members who wish to share mutual concerns and develop new skills in living. As leadership emerges, it is a short step to the development of the group as a self-help organization that can provide the core of a coalition for action.

Community counselors can work to encourage the creation of new people's organizations and to support the growth and effectiveness of ongoing activist groups.

3 Community Counselors Can Put Their Human Relations Skills at the Disposal of the People

If there is one common core skill that all effective community counselors have, it is in the area of interpersonal relations and communication. They can make a significant contribution by sharing these skills with people who are attempting to organize for change. Community counselors can act as consultants to such groups and can provide training in the skills that community members themselves see as important. Such activities might include:

a   *Provision of leadership training.*

b   *Analysis of communication patterns within the group.*

c   *Training in interpersonal skills that can help group members to function together as an effective unit.*

d   *Development of effective technieus of communication with other individuals and organizations.*

Community counselors may also be able to help people's organizations to develop expertise in research and evaluation—in gathering the hard data that they need to support their claims. Ideally, counselors can also share what expertise they may have in understanding social systems and the nature of change itself. Often, community counselors and the others who share their concerns and their goals must struggle to learn together.

In these instances, community counselors are plying the skills that are normally required in their work. They are, however, using them to advance the cause of people who are organizing to bring about change and to revise the ways in which power is distributed in the community.

4 Community Counselors Can Help to Coordinate the Efforts of Groups Attempting to Maintain Action for Change

Community counselors, when they are effective, have their fingers on the pulse of the community. Just as they are familiar with all of the agencies that provide direct services to individuals, they can also familiarize themselves with all of the groups and organizations that are attempting to bring about more fundamental changes. Just as they link individuals with agencies that provide part of the helping network, they can also link individuals and groups with organizations dealing head-on with issues that relate to identified needs.

Many agencies—particularly those serving the needs of special populations—act as clearinghouses for information and as home bases for a number of active groups. Community counselors can participate, along with others, in actions that are particularly relevant to the consumers of their services. Often, a number of organizations join forces to act in regard to a specific issue. Community counselors and their agencies must, at times, provide part of such a force for change.

5 Community Counselors Can Take Leadership to Bring About Change in the "Helping Network" Itself

When working with community members, counselors and other human service workers can assist in organizing, can act as encouragers and supporters, and can become part of the power base of those seeking social change. They must, however, allow leadership to arise from within the group that is attempting to help itself.

Community counselors can and must take leadership, however, in working to bring about change within their own agencies and institutions and among their own colleagues. The agencies and institutions, which make up the "helping network" that provides direct services to individuals, must change if they are to become more responsive to the needs of consumers and more aware of the need to maintain human dignity.

Some change is coming about through pressure that consumers are placing on agencies in their own behalf. There must, however, be a strong force for change operating within the helping network as well.

Community counselors must, themselves, organize into coalitions for change. Their dual targets include both the helping agencies in which they work and the organizations to which they and their colleagues belong. If they are organized, community counselors can act as consumer advocates within their agencies and can move their professional organizations toward positions of advocacy at the same time.

Delworth, discussing the misplaced assumption that paraprofessionals would become "guerrillas," bringing about change in their agencies, points out:

> . . . Little has come of the promise that paraprofessionals would create a real change in the delivery of human services, especially for minorities, the poor, and women. Many agencies remain as racist, sexist, and elitist as though paraprofessionals had never been involved in their operation. How could so many have had such a limited impact on the agencies in which they worked? What happened? (Delworth, 1974, p. 336).

What has happened in many instances is that paraprofessionals, like the concerned professionals before them, tried to bring about change alone, and found themselves isolated, powerless, and ineffectual. Paraprofessionals *can* fulfill the promise that they might make a difference, but only if they organize to the extent that they possess a real voice and a power base for change.

Paraprofessionals have the opportunity to build *new* organizations that are based on the premise that human service delivery must change. Professionals face the equally difficult task of changing the priorities of their own long-existing organizations and thereby making these professional organizations instruments of social change. A small number of concerned professionals could change the nature of professional associations representing thousands if they:

a *Met together to set priorities and selected a small number of major, but manageable, issues to be confronted.*
b *Set up task forces to deal with each of the issues to be confronted.*

c   *Identified resources* beyond themselves, *including change agents and organizations that might have an interest in the issue at hand.*

d   *Mobilized available resources to place pressure on the professional organizations.*

e   *Accepted only concrete actions as evidence of the organizations' changing priorities.*

In the human service professions, as in every community, change comes about, not just through the willingness of individuals to *fight*, but through their willingness to *fight together*, in organized coalitions.

6   Community Counselors Can Recognize Their Responsibility to the Powerless

Community counselors are not responsible *for* the powerless members of their communities; they are responsible *to* them. There are many qualities that community counselors as a group can bring to the movement for social change. There are just as many that individual counselors can identify as being unique in themselves.

Not all community counselors will want to become directly involved in social action for change. Such involvement implies, for one thing, a recognition that, when the needs of the powerless come into conflict with the desires of the powerful, one side should be supported against the other. The decision to leave objectivity behind and to take sides in a struggle is a personal one, and one that brings with it many risks. The community counselors whose personal values and perceptions lead them toward a commitment to social change will not find their work easy, nor will they find that their training has fully prepared them with the change agent's necessary skills. They can only adapt what skills they do have to the needs of the community and work to develop practical expertise in community organization and change. While training programs can move toward providing all human service workers with greater understanding of social systems and change, the concrete skills of strategy building and implementation tend to come with experience. Community counselors may find that others within the community are more skilled than they at selecting appropriate targets and goals, at devising effective tactics, at organizing and leading, and at influencing others. Community counselors can only give themselves to their communities and take every possible opportunity to learn from others and to become effective organizers of community action. The most difficult step is the initial commitment to change.

SUMMARY

Community organization efforts are built on the counselor's recognition that the well-being of clients depends on the quality of the social environment. Affecting that environment can be accomplished both through planning and through community action movements.

Social planning is instituted in a community in order to identify the community's needs for services, to set priorities, to allocate resources, and to develop facilities or programs to meet the needs that have been recognized. While traditional planning has been confined to small political or professional groups, community-based planning allows consumers and workers to be planners and decision makers. The model for community-based planning stresses well-coordinated helping networks, the opening of social planning agencies to broad participation, and continual communication among planning agencies, governmental bodies, direct service agencies, and community groups. An example of a movement toward such an effort is provided by the Community Congress of San Diego, Inc.

Community action movements work to organize people into coalitions that can give them vehicles for exerting power and bringing about substantial change. Such "people's organizations" seem to be most effective when they allow leadership to emerge from within the group, begin by attacking concrete and manageable issues, and use coalitions to combine the active involvement possible in small organizations with the large numbers that may be necessary to bring about change. An example of a group organized along these lines is The Woodlawn Organization, which represents the citizens of the Woodlawn area of Chicago.

Although counselors have not traditionally been closely involved in community organization efforts, they have much to offer, including a unique awareness of the problems faced by community members. They are in a special position to encourage and support new leadership, to share their human relations skills, to coordinate community efforts, and to bring about change in the helping network itself. Community counselors, like other groups, must organize if they are to deal successfully with the need for change.

ACTIVITIES TO ENHANCE UNDERSTANDING
OF CHAPTER 3

1   Look through a current newspaper published in your own local area.
    As you read, try to be alert to issues that might affect the clients of a
    community counseling program. Are there aspects of your communi-
    ty environment that might have a negative effect on individuals? Are
    there things going on that you feel should be changed? Assign pri-
    orities to the issues you identify, and try to come up with *one thing in
    your community that you would like to change.* (Try to come up with
    something that is specific and concrete, but big enough to make a
    difference.) Consider how you would go about making this change,
    taking into account the following questions.

    a. Can I, personally, get excited enough about this issue to get involved?

    *b. What other individuals or groups might share a concern about this issue?
        Where can I find mutual support and resources?*

    *c. What individuals or groups might be actively against this change? Is there
        some way to neutralize their efforts?*

    *d. Are there some smaller objectives that, if met, would help to bring about
        the desired change?*

    *e. What specific activities might do most to build support, eliminate opposi-
        tion, and begin to bring some success? Use your answers to these questions
        to design an approach to change. Be as specific as possible in laying out
        your plan.*

2   Consider again the hypothetical agency that you, yourself, have been
    designing. Are there things that you would need to do in order to
    make the community as a whole more responsive to the needs of the
    population you are serving? Does your program tend to deal with
    problems that could be prevented through community change efforts?
    Try to fill in the community organization facet in more detail.

CHAPTER
4
CLIENT
COUNSELING

Many individuals are, in the course of their lives, faced with the need for direct services. They may be facing immediate crisis situations or the need to respond to stressful events. Just as often, they simply need assistance in dealing with normal developmental tasks. When clients are "at risk," they are at points in their lives when direct interventions can prevent chronic problems. "People are members of risk groups not only because of individual characteristics they may possess but because they may be faced with situations that place high demands on adaptive capacity. . . . Altering some characteristic of the risk situation or event is . . . as likely to reduce risk as is a person-centered intervention whose purpose is to strengthen the coping capacity of the affected individual" (Heller, Price, & Sher, 1980). Regardless of the problem or issue being confronted, help should be immediately accessible and should be directed toward affecting the environment, as well as the individual.

PROACTIVE COUNSELING

When the community counselor works with an individual, he or she works with the whole person and also with the person's environment. Counselors have always recognized negative aspects of the individual's social surroundings. The question asked as part of a diagnosis has always been, "What aspects of the environment might be contributing to the cause of the problem?" Now we are learning to be just as aware of the positive aspects of the individual's world. We now ask an additional question: "In this person's everyday interactions with others, where are the possible sources of help and support?"

Most people have sources of help in their natural, everyday environments. They use these sources to satisfy many of their needs, including the following.

Physical needs, such as the need for food, shelter, and health care.

Psychological needs, such as the need for affection and esteem.

Social needs, such as the need for affiliation with a group or for a sense of being important to others.

Economic needs, such as the need for useful work and for a living wage.

Political needs, such as the need to feel some sense of power over events affecting oneself and one's community.

Growth needs, such as the need for stimulation and for opportunities to learn and create and to exhibit competency.

Everyone may share all of these needs, but different ones are important at different times for different people. Individuals are probably strongest when they have ongoing relationships that are varied enough and comprehensive enough to solve a number of problems and create a number of opportunities.

Caplan (1974) speaks of "support systems" as *enduring patterns* of interaction that help the individual to maintain a sense of self. "Social aggregates" are joined for a number of complex reasons.

> People have a variety of specific needs that demand satisfaction through enduring interpersonal relationships. . . . Most people develop and maintain a sense of well-being by involving themselves in a range of relationships in their lives that in toto satisfy these specific needs, such as marriage, parenthood, other forms of living and intimate ties, friendships, relationships with colleagues at work, membership in religious congregations and in social, cultural, political, and recreational associations, and acquaintanceships with neighbors, shopkeepers and providers of services; intermittent relationships of help-seeking from professional caregivers such as doctors, nurses, lawyers and social workers; and continuing dependence for education and guidance on teachers, clergymen, intellectuals, and community leaders . . . . In such relationships, the person is dealt with as a unique individual. The other people are interested in him in a personalized way (Caplan, 1974, p. 5).

Most people have support systems of this kind: networks of formal and informal relationships that they have developed in order to meet their needs. When community counselors deal with individuals, they work with them in the context of those support systems.

If an individual's normal associates cannot meet psychological, physical, social, economic, political, and growth needs—if, in other words, an adequate support system is missing—additional sources of support must be created. If aspects of the individual's environment are destructive—if they are interfering with the meeting of immediate personal needs—then those aspects must, if possible, be changed.

When community counselors work with troubled individuals, they must, of course, help them to examine, and perhaps to change, those aspects of their own behavior that are adding to their problems. Obviously, people have more control over their own actions than they have over the acts of others. If a problem can be resolved effectively on an individual basis, there is no need to change the environment.

Usually, however, the individual, the family, and the community are so closely related that the client's social system must be taken into account. Purely individual change may be impossible, impractical, or damaging to the individual's integrity. Then the need arises to do the following.

1 *Identify positive sources of help in the support system.*
2 *Create additional sources of positive support if needed.*
3 *Remove negative or destructive environmental pressures by:*
   a *Moving the individual away from them.*
   b *Directly confronting and changing them.*

Sometimes this process can uncover natural support systems that a number of individuals have in common. Strengthening these groups can mean preventing difficulty for more than one potential client. When community counselors work with neighborhood block clubs, with groups of co-workers, with extended families, with beginning self-help organizations, or with any other natural groupings, they can strengthen the sources of support available to individuals in their own communities, among people who care about them.

When helping troubled individuals, community counselors often find themselves working along with their clients to identify the most effective possible sources of support in the natural environment. This must be a joint process, because no one can tell an individual what his or her support system should be. Relationships are only supportive, and only helpful, if people experience them that way. There is no objective truth that can help us to distinguish between a "good" or a "bad" environment. It is the *interaction* between individuals and their surroundings that is important, and only the people involved can identify the situations in which their own needs are met.

This approach is different than that of traditional counseling, which might concentrate more fully on helping individuals to change themselves and their own attitudes and behaviors. If anything, community counseling is different simply because of the kinds of questions that are asked. Some examples may be drawn from specific kinds of situations.

A Runaway Youth

An adolescent has run away from home and finds himself alone and isolated in an unfamiliar neighborhood. He turns to the local runaway center, where a counselor might seek the answers to questions such as:

1   *Is the youth's own family a possible source of emotional support for him?*

2   *What changes in the family situation might make his home environment supportive enough for him to consider returning?*

3   *What changes in the youth's behavior might make the family situation more supportive for him? Can he make those changes and still be himself?*

4   *If family conflict cannot be resolved, what alternative living situations are available? Is there a family or a group home situation that he sees as potentially comfortable for himself?*

5   *How are relatives outside of the immediate family involved? Are there any potential sources of support here?*

6   *Have police authorities been involved?*

7   *Is there a possibility of economic self-sufficiency for the youth? What work skills does he have? What work opportunities exist or can be made to exist?*

8   *What are appropriate sources of financial aid for the youth or his family?*

9   *Does the youth have a group of friends with whom he identifies strongly? How can this support system be of help to him now?*

10   *What is the youth's school situation? Is that where the real conflict lies? Are there any people or programs in the school that can provide additional support? Are there negative factors that can be influenced to change?*

11   *Is there anyone else who has been trying to help the youth? Has some kind of relationship been established?*

These questions seem obviously appropriate, but it is surprising how many of them are left unasked in the immediacy of a crisis situation. Children don't run away in isolation; they run to something or from something. It is more than coincidence that many runaway centers, which initially concentrated on counseling or placement for individual adolescents, have now developed programs of group counseling for parents and for young people (Kolton, Dwarshuis, Gorodezky, & Dosher, 1973). What they are doing, in effect, is helping to build more effective support systems for their young clients.

A Physically Disabled Adult

A young, single woman has become physically disabled as a result of a recent accident. A period of hospitalization is now ending. A community counselor, taking a human services approach, would ask questions such as the following:

1   What living situation is appropriate for her? Is she able to live alone? Are family members available to provide attendant care? Must an attendant be hired?

2   What financial assistance is available, not only for her survival, but for attendants' salaries or for technical necessities? Is advocacy needed to obtain assistance?

3   What are her vocational goals? What work is she able to do? Are additional skills needed? What educational or training resources are available?

4   What is her relationship with family and friends? Have they been able to provide psychological support through the crisis period? How have they adjusted to her disability? Are they allowing her to be as independent as possible?

5   How can she maintain social relationships, and continue to enjoy recreation?

6   Does she need help and information in order to deal with what may be a crisis in her sexuality?

7   Does she have ready access to whatever legal and medical assistance she needs?

8   How can the greatest possible degree of physical mobility and independence be maintained?

In traditional approaches, one helper might deal with this woman's vocational goals, another with her physical needs, and still another with her psychological adjustment. Her needs for socializing and recreation might never be touched.

The community counselor sees the individual as a total person, interacting with a total environment. Her interactions make up her potential support system. The basic underlying question becomes: Is her former support system holding up under the pressure of change, or does she need additional, supplemental sources of help in order to have all of her needs met effectively? Where can additional support be found, and how can she be helped to make the most of the opportunities that now exist?

A Mature Woman Continuing Her Education

A woman who has devoted full time to raising a family and maintaining a household decides to return to school to complete an education that had been interrupted upon the birth of her first child. Her success, of course, depends on her own motivation, talent, and good fortune, but the environment does make a difference. The community counselor asks the following questions.

1   *Is her family supportive and enthusiastic about her new endeavor? If not, how can they be helped to understand the situation more fully?*

2   *Do her usual friends and associates understand her goals? Are some of them in similar situations, or do their values differ? Are they likely to encourage or discourage her?*

3   *Are there other women taking similar steps who might prove to be supportive new contacts?*

4   *How is her move affecting the family's economic well-being in the immediate present? Are sources of aid available?*

5   *Is the educational institution meeting her special needs by providing for day care, for flexible scheduling, or for vocational counseling?*

6   *Are extracurricular activities on campus geared solely toward young, resident students, or are there opportunities available that might be relevant for her and for other mature students? Can new and appropriate activities be designed?*

7   *What steps have been taken to integrate mature students into campus life? What kinds of interactions exist between age groups?*

8   *Who is taking responsibility for the household tasks to which she previously devoted her full time? Is the family pitching in? Are other helping resources available?*

9   *When she has completed her education, what job opportunities will she find? Are local hiring practices discriminatory against women or against middle-aged people? Are part-time or flexible careers possible? Can they be made possible?*

In this instance, what appears to be an individual step really involves the family, the educational institution, and the community. A change in this one individual's behavior places stress on all of her interactions with the environment. The support system, which might have been strong, is forced to adapt. If the former support system proves inadequate, new sources of help must be added to the environment, or some kind of change must take place.

Choice Points in the Change Process

When a counselor and a counselee work together to solve some problem or resolve some issue, they are dealing with a process of change. As an outcome of counseling, something must obviously be modified; otherwise, the people involved are back where they began.

Most counselors have always assumed that the objects of change should be the attitudes, the feelings, or the behaviors of the counselee. We are becoming more aware every day, however, that the obstacles that keep an individual from meeting his or her goals may be in the environment, rather than in the individual's own behaviors. One way to deal with this issue is to separate the cause of the problem from consideration of its solution. Even if environmental factors are clearly involved in the development of a problem, as when economic changes cause an individual's unemployment, "It may be important to separate responsibility for the *etiology* of the problem from responsibility for the *resolution* of the problem. Otherwise there is a danger that the individual will suffer passivity and helplessness from being portrayed as a victim of economic and social circumstance beyond his or her control" (Monahan & Vaux, 1980). This approach, which Brickman, Rabinowitz, Karuza, Coates, Cohn, and Kidder (1982) term the *compensatory model*, allows for recognition that the individual is not at fault for his or her predicament but can still take action to resolve it.

Counselors can also recognize that it is possible to resolve issues by directly attacking contributing factors that are external to the client. It is unrealistic for counselors to choose sides, with some insisting that most problems are within the individual and others just as sure that a destructive environment is usually to blame. In fact, sometimes individuals have the power to solve their own problems and sometimes they don't. It is helpful to look at the counseling process in terms of a number of choice points. These choice points are occasions when the counselor and the counselee, in concert, decide who has the power to resolve the issue at hand.

The First Choice Point   Figure 4.1 provides an illustration of the first choice point. As the counseling process has progressed, a specific issue has been brought to light. Working together, the counselor and the counselee attempt to clarify the alternative actions that might bring about a resolution. Every attempt is made to solve the problem through individual initiative. When a standstill is reached, the counselor and the counselee are forced to ask whether the counselee does, in fact, have the power to implement the best possible solution.

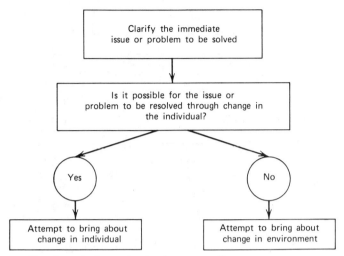

Figure 4.1 The first choice point in the counseling process.

If it is at all possible for the issue to be resolved through change in the individual, attempts are made to bring about that change. If it seems impossible at this point for the individual to grow—if some destructive force in the environment is placing an obstacle in his or her path—then attempts are made to bring about a change in the environment.

For example, if we return to consideration of the runaway youth discussed above, we can see that, early in the counseling process, the choice point is reached. The boy, with his counselor, must decide whether it is possible for him to return home and make a more satisfactory adjustment to his family by changing his own behavior. There is a good chance that this is all that is needed. Perhaps the youth can learn to communicate more effectively with his family, or make simple compromises in his behavior, or try to understand what his parents' expectations might be.

It is just as possible that the solution to his problem is not in his own hands. Perhaps his home or school situation is intolerable as it presently exists. In that case, attempts must be made to bring about appropriate changes in the environment.

Changing the Individual Suppose that a counselor and a counselee have decided that an individual might, indeed, have the power to change, and thus to solve the immediate problem. Figure 4.2 indicates the next choice point.

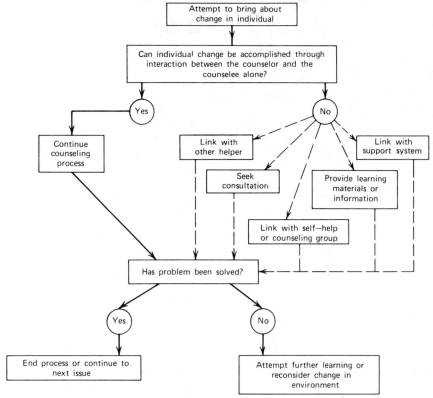

Figure 4.2   Choice point in individual change.

The next step must be to select the best method the individual can use to learn and, therefore, to change. Continuation in the one-to-one counseling process might be enough but, in some cases, other activities are needed.

It might be appropriate to link the individual more closely with other people in the natural support system or to work with the counselee in a group setting. The counselor might feel adequate to deal with the situation on a one-to-one basis, but only if consultation with a more specialized helper is also part of the process. It might become necessary to provide the counselee with additional opportunities to learn, such as programmed materials in decision making or participation in a seminar dealing with self-modification techniques.

Whether the counseling process alone is continued or other activities are involved, the counselor and the counselee finally evaluate the success of their efforts. If it seems that the appropriate learning has taken place and the problem can be solved, the counseling relationship is ended or the pair goes on to deal with another issue or problem. If the initial problem is still unresolved, they must decide whether additional learning is needed or whether, in fact, it will still be necessary to bring about some change in the environment.

Looking again at our example—that of the runaway adolescent—we can see that the youth might make the commitment to try to adjust to his school and home situations by changing his own behavior. How can he deal most effectively with the need to change?

Perhaps his goals can be achieved most effectively by continuing in the counseling relationship. Perhaps, however, there is someone in his "natural support system"—a friend, a relative, a teacher—who can assist him as well as the counselor could. The counselor might help him to plan for increased contacts with that person, knowing that ongoing relationships would be needed as close as possible to the situation where the difficulty originated.

Perhaps the youth and the counselor realize that new behaviors might be most effectively tried out among peers; the boy might be included in a counseling group made up of teenagers like himself. Perhaps, on the other hand, his primary problem involves conflict at school; he might be provided with educational or vocational materials to help him in the process of setting new goals.

The activities in which the youth becomes involved could include one learning process or a combination of several. Whatever method is chosen, the counselor and the counselee must finally evaluate their success. If the youth has changed all that he can change at this particular time and still experiences conflict at home or in school, some kind of intervention in those places must be considered again, or the youth can choose to adapt to a totally new situation.

Changing the Environment   When the counselor and the counselee tentatively decide that the solution to a problem lies outside of the counselee's own behavior, new questions must be asked. Figure 4.3 illustrates the nature of this choice point.

If the counselee does not have the power to solve the immediate problem, who does have that power? If change in the attitudes or behaviors of another person or group of people would solve the problem, the appropriate step might be to offer to consult with the individual or group,

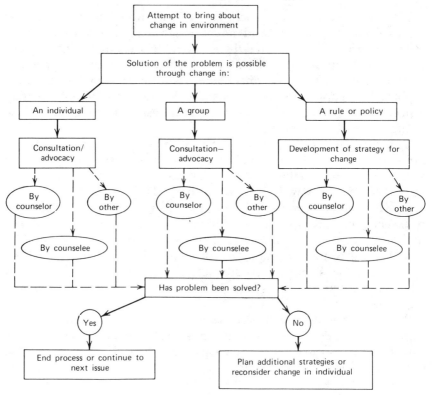

Figure 4.3   Choice point in environmental change.

or to speak up on behalf of the counselee. The person performing this task might be the counselor, the counselee, or another person, such as a citizen advocate or an official. If the solution to the problem requires an alteration in the rules or policies of some agency or institution, then a strategy for bringing about change must be devised. The appropriate person to take leadership in this process might be the counselor, the counselee, or another individual or group. The counselor is most likely to play an active role in confronting the issue if the rule or policy in question is having a negative effect on a number of people.

If change in the environment does take place and the problem has been solved, then the counseling process can be ended, or the counselor and the counselee can go on to deal with other problems or issues. If the problem has not yet been solved, they must plan additional strategies for dealing with the environment or consider once more the possibility that it is the individual who must change.

Our runaway youth might have been trying to escape from a severe conflict at home or in school. The aspects of the environment that he and the counselor might try to change would probably have to do with his parents or with school officials. Consulting with these individuals would be one way of helping the important adults in his life to make his normal environment more supportive for him. If those adults seem unwilling to participate in the change process, more active confrontations on behalf of the boy might become necessary. If the adults are willing to change their behavior but the conflict still exists, it might be necessary for the youth to consider again the part his own behavior is playing in the problem.

Change and Interaction Through all of the choice points in the counseling process, what is being selected is the area of major emphasis at any one time. When counselors help individuals to change, they are, at the same time, aware of the effects of the environment. When they concentrate on environmental change, they are aware of the individual's complex responses.

The interactive counseling process cannot, of course, be oversimplified. At each choice point, counselor and client consider the question of what kind of change—individual or environmental—could most effectively solve the problem at hand. They must also examine, however, the readiness for change being exhibited by the individual or by significant others in the environment. They first ask what change is preferable. They additionally ask what change is possible.

The important point is that community counselors need not choose between helping individuals and confronting the environment. They need not choose between being counselors and being agents of change. Those two roles constantly interact. Dealing with the environment can and should be an important part of the counseling process itself. Most important, this approach does not conflict with the compensatory model suggested by Brickman et al. (1982). While clients might recognize that the needed change is not just in their own behavior, they are learning to take a proactive stance in dealing with the systems that affect them. In this sense, their attitudes and behaviors might, in fact, begin to change.

COUNSELING ACCESSIBILITY

The opportunity for counseling should be a part of life in every community. When counseling is seen as a normal part of living, readily available to people without serious problems, self-referral comes early, when issues or problems can be easily resolved. When it is seen as a service that is distant and threatening, people tend to take advantage of the opportunity for self-exploration only when problems have already become severe. A goal of the community counselor is to make a personal growth experience easily attainable, no matter when or why an individual desires it. Only then can proactive counseling become a reality.

Enlarging the Pool of Counselors

It is becoming apparent that many people, in addition to professionals with academic credentials, can be trained to counsel effectively. If developmental counseling is to become a service that is delivered efficiently to members of the community, all available resources must be utilized. This means that counseling must be offered by a large number of people, including professionals, paraprofessionals, and volunteers. (We define professionals as individuals with graduate level training, emphasizing theory and research, as well as supervised experience in counseling or therapy. Paraprofessionals may also be career counselors. Usually, however, their academic work has been of shorter duration, with great emphasis on practical experiences and on-the-job training. Volunteers often have some career identity outside of their work as helpers, and volunteer their time in order to receive short-term training and to involve themselves in helping relationships.)

At one time, there was a reluctance among professionals to view their paraprofessional colleagues as counselors who could function effectively and independently in their own right. During the 1960s, great strides were made in this direction, so that now the role of the paraprofessional or nonprofessional counselor is widely accepted.

Of particular significance in the early stages was the work of Rioch, Elkes, Flint, Usdansky, Newman, and Silber, (1963) in training mental health counselors as a pilot study by the National Institute of Mental Health. Eight mature women, all of whom had raised families and were ready to embark on second careers, were trained as therapists to work with a variety of clients. Their training was intensive and concentrated specifically on counseling. The two-year program included:

1   *Supervised interviewing practice.*
2   *Observation of group, family, and individual therapy.*
3   *Lectures and discussions.*

4 *Outside reading and report writing.*

5 *Field placement with agencies in the community.*

This program was consistently evaluated as being successful on the basis of independent ratings of counselor effectiveness, measured changes in the clients who were served, and the fact that the individuals trained in the program were able to obtain and hold employment as counselors.

Rioch's trainees were educated, financially secure individuals who might work outside their own communities. But the 1960s also brought strong evidence of the effectiveness of "indigenous" mental health workers: nonprofessionals recruited from within a community and trained to serve their neighbors. The Neighborhood Service Centers, as described by Hallowitz and Riessman (1967), utilized mental health aides to provide a number of practical, direct services in the community. Their training was highlighted by the prevalence of on-the-job education. After a three-week initial training period, aides began to work at the centers. For two weeks, they worked half-time and received training and supervision half-time. After that, supervision was built into the normal, already ongoing program. It was apparent that this approach brought with it a new ability to serve larger numbers of consumers than could have been treated in a traditional mental health facility.

The Dona Ana Mental Health Services demonstration study, also occurring in the late 1960s, allowed for the provision of services in a community that had had no organized mental health facilities. The participants in the study, as described by Neleigh et al. (1971), were nonprofessionals who averaged 46 years of age and who were trained for second careers in mental health services. An important development in this instance was that they were trained, not solely as counselors, but as project leaders who would be able to create and maintain totally new service delivery systems. The responsibilities of the trained community project leader included those of leader and program developer, director, and coordinator, as well as counselor or therapist.

Since the breakthroughs made in the 1960s, carefully selected volunteers and new professionals have been trained to provide counseling services to virtually every kind of population. This trend increases the accessibility of counseling through sheer numbers of available counselors. At the same time, it might serve to enhance accessibility by allowing for a closer identification and a greater degree of trust between counselor and potential counselee.

A service approach that allows for a mixture of professionals and nonprofessionals brings with it a chance for workers with different kinds of expertise to learn from one another. Professionals are on hand to assist with training, supervision, consultation, and evaluation. At the same time, those professionals can learn a great deal from colleagues who may have more intimate knowledge of the needs of the community. Ideally, counselors and the consumers of their services can become more closely involved, with the result that the counseling service becomes more heavily used.

Providing Timely Counseling

The essence of easily accessible counseling is the hope that individuals may make use of the service at an early stage of problem development, when counseling can still be developmental instead of crisis centered.

One approach to this is the provision of accessible counseling for children, whose problems might be more easily resolvable than they would be if ignored until adulthood. Many mental health professionals envision the possibility of large-scale screening, using some measurement that could identify potential problems and then providing appropriate services for dealing with them. At this point, it seems that what little could be done to relieve impending symptoms would not outweigh the dangers of invasion of privacy and early labeling of "problem children."

Instead, voluntary participation in some kind of special personal relationship should become a real option for every child. Most schools have access to the services of psychologists, social workers, or counselors. Especially at the primary levels, however, there are seldom enough of these professionals employed to provide for more than brief personal contact with large numbers of children. More and more, aides and volunteers are being trained to fill this gap, and a body of research indicating their effectiveness is beginning to grow.

In Rochester, New York, for instance, 55 women who had been devoting their full time to homemaking were recruited to serve as child-aides (Cowen, McKim & Weissberg, 1971). In each of 11 schools, 5 aides worked in conjunction with mental health professionals, who were asked to decrease their time spent in diagnosis and treatment and to increase their time spent in consulting and supervising. The aides developed one-to-one relationships with primary grade children who had been referred by their classroom teachers. The interesting aspect of this study is that, in a period of three months, the aides saw 329 children 7583 times (an average of 23 contacts per child). In some schools, aides reached fewer children but saw each many more times; in others, a larger number of children was seen, but the number of contacts was fewer. In either case, many children were able — perhaps for the first time — to develop personal relationships with adults outside of their own families whose only interest was in helping them.

Many programs now in existence give mature women, who have raised or are raising families of their own, the chance to develop counseling relationships with children in the school setting. Another valuable counseling resource can be found among college students who wish to receive training and gain practical experience in working with children.

A good example of this kind of program is provided by Goodman (1972), who paired male college students with fifth- and sixth-grade boys. Half of the boys were seen as "quiet" and had problems such as isolation or withdrawal; half were "outgoing" and had difficulties such as being aggressive or hostile to others. Their helpers, the college students, were also divided into a "quiet" group and an "outgoing" group. Additionally, half of the counselors received training in weekly discussion groups, while the other half participated only in an initial orientation. The boys met with their counselors twice a week over the school year, to do or to talk about whatever they desired. Using a number of measurements of success, including parents' ratings of changes that they saw in their own children, Goodman found that the greatest degree of change took place among the boys who had been withdrawn or isolated, and that the most successful counselors were those who participated in ongoing traininng sessions.

As the use of nonprofessional adult counselors is becoming more widespread, so is the implementation of programs allowing children to counsel other children. Peer counseling at the secondary school level is becoming more common. Even more innovative is the extension of this concept into the elementary school. In a cross-age project described by Hawkinshire (1969), sixth-grade children who wished to participate served as helpers for four-year-olds in a junior kindergarten program. The older children received special training, which included the opportunity to visit and observe the junior kindergarten and to discuss and role-play sample problems in a seminar. An exciting facet of this project is that the researchers "found . . . older problem children to be excellent in working with younger children who, in many ways, [were] expressing some of the same behavioral symptoms" (p. 147).

Much of the research that has been done in this area emphasizes the provision of counseling for children with special problems. In fact, however, there is no reason that developmental counseling, or at least some kind of nourishing relationship, cannot be made available to *any* child. If aides and volunteers can work with disturbed children, they can also help utterly normal children to work through any current problems or decisions they might be facing.

Professionals, paraprofessionals, and volunteers can also help effectively functioning *adults* to deal with minor problems before those problems become major distractions. But counseling can only be timely if potential counselees are willing to use the service before they are faced with real discomfort. This, in turn, can only happen when participation in the counseling process is seen as a perfectly normal thing to do. That kind of image depends, to a great extent, on the setting in which counseling takes place.

Counseling in Accessible Settings

Counseling is only accessible if it is a normal part of community life, and it can become a normal part of community life only when it is located in or near the places where people live and work. Ideally, helpers could be on call in every neighborhood and in every work setting that employs large numbers of people. An "agency without walls" could train counselors who would then go to where the people are instead of waiting for their clients to come to them.

Now and in the immediate future, of course, counseling will continue to be provided in identifiable places. Those places will be utilized if they are both physically convenient and psychologically comfortable.

It is becoming apparent that decentralization is an important factor. It seems that physical facilities can be most effectively used when they are relatively small and scattered throughout a geographical area instead of being large and meant to attract consumers from all over a large community. Some of the importance of decentralization comes from the factor of community identification, some from the mere ease with which an individual can travel to a facility.

Within the facility itself, accessibility involves the kinds of experiences people can expect to have once they are there. If those experiences are to be both comfortable and comforting, several criteria must be met.

1 *Workers should be individuals who feel close to and accepting of the people they are there to serve.*
2 *There should be an adequate number of counselors, so that waiting lists and formal appointments can be avoided.*
3 *Procedures for becoming a client should be informal and uncomplicated.*

Crisis and Accessiblity

The quick accessibility of counseling is particularly necessary in dealing with crisis situations, and perhaps that is why the greatest strides toward immediate service have been made in this area. A crisis is a temporary stage in a person's life when his or her normal ways of dealing with the world are suddenly interrupted. The crisis may be the result of a number of problems adding up, or it might stem from a sudden life change. Regardless of the cause, people in crisis suddenly find that they are no longer on an even keel. They need help from other people — help in exploring the immediate problem, in finding the resources needed for its solution, in developing a practical plan of attack. Often, in their feelings of helplessness or tension, they need personal support and encouragement.

Although a crisis is temporary, the way it is handled can have long-lasting effects. When the difficulty is handled quickly and appropriately, the individual may grow from the experience, learning new problem-solving approaches and developing ways to avoid crises in the future. When a crisis is *not* faced and dealt with, the individual may emerge with ineffective methods of coping with the world. Problems may become chronic, or permanent.

In a crisis situation, then, timeliness is everything. A person in crisis needs immediate help, and that means assistance that is readily available. Crisis centers, which are now present in most cities, have *enlarged the pool of available workers* by using large numbers of trained volunteers. They have *provided timely services* by developing 24-hour telephone lines or walk-in facilities, so that helpers can react quickly and flexibly, with no waiting period. They have *created accessible settings,* often involving out-posts at crisis settings, such as hospital emergency rooms, or teams of helpers ready to go wherever they are needed. Still more could be accomplished in the area of crisis prevention by reaching out to people at earlier stages of crisis development.

To "intervene" is to enter into a situation and thereby change it in some way. Thus, in "crisis intervention" a helper is asked to enter the life of an individual in order to affect the outcome of a crisis being experienced. The intervention, of course, is temporary, with the desired end result being the individual's ability to develop all of the resources needed for a return to independence. Crisis intervention may take place in a center designed specifically for that purpose, or it may occur in an agency with a wider mandate for service. In either instance, the same basic principles apply.

McGee (1974) describes the *Community Model* for suicide and crisis services, emphasizing that the development and operation of such services must adhere to innovative principles of service delivery. If a program is to be termed "community based," it must include:

1 *Utilization of nonprofessional personnel.*
2 *Utilization of professional people as consultants.*
3 *An emphasis on prevention rather than treatment.*
4 *Avoidance of a pathology model.*
5 *Membership in a network of agencies.*
6 *Commitment to evaluation research.*

All of McGee's six principles are interconnected in terms of the assumptions on which they are based. The community model operates on the understanding that crises can be events in the lives of normal people who are faced with real stress and real environmental pressures. Intervenors need to know a great deal about the nature of crisis, but they do not necessarily need extensive knowledge of mental illness symptomatology. The job of helpers in crisis includes (Dixon & Burns, 1974, p. 122):[1]

1 Ascertaining what happened before the onset of crisis. What is the normal patterning of the person's life?
2 Putting the problem into perspective, helping the client to assess the situation in a realistic fashion, engaging in an active exploration of the problem and the identification of the most important information.
3 Helping the client in the identification of personal, institutional and other contextual sources of support.
4 A breakdown of the problem into manageable pieces and working through those one at a time, starting with those which can be worked on most directly or immediately.
5 Helping formulate new coping strategies.
6 Allocation of affect—helping person become aware of his own feelings and the possible feelings of others, including the expression of both positive and negative feelings.
7 Helping the person pace his efforts and thereby maintain control in as many areas of functioning as possible.
8 Helping the person to reorganize his life situation so as to avoid the reoccurrence of this or similar crisis situations in the future.

The approach to crisis intervention, then, is eminently practical, calling for tremendous stores of what might be termed "common sense skills."

[1]Copyright © *Journal of Community Psychology*. Reprinted with permission.

One of those common-sense skills is the ability to call on resources that can help people in crisis, not only to solve their immediate problems, but to prevent future stress. This requires awareness of, and close cooperation with, a network of other agencies or consultants that might be called on for assistance. Underlying all of these efforts is the need to evaluate every service given on the basis of its practical outcome.

The community model is in direct opposition to an approach based on a "pathology model," or the assumption that people in crisis are somehow disturbed or mentally ill. That basic assumption would have implications in practice. If it were assumed that all of such people's solutions are within themselves, it would also be assumed that they could only be helped to find those solutions through interactions with highly trained, professional specialists.

It is because traditional services failed to meet crisis needs that additional resources had to be developed. McCord and Packwood (1973) point out that:

> Most such centers and agencies provide their services only during the day and require that the person come to the office; they are not designed to handle bad drug experiences and other personal crises which can occur at any time and which require immediate attention. Crisis centers and hotlines provide help during the "uncovered" hours and are as convenient as the nearest telephone (p. 723).

Telephone counseling alone, however, has its own limitations. The centers that avoid face-to-face contact can deal with people in crisis only through verbal interchanges or referral to other helping sources. Although an initial contact, and even a beginning relationship, can be formed quickly, follow-through is difficult. It is becoming more apparent that crisis intervention, in addition to being highly accessible, must also be highly active. Physical movement to the source of crisis is being recognized as important, both in crisis centers and in the emergency components of innovative mental health centers.

High-Risk Situations

It is not possible to prevent every crisis. It is possible, however, to recognize the existence of common crisis-provoking situations and to reach out to people who are facing them. We know that there are specific life changes that place heavy demands on individuals as they try to cope with them. Recognizing this, we can provide the chance for people facing those changes to develop techniques for solving their current problems and to provide help and support for one another.

Holmes and Rahe (1967) have identified and ranked a number of life events that are particularly stressful, including:[2]

Death of spouse
Divorce
Marital separation
Jail term
Death of close family member
Personal injury or illness
Marriage
Fired at work
Marital reconciliation
Retirement
Change in health of family member
Pregnancy
Sex difficulties
Gain of new family member
Change in financial state
Death of close friend
Change to different line of work
Change in number of arguments with spouse
Mortgage over $10,000
Foreclosure of mortgage or loan
Change in responsibilities at work
Son or daughter leaving home
Trouble with in-laws
Outstanding personal achievement
Wife beginning or stopping work
Beginning or ending school
Revision of personal habits
Trouble with boss
Change in work hours or conditions
Change in residence
Change in schools
Change in recreation
Change in social activities
Mortgage or loan less than $10,000
Change in sleeping habits
Change in number of family get-togethers

Change in eating habits
Vacation
Minor violations of the law

Many of the highest-ranked life changes listed have implications for other areas of living, too. For instance, death or separation of spouse, a jail term, personal injury, retirement, or gain of a new family member may also bring about changes in financial status that might be crisis provoking in themselves.

Just as people are affected by identifiable life changes, they are also subjected to chronic, ongoing stressors that can also place strains on the ability to cope.

> Instead of searching for a specific underlying precondition associated with a particular pattern of maladaptive behavior, researchers have begun to focus their interests much more directly on stressful life events which appear to be capable of triggering patterns of maladaptive behavior in a proportion of the population that experiences those events. Thus, researchers have begun to shift their attention from "high risk populations" to "high risk situations" and events (Price, Bader, & Ketterer, 1980, p. 11).

Stressful situations can bring about a variety of physical, psychological, and social dysfunctions, but a stress reaction, in itself, is transient. "What follows after the immediate, transient stress reaction depends on the mediation of situational and psychological factors that define the context in which this reaction occurs" (Dohrenwend, 1978, p. 4). Whether individuals are able to withstand a high degree of stress depends, at least in part, on factors that can serve as buffers to protect the individual's sense of well-being. Such "buffers" include social support systems (Wilcox, 1981), the sense of having control over events (Bandura, 1982; Johnson & Sarason, 1979) and cognitive problem-solving skills (Shure & Spivack, 1982). People can develop what Kobasa (1979) terms *hardiness,* or the strength to withstand stressful situations.

We know that people faced with difficult life situations need to develop new and practical problem-solving strategies and approaches to everyday living. We also know that such people need close contact with others, new links to human beings who can provide support and encouragement. We can provide for these needs by creating self-help and educational opportunities for people currently facing volatile life changes.

What Sauber (1973) terms "anticipatory guidance for life crisis" can take the form of time-limited educational interventions or of less structured self-help networks. For instance, Chicago's Ravenswood Hospital Community Mental Health Center offers, through its Consultation and Education Department, "minicourses" of three to six weeks' duration for such groups as widows and widowers, newly separated individuals, new mothers, people preparing for retirement, and the recently unemployed. These courses provide the opportunity both for mutual support and for the sharing of concrete information about effective coping methods. Another strategy involves ongoing support groups, telephone outreach methods, and informal social groups for people dealing with such stressful events as loss of a spouse, family changes, or health problems.

In any community, it is possible to identify crisis situations that are especially prevalent and to organize around them. When a particularly stressful situation affects a large number of people, major interventions can prevent chronic problems and increase opportunities for growth. A good example of such an effort is provided by Atlanta's "Project C.A.N."

CLIENT SERVICES IN ACTION: PROJECT "C.A.N."[3]

Project C.A.N. (Community Action Network) was established in response to the distress created by Atlanta's Missing and Murdered Children's Crisis. The project was first suggested in 1980, after many Black children had been victimized. Project C.A.N. addressed the mental health aspects of the crisis, including stress, fear, personal safety, the gaps in community resources and support systems, and public neglect of children's needs. As a primary prevention and early intervention project, the program, under the direction of Dorothy Jeffries, focused on reducing environmental stressors and enhancing individual and community competence.

The mental health-related issues emerging out of the Missing and Murdered Children's Crisis were broad. The crisis created anxiety, fear of adults, and feelings of vulnerability for most children and their parents. Warnings to children concerning safety may have taught a distrust of adults, which could have long-term implications. The helplessness felt by adults might have affected children's sense of competence and initiative. "If it is not safe to be a child," how does that affect a child's self-esteem and beliefs about his/her environment?

Moreover, the crisis demonstrated a lack of mutual support and networking

[3]Adapted from Project C.A.N. Summary of Services, April, 1982. Reprinted with permission.

in the community. Many families chose to become isolated, rather than utilizing and forming support systems. Organizations and the media demonstrated a lack of sensitivity to the realities of the victims' communities.

In developing consultation, education, and outreach services, the staff assumed that effective coping with the sequelae of the crisis would improve the overall competence of children and adults. The primary emphases of the project included outreach to children and families in distress, community education, and training for parents and others with responsibility for care of children and adolescents. The project was also built on recognition that the effects of crises do not stop when the immediate danger is over. Children and adults still felt vulnerable, even when the media no longer reported stories of Missing and Murdered Children and a man had been convicted of two murders. The feelings engendered by the crisis continued to create distress, even as citizens and communities tried to forget it. Project C.A.N. continued to address the problems with educational and outreach programs, even after the arrest and conviction of an individual.

Project C.A.N., under the auspices of the Central Fulton Community Mental Health Center in Atlanta, Georgia, used a multi-faceted approach to dealing with this "high-risk situation."

1 Clinical Outreach Team

An interdisciplinary team of mental health professionals provided direct clinical services to children and families affected by the impact of the Murdered Children's Crisis. Services were provided directly to families and groups, with efforts coordinated with appropriate agencies in the immediate locales. The focus of therapy was on alleviating situational stress, facilitating the grief resolution process, and working out strategies to cope with the persistent nightmares and excessive fears experienced by the siblings of the victims and other children directly affected by the crisis. Treatment took place in the household of each family who requested the service, and appointment times were arranged so that the majority of the family members could be present.

In several cases additional work was done with individual children whose problems warranted special attention. These children were experiencing a range of symptoms including severe nightmares, excessive fear of strangers, decrease in school performance, bedwetting, acting out behavior and somatic complaints. The children were seen on a weekly basis in their school setting in conjunction with family therapy.

2 Groups for Children and Youth

A number of therapeutic groups were conducted throughout the city for children and youth. All groups were individually tailored to meet the needs of the agency or community group involved. Topics that were addressed in various groups included communication, cooperation, coping with issues of fear and safety, development of positive self-image for Black youth, anxiety and stress, values clarification, parental expectations, trust, anger, interpersonal conflict, and male/female relationships. Community resources such as the Minority Resource Center, Atlanta Public Schools, the Atlanta Public Library, and Planned Parenthood were used, with the ultimate goal being to assist community people so that groups could continue without Project C.A.N. staff.

3 Groups for Adults

Groups for adults normally met one time, and included presentations about Project C.A.N. Other topics included parenting, community involvement, networking as a resource for parents, identification of stress in children, parent/child communication, child development, children's perceptions of death, effects of television programming, and coping with issues of fear and safety. Groups/presentations were held at a variety of locations, including day care centers, churches, PTA meetings, health centers, tenant association meetings, mental health center citizens advisory council meetings, tutorial programs, police roll call, Metro Atlanta Boys' Club, and a number of other area public service agencies and community meetings.

4 Project I Can: Safe Summer '81

Ten graduate/college students, titled Community Educators, were hired with the assistance of the Atlanta Urban Corps to deliver a mental health-related summer program. Teams visited children's recreational centers and provided educational interventions designed to deal with such issues as self-esteem of Black children, values clarification, moral development, assertiveness, feelings about death and violence, identity, and decision making. Educators used a variety of approaches, including role playing, ice breakers, decision making exercises, identity exercises, experiences related to feelings, creative arts activities, brainstorming, discussions, and stress management training.

5 Literature for Children and Parents

Project C.A.N. developed materials as a strategy for reaching large numbers of community residents. These included:

a   Halloween Flyer: A flyer designed to address children's fears, to help adults recognize fear, and to outline safety precautions.
b   Holiday Message: The poem, "Children Learning What They Live," was distributed during Christmas week in poster form to schools, child care centers, recreational programs, and churches.
c   Parent-Child Community Flyer: A flyer, developed with the Police Department's Project SAFE, to encourage parents to communicate more with their children was distributed to every elementary and middle school.

d Valentine's Day Cards: Children were asked to draw valentine cards and write messages expressing concern for others. Copies of six cards were distributed by children to isolated people in the community.

e Comic Book About Fear: A comic book, based on thoughts and feelings expressed by 200 young adolescents, was designed for distribution to middle school children.

f Storybook/Workbook Concerning Feelings of Loss: The book, designed for young school-age children, encouraged understanding and expression of feelings.

These and other printed materials were used to reach children and adults who might not be touched by direct services.

6 Stress Training Program

Project C.A.N. developed a Stress Training Program to address the definition of stress and its impact, stress and normal development in children, developmental perceptions of death in children, signs and symptoms of stress, stress reduction, and available resources. The purpose of the program was to provide needed information to organizations and workers attempting to serve children and youth. The stress training was available to parents, day care teachers, school personnel, church personnel, human service agencies, community interest groups, youth serving organizations, and others.

7 Media Contacts

Project C.A.N. was involved in several media activities. One staff member participated in a Television Production Workshop that taught basic skills in producing public service announcements and short television segments. A Project C.A.N. open house was covered by local television newscasts and News Radio. In addition, interviews and filmed segments aired after the Wayne Williams conviction stressed the need for ongoing concern.

8 Networking

Networking was, from the beginning, a major goal of Project C.A.N. Although many direct services were offered, the objective of the project was to enhance the competence and self-esteem of the community as a whole. As the staff of Project C.A.N. puts it.

Networking is a voice of commitment which allows us to demonstrate our contribution and responsibility to have the city of Atlanta work for everyone, with no one or no thing left out. Community Action Network's task is to act as a clearinghouse and connect the services with each other and the total community (Project C.A.N., 1982, p. 28).

SUMMARY

Client counseling approaches are designed to help individuals and groups faced with the need for direct services. Such services include proactive, accessible counseling, as well as attempts to deal with high-risk situations.

Proactive counseling involves working with individuals and with their social environments. When proactive counselors work with clients, they attempt to build on sources of help in the support system and, when necessary, to resolve issues by directly confronting environmental factors. As the counseling process develops, counselor and client face a number of choice points at which they attempt to determine whether the issue can be resolved best through change in the individual or through change in the environment.

Proactive counseling should be seen as a normal part of living, with help readily accessible to individuals who might not yet have serious problems. Accessibility depends on enlarging the pool of counselors to include paraprofessionals and volunteers, as well as on the provision of services in convenient and non-threatening settings. Such accessibility is especially important for dealing with crisis situations before their effects lead to chronic difficulties.

Many crises can, in fact, be prevented. There are a number of stressful situations that we know place heavy demands on people's coping skills. People facing such crisis-provoking life changes can be assisted through the provision of self-help and educational opportunities. An especially noteworthy example of an intervention dealing with a high risk situation is provided by Project C.A.N., an Atlanta program designed to respond to distress brought about through the Missing and Murdered Children's Crisis.

ACTIVITIES TO ENHANCE UNDERSTANDING OF CHAPTER 4

1 Find a friend, colleague, or fellow student who is willing to work with you. Ask the individual to act as a counselee, either role playing an imaginary situation or sharing a real concern. Spend a few minutes exploring the issue with your "client" by using good listening skills and asking for clarification of any point you do not fully understand. When you think you have a good grasp of the problem, state it in your own words and ask whether your understanding is accurate. If it is,

you can now begin to consider available alternatives for resolution. Working together, the two of you should list a number of possibilities that you might explore if this were a real counseling situation. Include both methods for bringing about change in the individual's behavior and possibilities for bringing about change in the environment. In a real counseling situation, do you think you would be likely to explore these environmental factors as completely as you considered individual change technologies?

2 Consider again your own hypothetical community counseling program. For the client population you have identified, what would you do to make sure that counseling was accessible and that crisis situations could be prevented, or at least handled promptly? Design in more detail the client counseling facet of the program.

CHAPTER
5
CLIENT
ADVOCACY

W henever services are offered, emphasis should be placed, not on the recipient's weakness, but on his or her potential strength. An individual may seem to have many needs involving the services of the community counselor; perpetual dependence is never one of them.

These factors appear obvious but traditionally, mental health workers have had difficulty in their implementation. People seeking services have often felt a lack of power over their own lives, a sense that they were being forced to relinquish control over environmental contingencies to others.

> *How* we structure the services we offer to clients may have a significant impact on their perceived personal power. If services are structured in such a manner that experiences seem noncontingent to clients, we are encouraging learned helplessness and perceived external control—powerlessness (Stensrud & Stensrud, 1981, p. 301).

Clients who need specialized services may need assistance in making the environment more responsive to their individual or group needs. Such responsiveness depends on the ability of the community to place value on the contributions of all if its members and to develop helping networks that enhance clients' feelings of power and self-worth.

STRENGTHENING SOCIALLY DEVALUED POPULATIONS

When an individual suffers some "disability" or "impairment," whether mental or physical, he or she is labeled in terms of that quality, and the label carries with it an assumption of dependence and limited worth. When a person's past or present behavior leaves the social mainstream (whether through drug or alcohol abuse, delinquency, a history of institutionalization, or even the mere process of aging), a similar process occurs. Devaluing takes place when a person fails to exhibit "economic productivity" and, when the labeled person is very young, the powerlessness of childhood also takes its toll.

Almond (1974) describes the process through which an individual is labeled as "deviant," or different in some undesirable way. His or her behavior more and more brings about anxiety in others, until finally:

> The individual becomes characterized by his problem behavior. . . . As such, he may be dealt with differently; his deviance becomes the overriding

consideration and he may be arbitrarily deprived of certain rights and freedoms. Handling him becomes the special province of experts in his sort of deviance (Almond, 1974, p. xxiii).

Whether the "expert" involved is a doctor, a psychotherapist, or a jailer, individuals exiled to the province of professional care become separated from their peers and wholly or partially excluded from normal community life. The "overriding conditions" in their lives are emphasized to the point that, sometimes, those conditions *become* their lives.

Those whose labels become central to their interactions with others are, in effect, stigmatized.

> An individual who might have been received easily in ordinary social intercourse possesses a trait that can obtrude itself upon attention and turn those of us whom he meets away from him, breaking the claim that his other attributes have on us. He possesses a stigma, an undesired differentness from what we had anticipated. . . . By definition, of course, we believe the person with a stigma is not quite human (Goffman, 1963, p. 5).

In the long run, this kind of problem can only be resolved through changes in perception, through efforts to adapt society itself to new ways of dealing with everyone's real humanness. In the here and now, stigmatization is a reality, and one way of approaching it is through enhancing the strength of its victims.

When an individual or group has been categorized as likely to benefit from help in addition to that offered to the community as a whole, there is no doubt that some kind of labeling has taken place, if only through the procedure of identification itself. That does not imply that the group should be ignored but, instead, that a hoped-for end result must be a decrease in victimization and an increase in *self-valuing*.

When the community counselor works with socially devalued populations, he or she assumes that it is possible to:

1 *Place the stigma, label, or problem behavior in perspective as only one part of the individual's total being.*
2 *End the self-devaluing that often results from externally placed limitations.*
3 *Bring individuals who have been excluded into the mainstream of social and personal interaction.*
4 *Increase the power of the group to fight for needed social changes.*

It is unlikely that those goals could be reached solely through a relationship between an individual and a professional helper. Instead, the individual must be brought into contact with others, not only to be helped, but to have the chance to offer help. This is most effectively accomplished through self-help networks and through contacts with nonprofessional volunteers from the person's own community.

Self-Help

Dependence on professional assistance is part of the whole exclusionary process. The gap between the individual and his or her community is, if anything, widened.

When people have the opportunity to participate with others, however, their ties to the community are strengthened. When helping becomes a *mutual* occupation, each participant becomes aware of his or her value to others. In "self-help" organizations, people with common bonds have the opportunity to make contact with one another, to provide mutual support, to request or provide active assistance, and to deal with common problems in an understanding but realistic group. All decisions are made by the members, and the members are not divided into the categories of service givers or service receivers. All are both "helpers" and "helpees."

Steele (1974), p. 106), speaking of the self-help phenomenon in general terms, identifies several factors that seem to make such organizations effective.

1 Reference identification is to a peer group.
2 Attitudes are altered through emphasis on action and experience.
3 Communication is facilitated by peers; members do not have to overcome initial cultural, social, and educational barriers.
4 Opportunities for socialization are improved.
5 Group action, free and open discussion, and confrontation by peers help to remove individual defensiveness.
6 Because members are from the same community, they are better able to provide emotional support and understanding.
7 Status is not such a problem with peer group members as when different classes are represented.
8 In self-help groups some semblance of conditions existing in the outside world, appears in the group (Steele, 1974, p. 106)

These factors are particularly significant in the instance of people who have been excluded, for whatever reason, from society's mainstream. In the self-help setting, they can experience normal social contacts, as well as communication that is unhampered by irrelevant barriers. Most important, they can experience the opportunity for leadership. Although a self-help group or network might include professional or volunteer participation, or might even be the result of a human service worker's initial prodding, its potential for success is based on the active participation and commitment of its members. Those members must know that there is "room at the top."

The self-help organization is comparable to the "healing community," as described by Almond (1974). Almond sees the healing community as being therapeutic, both in terms of the interpersonal relationships among individual members and in terms of the social structure of the group as a whole. The therapeutic, or curative, aspects of individual relationships are defined by Almond as *"healing charisma,"* meaning that there is a specialness in the quality of person-to-person interaction, a social energy that helps members to experience themselves as people who can "actually become what they would like to become." The social structure of the group as a whole is characterized by *"communitas."* This means that individuals are not given status according to particular roles or titles but, ideally, that all of the individuals and all of their relationships are "charismatic" and joined by a basic "relatedness."

> The ideal of the healing community is for each individual and every interpersonal relationship to be charismatic. Communitas inspires charismatic feeling by emphasizing basic equality and integral relatedness among members; charisma strengthens the communitas by providing a form for relatedness that is special and not dependent on rigidly defined social structures (Almond, 1974, p. xxx).

When new members enter the community, they are encouraged to believe that the group and all its members are special, and that they can share in this quality. Full membership is valued and is seen as a result of behavior that is modeled according to the particular norms of the group. The same kind of behavior is expected from every member of the group, and it is through that behavior that an initiate becomes a full-fledged group member, a care giver instead of solely a care receiver.

The fact that each member of a self-help group becomes a *care giver* is the key to the efficacy of this approach. "Self-help converts . . . problems or needs into resources. Instead of seeing 32 million people with arthritis as a problem, it is possible to see these people as resources, service givers, for dealing with the everyday concerns of the arthritic. . . . At the same time, people will acquire a new sense of independence and empowerment as a consequence of dealing effectively with their own problems" (Gartner, 1982, p. 64).

One self-help network that works in accordance with this model is "Recovery, Incorporated," an organization for self-described "nervous and former mental patients."

> Recovery, Inc., is a systematic method of self-help aftercare developed by the late Abraham A. Low, M.D., to prevent relapses in former mental patients and chronicity in nervous patients.
>
> Recovery, Inc., is also a self-help organization, operated, managed, supported and controlled by patients and former patients trained in the Recovery method.
>
> Recovery groups located throughout continental United States and Canada meet on a regular weekly basis to provide training in Recovery's systematic method of self-help aftercare.
>
> The Recovery method consists of (1) studying Dr. Low's book, *Mental Health Though Will Training*, and other literature, plus records and tapes recorded by Dr. Low; (2) regular attendance at Recovery meetings; and (3) the practice of Recovery principles in one's daily life (Recovery, Inc., 1973, p. 3).

Recovery, Inc., has been growing since 1937. The initial impetus for the association, as well as its language and literature, were derived from a professional. Now, however, all leaders are lay people who came to the group as "patients." ("Patients" include people recently discharged from mental institutions, as well as others who identify themselves as under psychiatric care or as having symptoms such as anxiety or depression.) At weekly meetings, group discussion is combined with structured panel presentations during which members describe events and discomforts, contrasting old and new ways of dealing with them.

Recovery members emphasize the degree to which they have been helped through practicing the specific steps outlined by Low. It is likely, however, that they are also affected by the new awareness that they are not alone in their problems, by the chance to see successful behavior modeled by others like themselves, and by the realization that they, too, can assist others while helping themselves.

In addition to their regular meetings, experienced members also make presentations for the benefit of educational or community groups. This service provides a means for enhancing public knowledge and awareness concerning mental health, and emphasizes another strength of self-help groups: the chance to give people a collective voice that they would not have as individuals.

There is probably no group as traditionally voiceless as the mentally retarded, and their self-help groups also serve the dual purpose of helping participants while providing a means of communication with mainstream society. Wolfensberger (1972, p. 183) describes the Swedish experience with social clubs consisting of 30 to 40 retarded adults. Nonretarded adults participate, but leave planning and decision making in the hands of the retarded members as leadership emerges. Through these organizations, members have the chance to plan leisure activities in terms of their own desires, to develop social contacts with other people their own age, and to discuss common practical problems.

> Growing confidence was one of the results of the practical experiences gained. Also, the realization that they were sharing problems and interests with others helped the members in redefining to themselves their situation as retarded, as well as experiencing their awareness of being retarded in a new and dignified way. Through these clubs, the retarded were able to contact other organizations, other groups of young adults, and key social bodies dealing with leisure time activities in the community. They were also able to express and make known publicly their problems and endeavors, in newspapers and on television (Wolfensberger 1972, p. 183).

In Sweden, these experiences culminated in a national conference of the retarded, attended by representatives elected in their counties. After three days of work and discussion, consensus was reached on a final report covering topics such as leisure time activities, vacations, living conditions, education, and work. Nonretarded observers did not influence decisions, but were limited to the tasks of facilitation, note taking, and assisting in the editing of the final report. Retarded adults, when given the opportunity, have proven capable of helping themselves.

The physically handicapped are also coming into their own as voices to be reckoned with. Organizations like the Center for Independent Living in Berkeley, California give disabled or blind members the chance to share practical information; to give and get mutual support in the effort to maintain total independence; and to obtain comprehensive, coordinated services. Membership is open to all blind or disabled persons, while the nondisabled must obtain the signatures of four members of the Board of Directors in order to join.

In addition to providing a setting for mutual self-help, the C.I.L. reaches out into the total community. Educational programs provide a consciousness-raising experience for the general public; two radio documentaries, Stigma I and II, describe the feelings of the disabled, their perceptions of society's reactions, and the importance of organization for independence.

At the same time, unity gives the disabled a power base from which to work for needed changes in the physical and social environment. They can work for the attitudinal and legislative advances that can provide for fair housing and employment opportunities, the provision of accessible buildings and transportation, and the removal of physical barriers to free movement. They can fight for their own right to independent, unencumbered living.

The aged are also finding the need and the ability to fight. Social clubs, retirees' associations, and other organizations encourage senior citizens to make contact with one another, to increase their independence, and to break out of their isolation. The "Grey Panthers," in particular, has a strong social action component. Made up of autonomous local groups, with a national steering committee available for information and consultation, the Grey Panthers is providing an opportunity for seniors to help themselves. In addition to providing mutual self-help, these organizations lobby for issues such as the provision of preventive medicine through medicare, the improvement of decayed and deadening nursing homes, and the increased accessibility of public buildings and transportation. As their theme song states,

> "I'm a wrinkled radical.
> You'd better watch out for me."

Through self-help, many others are finding that they, too, are capable of helping themselves, and capable of expressing their needs to the total community.

The long-established Alcoholics Anonymous, with offshoots like Alanon and Alateen, allows alcoholics and their families to solve concrete problems while educating the public and assisting newcomers to solidify their commitments to change.

Parents Anonymous allows abusive parents to discuss their problems with people they can trust, while providing a means for prompt help and support when a crisis occurs.

Welfare rights organizations, as well as associations of ex-offenders, give a powerful voice to people whose social and economic contributions tend to be downgraded by the society at large.

Self-governance in penal institutions gives inmates some control over their own rehabilitation.

It seems that the self-help phenomenon does, indeed, help socially devalued populations to develop new ways of approaching their problems, voicing their concerns, increasing their independence, and making contact with others. While self-help can make a difference to many, it is important that such groups be brought into contact with their total communities, not only to be affected by them, but to affect them in return. It is necessary to avoid the pitfall of replacing individual isolation with group isolation. Most of the self-help groups mentioned in these pages provide some kind of outreach into the mainstream society, in addition to the basic presence of the healing community.

In the long run, other bridges must be built. The community counselor can help to build them, and one way is through the establishment of programs using volunteers.

Volunteerism

At one time, the use of nonsalaried volunteers to provide a variety of services seemed necessary because of the limited number of professionals available to deal with multiple problems. It is becoming more apparent that volunteers also have much to offer that is unique to them. Frequently, they can offer a depth of personal involvement, a freshness of approach, and a link to the community that salaried personnel could not duplicate.

Volunteerism is growing far beyond the traditional notion of "doing things to help others less fortunate." Under the traditional definition, the distance between the helpee and the helper might have been as great as that between a client and a professional mental health worker. As Cull and Hardy point out (1974, p. 112), even service-oriented volunteerism is changing. "At the very least there is a trend away from the concept of 'doing for' toward the concepts of 'doing with' and 'helping to help themselves.' "

This orientation is particularly important when we consider volunteer assistance in working with socially devalued populations. Such populations can, indeed, help themselves. Volunteers are needed because of their ability to provide links between the individual or group being helped and the community as a whole. They can do the following.

1 *Provide for two-way communication between an excluded population and the community at large,*

2   Assist in shedding light on the particular concerns of the group being served,

3   Mobilize community support for needed programs and changes.

The best efforts allow volunteers and those they are serving to work together, grow together, and learn together. The best programs do not replace self-help, but complement it.

Often the degree to which such efforts can be totally cooperative comes as a surprise. Wolfensberger (1972, p. 182) describes a three-day course during which retarded adults and volunteers take a trip to a city away from their homes.

> The nonretarded often arrive with the thought that they are to be the teachers, and the retarded will be their pupils. However, soon after arrival, all participants discover that they are taking part in a course common for all. As tourists, they are all going to learn and be enriched through new experiences and meeting new people. All are given the same amount of money for budgeting their weekend needs and activities, such as meals, shopping, sightseeing, and entertainment. When they are exploring the city in small mixed groups of three or four persons (which are changed at certain intervals), they gradually learn not only about the life and assets of this new city, but they also learn from being together. They find out about public transit, price levels of various restaurants, the amusement possibilities for their Saturday night, and the interesting sightseeing places for the Sunday morning walk.
>
> Through these experiences, occasional lectures, and comparative reports and discussions, the non-retarded gradually learn more and more about the proper ways of being together with the mentally retarded, as well as vice versa; and when they later listen to the report from the retarded, and to their reactions to the attitudes of the nonretarded they have met, the nonretarded (volunteers) commonly experience that they were the pupils and the retarded the teachers.[1]

Volunteers in programs such as the one described above certainly provide "help" to others. Just as certainly, however, they return home with new knowledge and new perceptions that enable them to help their communities, too. While the retarded group is being strengthened, the very process of stigmatization is also being attacked.

[1]W. Wolfensberger, *Normalization: The principle of normalization in human services.* Copyright © National Institute on Mental Retardation. Toronto, Canada, 1972. Reprinted by permission.

A similar thing seems to happen when volunteers become involved in corrections. Some of the most common capacities include developing personalized relationships with juvenile offenders, probationers, or prison inmates; locating job possibilities for ex-offenders; providing tutoring, vocational training, or other educational opportunities for prison populations; helping to create recreational programs or other services within prisons; and working with the families of inmates.

But, more important than the specific service being offered, is the willingness of the volunteer to recognize that correctional facilities are a community responsibility and that offenders are a part of the community.

> Both the offender and the community must become the focus of correctional activity. With this thrust, the reintegration of the offender into the community comes to the forefront as a major purpose of corrections. . . . The necessity of interplay between the correctional system and other parts of the public sector demands civic participation to degrees not foreseen even a few years ago.
>
> The new reintegration goals for corrections include the concept of "bridging": the establishment of positive links between the offender and free society (Dye & Sansouci, 1974, p. 133).

Volunteers create those "positive links" through their presence and through their recognition of the humanness of the offender. As this concept grows, the corrections process can be removed from its traditional isolation, and the victims of that process can be removed from theirs. At that point, the community at large can no longer turn away from problems that have long been allocated to the territory of mythical experts.

There are no "experts" who can solve the problems of the stigmatized. Too many of those problems lie in the attitudes of the community itself; therefore, it is up to the community to seek solutions. Many citizens are beginning to recognize that responsibility and to seek part of the action.

All of these attempts at developing effective programs of volunteerism veer sharply away from traditional forms. The volunteer can no longer be viewed as someone with excessive leisure time, someone who can fit in to perform whatever task has been left over or overlooked. What the volunteer has to give is as valuable as what the professional can offer, and this "new volunteer" has the right to expect new attitudes and opportunities.

1   Volunteers should be encouraged to examine their own needs and to develop work styles and assignments that can meet those needs most effectively.

2   *Volunteers should receive immediate training during an orientation period and then obtain in-service education that responds to the questions they themselves raise.*

3   *Volunteers should have the opportunity to use their work as part of their own career development, whether receiving academic credit or obtaining opportunities to move into paid human service positions.*

4   *Volunteers should be allowed to use their own creativity in developing roles and programs that meet the community needs they have observed.*

Volunteerism and self-help "may be the treatment of choice for many individuals whose need to become involved with other community members is greater than their need to become clients. When community members help themselves and one another, resources increase geometrically" (Lewis & Lewis, 1983, p. 101).

MAINTAINING A RESPONSIVE HELPING NETWORK

Self-help and voluntary groups form one part of the total network of care givers in any community. Clients sometimes need additional help, from agencies or institutions that have been designed to provide services. This helping network is a part of the social environment affecting community members, and counselors can affect this aspect of the environment by acting as links, as consultants, and as advocates.

In most communities, there are many agencies and institutions with the expressed purpose of providing services to enhance the well-being of individuals. Some examples of what might be termed "human service" settings include:

1   *Mental health facilities, which attempt to treat or prevent psychological problems.*

2   *Educational institutions.*

3   *Specialized agencies, which deal with specific problem areas (e.g., alcoholism, drug abuse, legal or medical problems, family conflicts, or retardation).*

4   *Population-oriented agencies, which provide services for specific groups, such as children, adolescents, or the aged.*

5   *Crisis or suicide prevention centers, which provide quick intervention in situations of personal crisis.*

6   *Employment or rehabilitation settings, which help individuals to gain the skills and opportunities needed for independence and economic security.*

7 *Alternative agencies, which have been set up by particular groups to provide an informal alternative to traditional agencies (e.g., women's centers, homosexual counseling services, participatory youth agencies, or organizations originated and run by minority group members).*

Any of these agencies may be government supported, charitable, or self-help; they may be large or small, formal or informal. They have in common the goal of providing helping services to their clients.

This goal may be shared by others, particularly those whose occupational roles give them a special power to help or harm others. Teachers, police officers, welfare workers, or employers, for instance, can provide important helping resources if they are sensitive to the human needs of the individuals they affect.

All of these individuals and agencies, in combination, can be seen as a *"helping network"* that makes up part of each individual's environment. But the "helping network" can only be helpful if it is truly responsive to the needs of the people it seeks to serve. And it can only be termed a "network" if all of its parts are interconnected. Community counselors can provide the needed links.

Linkage

Seeking help from the community when it is needed is the right of every individual. Yet the very process of asking for assistance can often be devastating and dehumanizing.

Taber describes the process a woman of the urban ghetto must survive if she is to obtain the services to which she is entitled.

> Her transactions with people representing formal social agencies and other social systems are usually experienced as destructive. In the interface with welfare, legal, medical, and other services, she receives attitudinal messages that are critical or punitive or, at best, patronizing. If she goes for therapy or counseling in a traditional psychiatric setting, she must accept another dependency role—that of patient. One of the conditions of receiving such help is usually that she admit to a problem within herself (Taber, 1973, p. 78).

This kind of process indicates a service network that is unresponsive to the needs that the individual, herself, can identify. But even if the individual care givers could be counted on to be open and humane, the procedures themselves might form a kind of obstacle course.

> Poor people, sick people, and disadvantaged people do not have the cultural, psychological or educational resources to thread their way without guidance through the tangle of agencies, procedures, regulations, restrictions and expectations in the complex mental health service delivery system. They do not need more finely sub-specialized technicians who work within a narrow range of highly developed skills—they need a single individual they can trust and who can help them to contact and work with many specialists and agencies now available (Community College Mental Health Workers Project, 1969).

In fact, the existence of highly fragmented services is not just difficult for "poor people, sick people, and disadvantaged people." It is difficult for *anyone.*

Many of the problems of fragmentation are being solved as agencies discover formal or informal means of developing cooperation among themselves. Services can be considered really coordinated, however, only when *consumers* are able to see the connections and find their way through the maze. And the helping network can be seen as responsive only when individuals are easily placed in contact with the services most appropriate for them—without having to lose any self-respect along the way.

Linkage versus Referral   To make a referral is to transfer a case from one helper to another. When an individual is referred to another agency, the new organization takes on responsibility for the client. The initial helper is no longer accountable. The referring agent, having carefully selected the service most appropriate for the client, may assume that the individual's needs are being met.

For instance, a crisis intervention team may *refer* an individual to another agency for long-term counseling once an initial crisis has passed. It is then assumed that the individual is getting whatever help may be needed to prevent future problems.

An employment counselor may *refer* a counselee to a drug or alcohol abuse center. It is assumed that the individual will return to the employment service once the drug or alcohol problem has been overcome.

A school official may *refer* a student to a child guidance center for help in dealing with emotional problems. While the school still has contact with and concern for the child, it is assumed that the child's urgent psychological needs are being met elsewhere.

In some situations, the individual's contact with the initial referring agent—the first helper—may be lost. Follow-up, while always considered desirable, is not necessarily built into the process. The special needs of the client might be met—but they might not. In effect, the chain is broken, and individuals may find themselves once again threading their own way through the service system.

In *linkage*, as opposed to *referral*, community counselors remain active ingredients in their counselees' lives, continuing their involvement through the referral process and beyond.

Programming for Linkage In some instances, agencies receiving referrals insist that the initial relationship be kept alive by requiring involvement of the referral source in case conferences. This approach ensures continuity in the client's relationships with service providers, while also providing training for people working in a variety of human service roles and settings.

In most cases, however, the agency making the referral must take some responsibility for avoiding duplication of effort and enhancing the provision of services. One approach that is becoming increasingly common is the presence of an agency whose main function is putting individuals in touch with appropriate services. Generally, the resources of such organizations are too limited to allow for ongoing relationships with clients. Instead, their work trends to be confined to providing information and making appropriate referrals. Referral sources are commonplace; linkage sources are rare.

The basis on which a linkage agency might work is modeled on a smaller scale by the Harbor Area Mental Health System in Boston, Massachusetts (R. E. Cohen, 1974). This mental health and retardation program involves a comprehensive mental health center, including inpatient care, as well as several community clinics that act as satellites. Linkage is provided by an "interface team." The Harbor Area interface team spans the boundaries between separate but related units of the same mental health system. The team includes members based in each unit.

> The functions of the interface staff have evolved to include: ensuring continuity of care of the patient; utilizing community clinic staff in finding alternatives to hospitalization or rehospitalization of patients; monitoring the flow of patients through the system; and overseeing a unified treatment plan for each patient, including precare and aftercare. To perform these tasks

team members have to be kept informed of all changes in patient status. This is made possible by a system of open and sanctioned communication between team members and professional staff in both settings and by formal procedures for planning transfers or discharges (R. E. Cohen, 1974, pp. 70 –71).

The existence of the interface team means that the progress of all clients is closely followed as they move from one service unit to another. When a patient is released after hospitalization, for instance, someone is waiting, ready to locate whatever services may be needed and to ease the transition from one kind of environment to another.

The fact that the units involved are administratively connected simplifies the linkage process. In other kinds of settings, helping services may be related loosely, or not at all. That makes coordination more difficult, but it also makes it more important. A number of independent agencies within a loosely defined helping network could send representatives to an interface team whose sole purposes would be to coordinate the efforts made on behalf of individual clients. There are organizations that have as their primary goal that of linking agencies with one another and with other community resources (e.g., the Community Congress of San Diego, described in Chapter 3). An interface team would serve, first and foremost, as an attempt to link *individuals* with available services.

The Human Link   Even without formal organizational mechanisms, linkage can still take place. It occurs whenever community counselors and the agencies or institutions that employ them see it as part of their role.

The community counseling orientation is one of dealing with the whole person in the context of his or her environment. Specialists who provide services dealing with one aspect of an individual's life do not hesitate to refer their clients to other specialists dealing with still other aspects. For community counselors, however, referral is often inadequate. Working with whole persons and their environments must mean acting as "expediters," as "advocates," and as "intermediaries." It means, in short, providing the needed human link between individuals and the helping network. This link may be needed because of the client's inability to make full use of available services. Just as often, it is needed because, unfortunately, *the helping network cannot always be trusted to be responsive.*

We have to assume that helpers want to be responsive. Reality tells us that, at times, an extra nudge from a colleague may be needed. When linkage is seen as everyone's responsibility, we may reach the time when no client is ever "lost in the shuffle."

Active linkage can ensure that every individual gains access to needed help. It cannot, however, provide any guarantees about the quality of the services received. Members of the helping network have the additional responsibility of assisting one another to increase their actual effectiveness. One way this can be accomplished is through consultation.

Consultation

A traditional and widely accepted definition of the term *consultation* is that provided by Caplan (1970, p. 19), who sees consultation as "a process of interaction between two professional persons — the consultant, who is a specialist, and the consultee, who invokes the consultant's help in regard to a current work problem with which he is having some difficulty and which he has decided is within the other's area of specialized competence."

As the concept of consultation has developed in practice, it is no longer necessarily true that only "professionals" become involved in the process. In reality, most members of the helping network find themselves acting at some times as consultants and at other times as consultees. On some occasions they give help to their colleagues; on others, they ask for it. This does not always depend on their official roles or specializations but, instead, on their practical knowledge of and competence to deal with specific aspects of human behavior.

The process of consultation, however, can still be identified in terms of several special characteristics.

1 *The consultee asks for help.* If a relationship between two people is to be termed "consultative," participation must be voluntary. An individual recognizes the existence of a real or potential work problem and requests assistance from someone seen as competent to offer it.

2 *The consultant does not have power over the consultee's actions.* The relationship between the consultant and the consultee is a cooperative one. Just as the consultee can decide to participate in the process or to avoid it, he or she can also follow the consultant's suggestions or reject them. The two participants work together to solve immediate problems and to increase the consultee's skills. The final decision concerning actions and solutions is the responsibility of the person who asked for help.

3 *The consulting process is educational.* Often help is requested because of an immediate situation. Yet, "the twin goals of consultation are to help the consultee improve his handlings or understanding of the

current work difficulty and through this to increase his capacity to master future problems of a similar type" (Caplan, 1970, p. 29). The consultee may learn to work more effectively with a particular kind of client or a special kind of problem. Just as important, though, is the fact that he may learn to be more proficient in the skills needed to solve problems and make decisions.

4 *Concentration is on the consultee as a worker.* To be effective, the consulting process must deal with the consultee's feelings, attitudes, and values. The relationship is similar to a counseling relationship, but the desired end result is different. The consultee's personality is dealt with primarily in terms of its effect on his or her work as a helper. The goal is to increase the consultee's effectiveness in this one specific aspect of living.

5 *Focus is on a third individual or group.* The long-range beneficiary of the consultation process is the individual or group to be helped by the consultee. Although the consultee may learn a great deal through participation in the process, what is learned is meant to be applied in relationships with others. Those others may be current clients or groups that might be helped in the future. In either case, some focus is placed on the nature of that invisible third person, who might not be present during consultation, but who is nevertheless an important part of its content. The process has been illustrated graphically by Singh (1971, p. 10) as follows on page 180.[2]

As this figure indicates, the consultative process involves two-way, equal communication between the consultant and the consultee, with focus

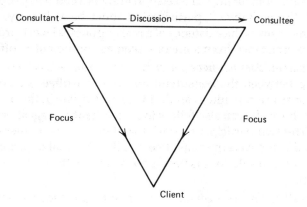

2Copyright © R. K. J. Singh, 1971. Reprinted with permission.

being placed on a third party: the individual or group identified as the consultee's client.

The client may be an individual whom the consultee is actively facing in a current situation; then consultation concentrates on immediate, "here-and-now" issues. The basic question is, "How can I be more effective in my interactions with this particular individual?" What is learned through consultation may have the added effect of helping the consultee to be more effective with other clients, and thus of preventing future problems.

Sometimes consultation is more purely preventive. The consultee may want to develop more skill and knowledge in order to work effectively with a particular type of client or a range of potential problems. The question then becomes, "How can I learn *now* to work more effectively with a number of individuals I have yet to meet?" When "preventive consultation" has taken place, many urgent problems, unwitting mistakes, and last-minute "crash courses" can be avoided.

"Here-and-Now Consultation" Whenever helpers try to provide services to people, there are certain to be times when they feel some lack in their own skill, knowledge, training, or objectivity. There are bound to be times when they feel that others could handle a problem more competently than they. This happens to *everyone* — no matter how skilled, how competent, or how well trained. Any case can take an unexpected turn and leave the helper feeling uncertain.

On occasions such as those, a helper's first instinct — often out of desperation — is to "refer the case" to someone else, to link the client with another, more specialized helper. Sometimes this is necessary. Just as frequently, however, what the original helper needs is support, encouragement, and practical assistance. What the helper needs is ready access to a consultant.

The consultation process may not provide all of the answers, but it can increase the confidence of the consultee. Then a relationship that has already been formed can be maintained without interruption.

Cross-consultation Community counselors in human service agencies can ensure smooth access to consultation by setting up cooperative, interagency mechanisms. A coordinated network of helping organizations has a never-ending supply of human resources, a pool of individuals who can be turned to when help is needed. Instead of identifying a small group of "experts" to serve as consultants to a large group of potential "consultees," agency workers can recognize that every one of them has expertise to share, and that every one of them might, at some time, need to ask someone else for assistance. What results is "cross-consultation" among cooperating equals.

Youth workers accustomed to dealing with young people on an individual basis can handle family situations when it becomes appropriate. They can handle them because a consultant from a family service agency is on hand to provide guidance and help to evaluate the process.

Developmental counselors whose clients become involved in severe personal crises can see them through. They can see them through because someone experienced in crisis intervention supplies information about the stages in crisis development and appropriate strategies for dealing with them.

Counselors who have never done so before can work with disabled individuals when they encounter them. They can work with them because a rehabilitation counselor is able to provide guidelines about special needs and problems that might emerge.

Employment counselors faced with elderly job applicants can provide the needed services. They can provide them because someone from a neighboring Senior Citizens Center encourages them to see, and perhaps to sell, the individual's strengths.

Volunteers working in alternative human service agencies can deal with individuals whose personal problems are complex. They can deal with them because someone with extensive psychological training can help them to clarify the situation and to decide on the nature of their own involvement.

Professionals having difficulty communicating with particular kinds of clients can continue to serve them. They can continue because someone from the community is able to interpret and explain possible conflicts in values or life-styles.

There is no end to the possible examples one might list. What is important is that everyone who has been available to *give* help will, at some time, *receive* it from someone else. Everyone involved in the helping services has an identity both as a consultant and as a consultee.

The Informal Helping Network   It must be remembered that there is also a large group of potential consultees outside of formal human service agencies. Many people have jobs that place them in close contact with others, or even in positions in which they have a degree of power over other people's lives. Ideally, they can form part of an informal helping network.

Access to consultation for such workers means that they can be helped to make their influence more positive and more sensitive to the needs of those whose lives they touch. It also means that many problems can be handled in the individual's normal setting, without the need for direct services from a helping agency.

An employer who has just hired an ex-offender or an ex-mental patient, for instance, may tend either to overemphasize the new employee's difference from others or, on the other hand, to be unaware of real issues, such as the question of confidentiality. A consultant can help such an employer to find the responsive middle road.

A teacher in a public school may encounter a student who has unique learning problems or an unusual set of behaviors. Access to a consultant means that the teacher can devise, try out, and evaluate new approaches, while becoming more aware of his or her own attitudes toward the child. The presence of the consultant's support may mean the difference between effectively teaching the child in the normal classroom or depending on the existence of special education facilities.

A police officer, providing the first contact with an individual or group in crisis, can make a more constructive contribution if he or she has access to appropriate information about the psychological aspects of a situation and the most effective methods of communicating personal concern.

In these and other situations, the presence of a consultant helps community members to deal with difficult problems in the normal settings in which they occur. If participation in the process becomes widespread, many of those problems can actually be prevented.

Preventive Consultation   In preventive consultation, the consultee asks for help before an immediate problem has to be approached. Any member of the helping network may recognize the need to develop new skills and fresh awareness and ask for assistance before being faced with a pressing need.

The employer who is planning to hire ex-offenders or ex-mental patients (or people who are mentally or physically handicapped) asks for guidelines before the policy is actually implemented. Such employers do not wait for the first problem to appear, but prepare for it in advance. Then they know that they can be responsive to their employees' real needs.

The teacher who is not experiencing serious difficulty with any one student asks for help in developing more effective methods of responding to all children. When such teachers are faced with problems that they might once have felt inadequate to handle, they have a store of self-awareness and flexibility that can allow them to adapt to special needs as they arise.

The police officer, knowing that crisis situations will be faced frequently in the future, asks for training in needed communication skills. Such police officers can then more effectively calm family crises or provide personal support for suicide attempters.

When consultation is preventive, it can often be done effectively in groups. Several teachers, for instance, can participate in a series of meetings with a consultant. In those meetings, they can discuss their own attitudes as teachers in addition to receiving help in understanding and working with specific children. Group procedures use time efficiently, but even more important is the fact that more resources are added to the consultative process. Every group member is, in effect, a consultant to every other group member, and relevant experiences can be shared in a setting where people are open to one another's ideas.

Consultation Versus Advocacy   The entire concept of consultation is based on the assumption that the consultant and the consultee are equals, each respecting the other's skill and expertise. This assumes some commonality in values and in goals, some sense that an action contemplated by the consultee is likely to be accepted by the consultant. Each participant in the process has faith that the other is trying to approach clients (or students or employees or citizens or patients) in a constructive way.

Sometimes, however, human beings are destructive in their approaches to others. Sometimes the rights of individuals are ignored. Sometimes people with power over others fail to respond effectively to the needs that they should be perceiving.

When community counselors face such situations, they see their responsibility as one of actively protecting the rights of the less powerful. The process in which they must engage is one not of consultation, but of advocacy.

Advocacy

Advocacy is the act of speaking up on behalf of individuals or groups who lack the power to defend their own rights. When community counselors see the rights of individuals being impinged on, whether by other people or by institutions, they know that they must take action. Sometimes oppressed individuals or groups can be strengthened to the point of being able to protect themselves. In the interim, however, community counselors do not turn their backs on situations of conflict that might develop. They act to protect those who need protection, to defend those who need defense, and to limit the power of those who abuse their strength. In advocacy, there is no question of objectivity: the community counselor is on the side of the human being who is being misused.

"Here-and-now advocacy" arises in response to an immediate situation. The community counselor observes an injustice, evaluates the situation, and acts to right the wrong being committed.

"Preventive advocacy" develops out of a recognition that entire groups of people may be at society's mercy. Action on behalf of the group as a whole prevents injustice against individuals by creating attitudes and mechanisms that make justice and respect for others the norms.

Community counselors do not always have to work alone, against the odds. Many others are available to serve as advocates. "Citizen advocacy" is a movement that encourages and makes possible voluntary action in protection of the rights of others.

"Here-and-Now Advocacy" Unfortunately for those who value peace and quiet, many occasions of injustice are encountered all too close to home. The incidents we are most likely to observe at first hand are often those that occur in our own institutions and agencies. It might be easier to let things pass, but abuses of power are just that much more difficult to stomach when they stem from agents of what we see as the helping network.

Wineman and James point out the challenge for advocacy that exists whenever individuals are placed in a captor versus captive situation.

> There are prisons with and without walls. A prison is here defined as a social arrangement in which a captor-captive relationship exists. Public assistance, probation, and parole agencies are prisons without walls. All forms of incarceration—jails and mental hospitals—are virtual prisons. And the American public school system chronically oscillates between potential and actual prisonhood.
>
> Captor-captive states are inherently inimical to the human condition because they jeopardize the humanity of both captor and captive. Yet they appear to be inevitable in most complex societies. The degree of civilization of a society is demonstrated by how it treats its various classifications of captives, by the extent to which it displays a consciousness of its destructiveness, and by its readiness to undertake counter-measures against dehumanization (Wineman & James, 1973, p. 217).

Whenever people have immense power over others, they may be termed captors. And whenever others must submit to that power without being able to choose, they can be seen as captives. People whose element of choice is consistently taken away from them — mental patients, retarded adults, some nursing home residents, all children — are perennial captives.

What Wineman and James see as the "dehumanization" that accompanies captivity includes such matters as physical brutality; psychic humiliation, including shaming and the arbitrary use of authority; forms of punishment that are damaging to the individual; and violations of privacy.

The fact that these things happen to precisely the individuals who have no way out of a situation means that they, as captives, must be protected. They must be protected by people who have more freedom to initiate action and who have easier access to the captors. They must have, as advocates, people who have not allowed themselves to become either captors or captives in institutions where it may be assumed that everyone must be either one or the other.

But there are two sides of the coin. Just as advocates are needed to fight *against dehumanization,* they are also needed to fight *for humanization.* People don't just have the right not to be mistreated. They also have the right to grow, to develop their own creativity and their own values, to have access to whatever benefits our culture may have to offer, and to increase the number of choices in their lives.

When community counselors see individuals being confined and constricted, they seek to affect the situation, whether that means fighting to change a policy or acting to make individuals in authority accountable for their actions. They fight, not just to eliminate negative constraints, but to create positive opportunities.

When community counselors in school settings encounter situations in which children are being unfairly punished, they confront the school authorities. They also confront those authorities when children are denied the opportunity to learn in warm, exciting classroom environments.

When community counselors see their clients treated without dignity by governmental agencies, they confront those agencies. They also fight for the right of access to services.

When community counselors see individuals denied their right to privacy in residential institutions, they act to safeguard that right. At the same time, they fight for the right to a comfortable and stimulating environment.

Wherever community counselors may work, they are bound to encounter situations that arouse their anger and their frustration. Unlike many others, they do have the power to do something about it, if for no other reason than that they are adults and colleagues. Sometimes a verbal sharing of concern with a person in authority is all that is needed. Sometimes ills in the organization must be exposed, and groups must be organized to confront them. Whatever happens, the situation is never comfortable and never easy. Yet community counselors must know that they have tried. Otherwise they, too, are captors; they, too, lose some of their own humanity.

It is difficult—even impossible—to present guidelines for the implementation of here-and-now advocacy. No one person can tell another what situations should provoke anger, how far one should go in confronting authority, or how many risks should be taken. In the long run, the nature of advocacy in any situation is based on the conscience, and the consciousness, of the individual involved.

"Preventive Advocacy"   Preventive advocacy is not stimulated by an immediate crisis. Instead, the community counselor recognizes a situation that could potentially deprive individuals of their rights and opportunities and acts on the environment before individual clients are damaged.

This most frequently occurs when a population is identified as having special needs that should be met by the environment, as needing support in attempts to protect themselves against impingement on their freedom. Acting on behalf of the group as a whole can prevent much damage that might later occur to individuals.

One example of this is the growth of a movement for *child advocacy.* Although other institutions or agencies may be involved, much attention seems to be centering around schools. Instead of waiting for individual crises to arise, many child advocates actively question the relationship between schools and children.

> . . . We believe that too often the agencies that exist to help children actually end up hurting them instead. When schools and other institutions become too inflexible, too insensitive, when they demand conformity at any cost, then confrontations are bound to occur. . . .
>
> An emerging point of view—child advocacy—. . . proposes that confrontations between schools or parents and children must be scrutinized not only from the traditional point of view—that of blaming the child—but also in terms of the milieu in which the battle occurs. . . . This transformation would require schools and other public agencies to carefully examine the "why" behind their own rules (Silberberg & Silberberg, 1974, p. 39).

Child advocates try to prevent damage to individuals by fighting against policies and practices that are dehumanizing to all children. At the same time, they are available to represent individual children in situations that they may be powerless to overcome. "They intercede on behalf of the child with the schools, courts, the welfare system and other agencies that were originally designed to help the child, but often aid in his destruction" (Silberberg & Silberberg, 1974, p. 39).

Advocacy movements are also forming around the concerns of a number of other specific populations. Depending on the priorities and needs of their own communities, community counselors have become involved in preventive advocacy in a number of areas, such as the following:

- Joining those who seek the removal of physical barriers that keep the handicapped and the aged from making full use of all community facilities.

- Working to realize alternatives to incarceration for those found guilty of breaking the law, to create self-governance in prisons, and to ensure equal employment opportunity for ex-offenders.

- Fighting for the rights of mentally handicapped citizens to enjoy normal lives in their own communities.

- Cutting through governmental bureaucracy to ensure that people forced to depend on welfare, unemployment compensation, or Social Security checks can obtain what they have the right to receive without being forced to give up privacy and self-respect.

- Fighting for affirmative action in hiring practices.

- Advocating bilingual education and communication in communities where it is appropriate.

- Confronting *whatever* unreasonable limitations are placed on individuals or groups within the counselor's community.

No one community counselor can do everything. Each must decide on a course of action in terms of his or her work setting and the needs of the particular community being served. Fortunately, workers in agencies and institutions do not need to bear the entire burden of advocacy alone. There are many citizens who are willing to involve themselves in the lives of others.

Citizen Advocacy   Wolfensberger and Zauha (1973, p. 11) define citizen advocacy as "a mature, competent citizen volunteer representing, as if they were his own, the interests of another citizen who is impaired in his instrumental competency (meaning the ability to solve practical problems of everyday living), or who has major expressive needs which are unmet and which are likely to remain unmet without special intervention."

Normally, citizen advocacy involves a continuous, one-to-one relationship between an advocate and a "protege," with the advocate representing the interests of his or her protege in whatever way might be necessary. The relationship may be one of friendship. The added dimension is that the advocate serves as a bridge between the impaired person and the environment, constantly seeking to ensure that the protege's needs are effectively met.

Citizen advocacy is not just a concept, but a living reality. For instance, the Capitol Association for Retarded Children, in Lincoln, Nebraska, operates an advocacy office that recruits, selects, orients, guides, and reinforces citizen advocates. This is in keeping with the "Nebraska Plan," which requires that each retarded person should have a relationship with a personal advocate to represent his or her interests.

In addition to individual advocacy, there are also a number of other approaches that may be appropriate for citizen volunteers. Wolfensberger and Zauha (1973, p. 35) categorize them as[3]

Generic or Class Advocacy

A person may play an advocacy role for an entire category of persons, such as the poor, the retarded, etc. An example here is a person such as Ralph Nader who has acted as an advocate for the consumer.

Collective or Corporate Advocacy

. . . A group of individuals covenant between themselves to represent the interests of an entire category of persons. Examples are the many voluntary citizens' groups, such as the associations for retarded children, United Cerebral Palsy, etc.

Group Advocacy

. . . involving a highly specific and circumscribed group of impaired proteges and a highly specific and circumscribed, but usually informal, group of citizens. Examples are a women's church club which "adopts" the residents of a home for the aged, or of a living unit in an institution for the retarded; a service club which dedicates itself to the role of a citizens' watchdog group over a particular public agency such as an institution; and a legal firm which provides free services to a specific group of persons, such as the poor of a certain neighborhood.

[3]Copyright National Institute on Mental Retardation, 1973. Reprinted with permission.

Multiple Advocacy

One citizen or family may play advocacy roles to more than one protege. . . . As long as only a few proteges are involved, such arrangements can still preserve the sustained one-to-one relationship so crucial to effective individual advocacy.

Dispersed Advocacy

. . . Several citizens might divide advocacy functions in regard to a protege among themselves. . . .

Crisis Advocacy

An impaired person and /or his family may experience a sudden crisis that requires immediate and extensive attention. During such a crisis, there may be no one with the time and calmness to contact the relevant persons and agencies that may be involved or that may render help. . . . In such a crisis situation, an advocate can step in and act as coordinator, legman, and back-up. He may provide transportation, attend to certain undone but important function, and can see to it that the agencies do not play runabout games.

Youth Advocacy

. . . A teenager might select another impaired or disadvantaged teenager or child as a special friend; or a group of teenagers, such as a youth club, might assume a special socializing or friendship function vis-a-vis a group of impaired children or fellow teenagers.

The Advocate Associate

Many professionals, agency personnel, and other individuals in influential positions are likely to embrace the advocacy concept without, however, actually playing direct, individualized, sustained advocacy roles. Instead, they can act as apostles of the concept, as change agents within their own agencies, and as members of committees for the advocacy office. . . .

The community counselor may, in fact, be an "advocate associate," helping to create and maintain programs of citizen advocacy. This may mean involvement with an advocacy office that coordinates one-to-one relationships, or it may mean participation in a group or collective endeavor. There is room in an effective advocacy organization for both volunteers and professionals.

In many ways, citizen action combines both "here-and-now advocacy" and "preventive advocacy" in an attempt to represent those who might not have the power to represent themselves. As long as such individuals and such populations exist, advocacy is everyone's responsibility.

CLIENT ADVOCACY IN ACTION: CONSENSUS BUILDING IN THE STATE OF WASHINGTON

In Washington, advocates working in behalf of developmentally disabled citizens are attempting to build consensus around common recognition of the needs and rights of persons with special developmental needs. Statewide organizations with specific advocacy concerns include the Developmental Disabilities Planning Council, the Protection and Advocacy System ("The Troubleshooters"), the Disabilities Political Action Committee, the Washington Assembly for Citizens with Disabilities, and the Developmental Disabilities Research and Information Coalition.

Developmental Disabilities Planning Council

Public Law 95-602 makes it mandatory for any state receiving federal funds to establish a state planning council to serve as a systems advocate for developmentally disabled persons. The function of each Council is to set broad policy, determine priorities among service needs and set goals and objectives for the State program of service for persons with developmental disabilities (Federal Register, 1980). In Washington, the thrust of the Planning Council, under the directorship of Dr. Stephen Schain, has been to affect the attitudes and values underlying the service delivery system, to encourage the development of community-based, normalized programs for developmentally disabled citizens, and to build consensus based on broad citizen and consumer input. These accomplishments are based on planning, legislative, and funding activities.

Using planning and administrative funds, the Council has been able to influence community alternative living efforts through the sponsorship of visits by nationally and internationally recognized experts who have consulted with local service providers about the development and implementation of normative projects. Even more impact on the attitudes and values underlying service activity has been brought about through the funding of a number of Normalization and Training Workshops. These efforts, provided in a number of locations around the state, have served to increase staff and citizen sensitivity and knowledge in applying the principles of normalization of train ng them in the use of the evaluation tool PASS (Program Analysis of Service System).

The ideals of normalization, community-based programming, and citizen advocacy have also been enhanced through a number of projects funded through the Planning Council's authorization under Public Law 95-602 Formula Grant Funds. In Fiscal Year 1980 alone, dozens of projects focused on such efforts as increasing public understanding and acceptance of developmental disabilities; developing living alternatives for institutionalized children; providing for rural, minority and self-advocacy efforts; developing model programs for community housing; training graduate students to broaden their understanding of developmentally disabled persons; monitoring and evaluating protection and advocacy services; increasing statewide mental health services; and piloting programs to enhance adoption of developmentally disabled children (Developmental Disabilities Planning Council, 1981).

Protection and Advocacy System

The Protection and Advocacy System is also federally mandated and is independent of any service delivering agency, public or private. The System, through its home office in Seattle and a network of affiliate offices, serves a number of related purposes, including the following:

1 Ensure the adequacy and comprehensiveness of Protection and Advocacy services to developmentally disabled persons throughout the state.
2 Improve the attitudes of families, service providers, public officials and the general public toward developmentally disabled citizens.
3 To be available and accessible to developmentally disabled consumers for the appropriate teaching and training of self advocacy.
4 Ensure programs which protect civil and human rights of developmentally disabled persons (Developmental Disabilities Planning Council, 1981).

The central office of the Protection and Advocacy System works toward these purposes by recruiting and training troubleshooters /advocates, maintaining a statewide communication system, providing technical assistance to affiliated advocates, providing support services to advocates, and maintaining a recordkeeping system for documentation of services provided. The statewide network of advocates promotes self-advocacy, recruits and develops volunteer advocates, provides public information, promotes personal and citizen advocacy, conducts investigations for persons who are being abused, assists students and parents in individual planning processes, and assists in citizen monitoring of programs related to developmental disabilities. In concert with other statewide organizations, the Protection and Advocacy System informs the public and improves communities' understanding for handicapped persons.

Disabilities Political Action Committee

The purpose of the Disabilities Political Action Committee (D-PAC) is to impact the political /electoral process. D-PAC raises money for contributions to candidates and uses contributions to assist in the election of legislators who support adequate funding and services for special education and human services. The organization also utilizes contributions to support ballot issues affecting habilitation rights and services. In general, the functions of D-PAC, which does not intend to be a single-issue political action committee, include:

1 Political contributions to legislative candidates.
2 Political contributions to ballot issues.
3 Political endorsements of legislative candidates.
4 Political endorsements of ballot issues.

Washington Assembly for Citizens with Disabilities

The Washington Assembly for Citizens with Disabilities (WACD) also plays a role in the political process, rating candidates and endorsing issues. It also organizes community political activity for and against legislative issues regarding habilitation rights, services and related issues.

The goals of WACD include the following:

1 Increase community support for developmental services.
2 Increase citizen participation in the political process to obtain and maintain developmental and support services.
3 Build a broad base coalition to support adequate human service systems.
4 Improve the quality and quantity of services to citizens with disabilities by working for the continued development of a comprehensive service system which promotes: (a) protection of individual interests in the areas of health and human and legal rights, (b) community presence, (c) community participation, (d) competency building, and (e) status enhancement.

WACD accomplishes these goals through such functions as voter registration and education, coalition building, legislator ratings, candidate questionnaires, community organization, issue endorsements, hotline operation, lobbying, and statewide communication efforts. The Assembly is based on representation from statewide groups dealing with every type of disability or handicap.

Developmental Disabilities Research and Information Coalition

The purpose of the Developmental Disabilities Research and Information Coalition is to provide information to the community, the legislature, administrative agencies, and others related to developmental disabilities issues.

The Coalition does not engage in political activity except to provide issue information. It is a research body.

The overall goal of the Coalition is to provide a nonpartisan forum for generating information on budgetary and related issues affecting special education and human services for citizens with disabilities. This goal is accomplished through such functions as research, analysis, dissemination of information to legislature and citizenry, and utilization of a Coalition newsletter.

Each of the statewide organizations dealing with advocacy in Washington thus plays a unique role in the effort to encourage self-help and volunteerism, to build an effective helping network, and to safeguard the rights of citizens with special needs.

SUMMARY

People who need more intensive services than those provided to the population at large may also need assistance in making the environment more responsive to their individual or group requirements and rights. Community counselors place strong emphasis on helping to strengthen populations which have been, in some sense, "socially devalued." Since dependence on professional assistance may actually accelerate the process of stigmatization and devaluing, efforts are made to encourage self-help and volunteerism, to build bridges between individuals and their communities.

The community counselor also recognizes that the "helping network" is part of the social environment affecting community members. Efforts are made to increase the responsiveness of the helping network by providing linkages among agencies, by consulting with other helpers, and by advocating on behalf of individuals or groups. A good example of a concerted advocacy effort is provided by the statewide organizations working for the rights of developmentally disabled citizens in Washington.

ACTIVITIES TO ENHANCE UNDERSTANDING OF CHAPTER 5

1 It is difficult to understand the process of social devaluation without actually experiencing it. Although you can never duplicate the experience of another individual or group, you can attempt, at least temporarily, to learn something about how stigmatization feels. Choose

one population that you can identify as "socially devalued," preferably one that you hope to work with professionally. Find a way to experience what a member of that population might face as a part of everyday living. Spend at least part of one day seeking services or relating to others as though you had a disability that you have not experienced before. Think about the differences between your usual interactions with others and your interactions when you are perceived as disabled.

2 Considering again the hypothetical agency or program that you have been creating, try to fill in the fourth facet: client advocacy. How would you go about improving the responsiveness of the community and the helping network to your clients' needs?

CHAPTER
6
COMMUNITY
COUNSELING IN
EDUCATIONAL
SETTINGS

T he counselor who works in an educational institution can still be a community counselor. The school counselor, in fact, is responsible to *two* separate but interlinked communities: that of the school itself and that of the neighborhood or locality in which the institution is located.

We have defined *"community"* as *a system of interdependent persons, groups and organizations that:*

1 *Meets the individual's primary needs.*
2 *Affects the individual's daily life.*
3 *Acts as intermediary between the individual and the society as a whole.*

The school or college, then, can be seen as a community, and the counselor has a responsibility to deal with that environment as it affects the people who work and study there. At the same time, the school is located within a larger community. The counselor must deal with that community, too, with particular regard to recognizing its helping resources and providing assistance to community members who are also parents.

In an educational setting, perhaps more than in any other kind of agency or institution, the community counselor can create opportunities for positive human growth and development instead of concentrating on the remediation of existing problems. The school community itself is an environment that has the potential to concentrate on no other goal but creating the best possible setting for learning and growth. The community counselor's task is to make that potential a reality, both by providing dynamic, growth-producing programs for students and community members and by bringing about changes in the environment so that the school develops an appropriate climate for learning.

Just as in other settings, the community counselor creates and implements the following services.

1 *Direct community services that provide developmental learning experiences for students and community members.*
2 *Direct client services that provide special experiences, such as individual and group counseling, for students or community members.*
3 *Indirect community services that attempt to influence the learning climate of the total school.*
4 *Indirect client services that attempt to make both school and community more responsive to the needs of individual students.*

These four facets of community counseling can be adapted to meet the special needs of elementary and secondary schools and colleges and universities.

ELEMENTARY AND SECONDARY SCHOOLS

In this country, elementary and secondary schools touch the lives of all of our citizens. Free, compulsory public education means that most individuals have experienced schooling at some time in their lives. It also means that the school is a central, recognized institution in virtually every community.

The fact that such educational settings are so central to the society gives community counselors in elementary and secondary schools a unique opportunity to affect their world. It also creates a very difficult challenge to meet the needs of many people in many ways. A beginning can be made through the creation of a multifaceted approach to counseling. The direction that such an approach might take is illustrated in Table 6.1.

Direct Community Services

Direct community services are meant to provide growth and learning opportunities to a broad range of individuals instead of to those who have been identified as needing special services.

In school situations such programs can be offered to the community at large. The school possesses a unique combination of personal and physical resources that can be put at the disposal of the community to meet the educational needs that adult citizens have identified as important for themselves. The school can provide leadership in identifying innovative educational programs, can respond to the requests of community members themselves, and can place special emphasis on the development of learning situations for adults that might, in turn, affect the lives of children.

During the school day itself, students must have the chance to develop, not only academically, but also personally. In a school attempting to deal with the student as a whole person, the curriculum allows students the chance to learn about themselves and their relationships with others. In some instances, community counselors may create and implement special programs available to any students who wish to participate. More often, however, attempts are made to integrate education toward personal awareness and skills into the total curriculum. Community counselors do the following.

Table 6.1
Community Counseling in Elementary and Secondary Schools

	Community Services	**Client Services**

Direct	Educational programs dealing with:
	  Career development
	  Personal and interpersonal understanding
	  Value clarification and decision making
	  Intergroup conflict resolution
	  Community and parent education
		Accessible individual and group counseling, using professionals, community volunteers, and trained peer counselors

Indirect	Advocacy in behalf of children and youth Encouragement of effective learning climates Development of flexible and democratic institutions	Case advocacy, both within schools and in regard to community agencies Consultation with administrators, teachers, parents, and members of the community's helping network Linkage with community agencies.

1   *Go into the classrooms themselves, both to teach and to provide demonstration models for teachers.*

2   *Help teachers to select among available materials and to plan and implement new programs.*

3   *Provide assistance in working new subject areas into the curriculum.*

4   *Use resources from the community to enhance the school's educational program.*

5   *Encourage and support teachers in their attempts to create totally new learning experiences adapted to the needs of their own students.*

6   *Help groups of students to develop educational programs in accordance with their own goals.*

These kinds of approaches are opening classrooms to the consideration of many aspects of the human condition—aspects that often went unmentioned in the past. Counselors deal with aging education (Colangelo & Rosenthal, 1982), alcohol prevention (Spoth & Rosenthal, 1980), social problem solving (Alpert & Rosenfield, 1981), assertiveness (Jean-Grant, 1980), premarital education (Martin, Gawinski, Medler, & Eddy, 1981), democratic values (Hayes, 1982), moral development (Kohlberg, 1981; Mosher, 1980), and affective education (Dinkmeyer & Dinkmeyer, 1980). Topics such as career development, personal and interpersonal understanding, value clarification, decision making, and intergroup relationships are now as much a part of the school's curriculum as any subject matter or academic discipline.

Career Development   There is an ever-increasing recognition that career development is a lifelong process of discovery as individuals continually integrate new information about themselves and about the environment. Attention to career development cannot be confined to any one age or grade level, nor can it be separated from the totality of the individual's learning and growth. Career education is, in more and more schools, being integrated into the total curriculum in an organized, sequential manner. A model for this kind of program is provided by the United States Office of Education in terms of objectives for each level (Hansen & Borow, 1973, pp. 197–198).

Grades K–6:

To develop in pupils attitudes about the personal and social significance of work.

To develop each pupil's self-awareness.

To develop and expand the occupational awareness and aspirations of the pupils.

To improve overall pupil performance by unifying and focusing basic subjects around a career development theme.

Grades 7–8:

To provide experiences for students to assist them in evaluating their interests, abilities, values, and needs as they relate to occupational roles.

To provide students with opportunities for further and more detailed exploration of selected occupational clusters, leading to a tentative selection of a particular cluster for the depth exploration at the ninth-grade level.

To improve the performance of students in basic subject areas by making the subject matter more meaningful and relevant through unifying and focusing it around a career development theme.

Grades 9–10:

To provide in-depth exploration and training in one occupational cluster leading to entry-level skill in one occupational area and establish a foundation for further progress, leaving open the option to move to other clusters if desired.

To improve the performance of students in basic areas of instruction by making the subject matter more meaningful and relevant through unification and focus upon a career development theme.

To provide guidance and counseling for the purpose of assisting students to select an occupational specialty for eleventh- and twelfth-grade levels with the following options: intensive job preparation, preparation for postsecondary occupational education program or a four-year college program.

Grades 11–12:

To provide every student with intensive preparation in a selected occupational cluster or specific occupation, or with preparation for job entry and / or further education.

To provide guidance and counseling in preparation for employment and / or further education.

To insure placement of all students, upon leaving school, in either a job, a postsecondary occupational program or a four-year college program.

To maintain continuous follow-up of all dropouts and graduates and to use the resulting information for program revisions.

A strength that can be found in this and in similar models is the attempt to integrate career development so completely into the educational program that all subject matter is influenced. It is also important that recognition of career development begins in the early grades, with emphasis on helping children to become aware of vast alternatives in the environment and to develop in their own awareness of themselves as workers. Much can be accomplished in this regard by giving children the opportunity to explore their community through field trips; by bringing the community into the school through guest speakers and role models; by giving children "hands-on" experiences with new kinds of tools and implements; by describing a number of occupations through interesting audiovisual or graphic means; by working career information into reading and arithmetic lessons; and by giving children the chance to talk and write about themselves and their experiences.

But while the elementary school career development experience is meant to be enlarging, the USOE model, like most others, tends to prescribe a narrower focus in the later grades. In a world as rapidly changing as our own, it might be inappropriate to ask young people to narrow down their choices, even to a job cluster or category. Even at the high school level, attention should still be paid to allowing students to experience as much as possible of the community, creating opportunities for field and school experiences that bring education and work much closer together than they have been in the past. Many career development models assume that employment will play a central part in everyone's life. In fact, that is open to question, and students should be given the chance to read, write, and talk about the place of work in the individual's total style of life. In the long run, their *own* perceptions of themselves and the world of work are the ones that will affect their lives.

Personal and Interpersonal Understanding   Educational programs should also help individual students to increase their understanding of themselves and to enhance their skills in dealing with other people. This kind of personal development is a lifelong process. Opportunities appropriate to the maturity level of students should be designed, beginning with the elementary school population and continuing on through the high school curriculum.

Ideally, teachers and counselors should be able to create learning experiences that meet the needs of their own students as those needs emerge. In reality, however, teachers are often more accustomed to dealing with thoughts than with feelings, more comfortable coping with intellectual development than with personal development. Sometimes they feel more secure having a structured curriculum to provide guidelines, especially at the beginning. A few effective programs, particularly at the elementary school level have emerged to fill that gap, including some of the more popular listed as follows.

1   *The "DUSO" Kit.*"Developing Understanding of Self and Others" (American Guidance Service, Inc.) was developed by Dinkmeyer for use with the primary grades. The kit utilizes a variety of materials, including puppets, stories, pictures, and records, to provide back-

ground for a developmental series of experiences. The materials themselves provide the impetus for group discussions aimed toward helping young children to become more aware of their feelings, goals, values, and behaviors, as well as those of other children.

2   *Focus on Self-Development.* This multimedia series (Science Research Associates) includes fiimstrips, records or cassettes, photographs, and activity books. Materials for the kindergarten and early primary levels focus on awareness of self, others, and the environment. Stage two, for grades two to four, concentrates on responding, particularly in interpersonal situations. Stage three, for grades four to six, highlights involvement, with stress on the exploration of personal values.

3   *Dimensions of Personality.* Dimensions of Personality (Pflaum/Standard) is a series of texts and activity sheets to be used with children in small groups. Children read or listen to textbook material and then participate in programmed, group-related activities. The series is adapted according to grade level, with topics such as "I Can Do It" (grade two), "I'm Not Alone" (grade five), and "Becoming Myself" (grade six).

4   *Methods in Human Development.* The "magic circle" approach, developed by Bessell and Palomares (Institute for Personal Effectiveness in Children), provides for greater flexibility in implementation, but also calls for more skill on the part of the teacher or counselor in leading free discussions and modeling active listening. Children, in the "magic circle," discuss topics related to mastery, awareness, and social interaction. These discussions become part of the daily classroom routine, helping children both to increase their understanding of themselves and to relate more effectively with other children. Programmed materials outline discussion topics and also provide suggested activities.

At the elementary school level, such programs can easily be integrated into the normal school day. At the secondary school level, there is more fragmentation in the individual student's educational program. Since classrooms are not "self-contained," students experience a number of different teachers and a variety of classroom settings. Curricula dealing with personal and interpersonal understanding can be developed specifically for courses in psychology or related subjects. Such material can also be integrated into many academic courses. The study of history or literature, for instance, comes to life when young people have the chance to relate what they are learning to the reality of their own lives, their own feelings, and their own perceptions.

Value Clarification and Decision Making One aspect of self-understanding that is gaining more and more recognition is the process of value clarification. The things that an individual really values—really wants and cares about in life—affect every decision that is made. Exercises in value clarification do not attempt to teach a specific value or group of values. Instead, they help individuals of all ages to become more aware of their unique set of values and the ways in which they are affected by them.

Simon and Clark (1975, p. 35) summarize the process of value clarification in terms of the following steps.

Choosing

1 Choosing freely.
2 Choosing from among alternatives.
3 Choosing after thoughtful consideration of the consequences of each alternative.

Cherishing

4 Cherishing, being happy with the choice.
5 Being willing to affirm the choice publicly.

Acting

6 Doing something with the choice.
7 Doing it repeatedly, in some pattern of life.

A value has really been clarified, then, only when the individual has the chance to choose it freely, to affirm it, and to act on it. Helping young people to clarify their values involves a set of procedures that begins with the opportunity to make free choices in nonthreatening situations. Gradually, they can begin to ask themselves ever-deepening questions. When they have reached the point that they are willing to commit themselves to an idea, they must be given the chance to act on that idea—to make it a part of their lives.

The process of value clarification can become an integral part of the student's educational development. Exercises that aid in the understanding of values and attitudes can be adapted to any age level, so that the process can be developmental and follow a logical sequence. The youngest child or the most mature adult can learn from some of the following exercises.

1 Using words, pictures, or collages to describe aspects of themselves and their feelings.

2   *Forming an opinion in response to a concrete question and then defending that opinion.*

3   *Becoming aware of the range of possible responses by participating in a voting process.*

4   *Generating lists of alternative responses to a creative question.*

5   *Listing valued activities or objects and then categorizing them according to given questions.*

6   *Deciding on opposite responses to controversial questions and considering all the alternatives that might fall between.*

The process of value clarification is enhanced and deepened as students become aware of the vast range of alternatives from which to choose and as they realize that there is no one "right answer" to any of the questions they are confronting. As values become clarified, the teacher or counselor can begin to encourage further commitment and action.

Value clarification is basic to the process of decision making, and it is apparent that the art of making effective decisions is one that can, indeed, be taught. It is important that opportunities to practice decision making be provided from the earliest elementary school days, so that when students reach important choice points at the secondary school level, they are already accomplished at discerning their values, considering their alternatives, and planning in accordance with the consequences that their actions will hold. A particularly useful program is "Deciding" (College Entrance Examination Board), which was developed for use at the junior high school level. Through a series of practice exercises, story examples, and background reading material, the program gives students the opportunity to examine the place of values in decision making, to learn to locate and use relevant information, and to identify appropriate strategies for action. Content areas include the following.

Identifying critical decision points.
Recognizing and clarifying personal values.
Identifying alternatives and creating new ones.
Seeking, evaluating, and utilizing information.
Risk taking.
Developing strategies for decision making.

Although the simulations and exercises used in this program are most appropriate for the junior high school age level, the kinds of topics covered are meaningful both for much younger children and for high school-age youth. The opportunity to practice making decisions is one that should be offered developmentally, throughout the years of schooling.

Intergroup Education   Largely through legislation and court order, schools are becoming environments that bring together young people of differing races and ethnic backgrounds. Unfortunately, in most schools little has been made of the opportunity for children to learn from one another, to bring conflicts to the surface so they can be resolved, or to use intimate contact to break through long-standing stereotypes and prejudices. Instead, students share in essentially passive pastimes, having little opportunity to work together toward the resolution of problems that have real meaning for them. They receive little encouragement for interaction, either from their parents or from school teachers and administrators who are often paralyzed by fear of overt conflict. Thus, many young people tend either to avoid contact with students outside of their immediate group or to participate in conflict situations that are violent or destructive.

Particularly with younger children, much can be done to provide opportunities for close interaction and for the active, positive resolution of conflicts based on lack of knowledge. Difficulties can be prevented and positive learning can occur when small groups of children have the chance to share their ideas and feelings and to work interdependently toward a common goal. It is important, however, that emphasis be placed on activity instead of on abstract discussions that range far afield from young people's immediate concerns. Conflict among groups can, in itself, be a creative force for learning when young people have the chance to define the areas of disagreement and to work, with adult support, toward effective resolution. This kind of creativity cannot occur when adults try to bury conflict or to pretend it doesn't exist. It cannot occur when the normal school day does not purposefully create the settings and opportunities for real personal interaction. Time must be alloted—both within classrooms and through extracurricular activities—for children to seek and find one another, and that only happens when adults see fit to make it happen.

Parent Education   Although many schools act as centers for adult education, offering a variety of learning experiences to community members, a major focus should be placed on education toward effective parenting. Community counselors in many schools participate in the planning and implementation of courses or study groups that can help parents to function effectively and that therefore have indirect effects on the students themselves.

Working in groups gives parents the chance to share their feelings, frustrations, and successes with one another and to provide support in what can be a difficult process for many. It is important to concentrate on the development of programs that are offered to any parents who wish to participate, not just specialized experiences for the parents of children with "problems." In many instances, these kinds of programs are helpful, regardless of the specific topics being discussed. There are, however, structured programs that can help in the initiation of parent classes based on tested guidelines.

One possibility is the "parent study group," which gives groups of parents the chance to share their reactions to specific reading material. Some groups use the text *Raising a Responsible Child: Practical Steps to Successful Family Relationships* (Dinkmeyer & McKay, 1973), while others use *Children the Challenge* (Dreikurs & Soltz, 1964). These texts also include study guides or leadership manuals, making it possible for parents themselves to lead the discussions without a professional leader. Topics such as the goals of children's behavior, the processes of communication and encouragement, and effective family problem solving are discussed, with group members encouraged to help one another deal with immediate, practical concerns.

Another increasingly popular program is that provided by Parent Effectiveness Training (Gordon, 1971), which is taught by instructors trained in the apecific method. In a series of discussion sessions, parents are exposed to the P.E.T. theory of effectiveness in human relations. The course content provides for the following (Gordon, 1971, p. 49:[1]

1 Parents are taught to differentiate between those situations in which the child is making it difficult for himself to meet his own needs as a person, separate from the parent, and those situations in which the child is making it difficult for the parent to meet his own needs.

2 Parents are given skill-training in those forms of verbal communication that have been shown to be most effective in helping another person overcome difficulties in meeting his own needs. Parents are actually taught the particular forms of communication utilized by competent professional counselors. . . .

3 Parents are given skill-training in those forms of verbal communication that have been shown to be most effective when one person wants to

[1]Copyright © Thomas Gordon, reprinted by permission.

influence another person to modify behavior that is interfering with the needs of the first person—methods of confrontation that have low probability of producing guilt and resistance and high probability of maintaining the other's self-esteem. . . .

4 Parents are then given skill training in specific methods of preventing conflicts between parent and child—such as enriching or modifying the child's environment, preparing the child ahead of time for change, conducting participative decision-making meets for setting rules and policies that will govern children's behavior in future situations.

5 Parents are taught the hazards and harmful effects of using either of the two "win-lose" (power-struggle) methods of conflict resolution—Method I (parent wins and child loses) or Method II (child wins and parent loses).

6 Parents are then given skill training in using a non-power or "no-lose" method of resolving all conflicts between parent and child—our "Method III," whereby parent and child mutually search for a solution that will be acceptable to both, thus eliminating the necessity for the parent to use his power to force submission on the part of the child.

Although P.E.T. can only be provided by licensed instructors, opportunities for leadership training are offered constantly throughout the country.

In parent education, as in the development of programs for children themselves, counselors and teachers can utilize guidelines prepared by others or develop curricula to meet specific local needs. In the long run, prepared programs can only provide a beginning.

Direct Client Services

For many children, classroom group experiences will provide all of the personal assistance they need or want in a school setting. As they struggle toward maturity, however, young people often encounter situations in which they need extra help and support. Just as often, they seek the chance to explore in greater detail their own feelings about themselves and their world. The chance to participate in a one-to-one or small group counseling process must be open to all young people instead of being limited to those who have somehow been labeled as having unusual problems. "Developmental counseling" is a highly communicative relationship, in the course of which the counselee can do the following.

1 Learn more about himself or herself through self-examination.

2 Learn more about the environment and its effects.

3   *Set realistic goals.*
4   *Try out and evaluate new ways of behaving.*
5   *Solve immediate problems while learning long-range problem-solving skills.*

This kind of process is particularly important to children and adolescents as they strive to find their personal identities, to reach an understanding of their environment, and to develop skills in relating to others. Their struggle for independence and individuality brings with it the need to develop their own unique value systems and goals. As their search goes on, they must also contend with the immediate, practical pressures inherent in family, school, and peer group situations.

Students have the right to expect that someone in the school setting be ready to devote time to helping them through these important aspects of their personal growth. They have a right to expect immediate, informal access to a counselor, whether they desire long-range developmental counseling or short-term assistance with a situational problem.

Counselors must, of course, set a high priority on being readily available themselves to provide individual counseling and support when it is needed. Effective counseling tends, however, to create a still greater demand for the service. As this occurs, counselors must look beyond themselves for the resources that can meet this demand. They must also make counseling more readily available by training others to serve in the counseling capacity.

A pool of potential helpers can be found among teachers, volunteers from the local community, and the students themselves. Motivated members of any of these groups can be trained, in a relatively short time, to provide helping services under the counselor's general supervision. Particularly when students are trained as "peer counselors," there are added benefits. The number of available helpers is enlarged, and counseling also becomes more accessible because, for some young people, going to another student for help is preferable to seeking assistance from an adult. To physical accessibility is added the psychological accessibility of shared experiences and mutual concerns.

Whether the helpers being trained are elementary or secondary school students, community members, or teachers, the training process itself is essentially the same. Potential helpers—usually working together in a small group—generally have the opportunity to:

1   *Discuss the kinds of issues with which they are likely to be confronted as helpers.*

2   *Discuss their role as helpers.*

3   *Observe demonstrations of the helping process.*

4   *Evaluate the interaction being observed, in accordance with clear criteria.*

5   *Practice the helping process repeatedly, under supervision.*

6   *Receive feedback concerning their helping skills.*

7   *Give feedback to other group members concerning their helping skills.*

8   *Evaluate their own strengths and weaknesses as helpers.*

Even after the initial training period, helpers in action should have the opportunity for ongoing training and supervision, particularly as their participation in the real helping process brings new questions and concerns to the surface.

If programs are to be effective and far-reaching, the community counselor must act both as an accessible helper and as a trainer and supervisor of others.

Indirect Community Services

Counselors in school settings are intensely involved in meeting the needs of children and youth. This involvement makes them exceedingly aware of the degree to which the community provides a nourishing, responsive environment for young people's growth. Thus, counselors often find it necessary to engage in class advocacy in behalf of children. This may involve confronting policies that discriminate against young people or urging the community to create needed programs. Counselors have often been involved, for instance, in bringing about changes in police or court policies regarding youth; in helping community agencies to become more sensitive to the needs of children and their families; in striving for the creation of social or recreational programs for the young people of a community; or in encouraging local businesses to create meaningful job opportunities for students.

More often, however, the immediate environment of the school itself must be made more responsive to the needs of the students it was created to serve. In an ideal situation, when educational leaders are open to change, the counselor can act as a consultant, encouraging the development of democratic decision-making mechanisms and enhancing communication among students, teachers, administrators, and community members. The counselor can play an important role in formulating policies and procedures that can make the school a creative, open, living institution. Unfortunately, schools as institutions are often reluctant to change, and the means to bring about increased responsiveness must sometimes revolve not around consultation, but around political action. Aubrey, discussing the elementary school setting in particular, states:

> The desires and aspirations of many elementary school counselors are constantly thwarted by many nonnegotiable factors within the educational system. These nonnegotiable factors are institutional constraints that have been ingrained and long-established by custom and tradition, e.g., the ultimate authority of the principal in instructional and noninstructional matters, the inviolate sovereignty of the teacher in his classroom, the rigid time schedule in schools, the inflexible methods in the grouping of children . . . , the premium placed on docility and conformity, and so on. In the course of time, they become sanctioned and therefore present themselves to counselors as routine procedures, structural patterns, organizational practices, hierarchical processes, and conventional observances. Collectively, these school heirlooms represent tremendous impediments to counselors wishing to innovate programs and practices for children. Without power, a viable means of influencing the school policy makers, counselors have little or no chance of effecting changes for children (Aubrey, 1972, p. 90).

Stating that "power is the key to unlocking closed doors and allowing innovation, vigor, and vitality into the musty corridors of education" (p. 92), Aubrey suggests that the counselor, in order to be effective, must develop power bases among teachers and parents. Positive changes that could not be accomplished by counselors alone can be brought about through the concerted efforts of counselors, teachers, parents, and other school and community members. These power bases can begin to develop when counselors take the leadership in bringing members of various groups together to work on projects related to their common concerns.

At the secondary school level, a significant power base for change consists of the students themselves. While the community counselor acts as a student advocate, he or she may also organize and train students to act as advocates for themselves.

> If students are able to create and participate in new governance structures which represent their interests—and the competing interests of other school groups—our belief, supported by much practical experience, is that the living and learning processes in such schools will be more humane, more creative, and closer to national educational goals. It is not simply that the students' sense of control over their fate, so closely allied to other educational out-

comes, increases. It is that the educational activities which ensue are better ones (Chester & Lohman, 1971, p. 210).

The school environment can become more responsive and more stimulating when power is distributed widely and when many individuals and groups play an active part in decision making. The counselor can be a key to the creation of those kinds of processes.

Indirect Client Services

The counselor is also a key person in the relationships between the school and local community agencies. Often, individual children need services that are more specialized than those which a school can offer. Such services may be medical, legal, social, psychological, or vocational. In any case, the counselor can act as a link, helping in the location of the appropriate agency, and then following through by maintaining a close association with the child's new helper. It is important that this ongoing linkage take place so that the student's school program and the outside help being received are complementary and so that all of the helpers in the child's life are working in the same direction. The counselor is in a good position to act as a coordinator, working closely with school administrators and teachers, parents, and the community agency being utilized.

Ongoing linkage between school and community agencies can mean that individual children are helped more effectively. It can also provide the basis for joint agency-school educational endeavors. For instance, the state employment service can play a significant role in developing relevant vocational services in the school, while counselors working with youth or drug counseling agencies often have much to offer in the creation of school-based drug education course. Other community members, such as participants in civic organizations or business leaders, can also make great contributions to the school program if they have been effectively linked to the school through the counselor's outreach.

In instances such as these, community members are actually serving as consultants to the school. Just as often, community counselors themselves are called on to act as consultants, both within the school and outside, in the local community. Counselors who are employed in schools are often viewed as people who are aware of the needs of children and youth. For this reason, they are frequently asked to assist in the development of community programs or services for youth or to aid in the development of skills among workers who tend to have close contact with young people. Many counselors, for instance, maintain effective liaisons with the local police officers who work primarily with youth.

Of even greater importance is the counselor's role as a consultant to other people within the school itself. Counselors must work closely with administrators, teachers, and other school personnel to make school practices and policies responsive to the needs of all children and to ensure that the special needs of individual students are met.

The consulting process is, of course, a voluntary one, so consultants providing a service for teachers must respond to the priorities that those teachers set. Teachers tend, for instance, to ask for help in dealing with individual children, immediate problems, or special situations. Often, however, this can pave the way for the development of a relationship through which the teacher can be helped to create more effective learning climates for *all* children. Through consultation, teachers can be helped to examine their current situations, to generate new ideas, to consider their alternatives, and to select and evaluate new plans for action. Consultants cannot really solve their consultees' problems. They can, however, help teachers to examine the values, the goals, and the behaviors that they bring into their relationships with young people. While consultants can be helpful and supportive, final decisions for action must be made by consultees, according to what works for them.

It is being recognized more and more often that this kind of consulting process can work most effectively with *groups* of teachers instead of with just individuals. When teachers can participate in a group process, they gain still more support and have the chance to share many more ideas than might be devised individually. One approach being used widely is the "C" Group (Dinkmeyer & Dinkmeyer, 1979), which includes *consultation, collaboration, communication, clarification, change,* and *commitment.* The "C" group gives teachers the opportunity to help one another and to provide mutual support as group members attempt to examine their own values and their own behaviors in relation to children. The process of consultation is thus strengthened by the presence of a number of consultants and by the chance for an individual teacher to be both consultant and consultee. A group of teachers, pooling their knowledge, learn more about themselves and, at the same time, more about children.

The consulting process assumes, of course, that the consultee is anxious to learn, to change, and to become involved in the kind of self-examination that is needed for behavior to be affected. The counselor cannot always wait for such a situation to occur. Often, there is a need to take action in behalf of an individual child. Children are often powerless to bring about changes in their own environment. There are many situations in which they need advocates who can confront the significant adults in their lives, either to pave the way for the creation of positive programs or services or to halt policies or actions that may be detrimental to their development. Child advocacy and youth advocacy are growing movements. Counselors in school situations know young people and know the kinds of environmental pressures they face. They are in the position to take immediate action when it is necessary to defend the rights of youth, whether it is a community agency or a school official that must be confronted.

In the school setting, counselors must be accountable — first and foremost — to the students they serve. Their responsibility involves providing services that aid young people in their development toward healthy, independent maturity and, at the same time, taking action to provide an environment that nurtures growth and creativity.

COLLEGES AND UNIVERSITIES

In higher education, two long-standing traditions are gradually being broken down.

The first tradition is that of the university as an island in the midst of a community, isolated from the life of the town or city surrounding the campus. This tradition is being eradicated, both by attempts of college personnel and students to reach out to the world around them, and by community members' growing interest in the higher education institution and its role in community life. Significant leadership has arisen through the growth of community colleges, whose very title speaks to a new role and a new mandate for higher education.

The second tradition involves the college counseling center as another isolated island — this one in the midst of the college or university campus. This tradition, too, is being broken down, as counselors search for the ways that they can reach out to the populations they seek to serve and make a real difference, not just to a few students, but to the total campus community.

The counselor in a college or university setting must now be a true community counselor. This involves dealing with the college campus as an environment that affects every student and staff member. It also involves helping to bridge the gap between the institution and the community that surrounds it. Those tasks can be very complex, particularly in large, urban institutions that have long been lacking the human touch. The thrust that community counseling might take in the college or university setting is illustrated in Table 6.2.

In many instances, programs developed for the campus itself and those applied to the community at large run in parallel lines. Raines (1972, p. 148) points out the commonalities between services oriented toward students and those offered to the off-campus community.

Conceptually both programs: (a) share a concern for human (self) development; (b) seek to adapt activities to the needs and interests of the clientele they serve; (c) acknowledge the importance of development of the whole person rather than single compartmentalized segments of personality; and (d) recognize the importance of creating environments that are conducive to individual and group development. In day-to-day practice both programs conduct similar activities and utilize similar human relationship skills. . . . The essential differences between the two programs are more operational than conceptual. Student personnel programs focus on *campus* life and a more traditional clientele (though this is changing) while community service programs focus on *community* life and a *non-student* clientele.

Table 6.2
Community Counseling in Colleges and Universities

	Community Services	**Client Services**
Direct	Educational programs as community outreach	Outreach counseling
		Crisis intervention
	Skill-building programs using self-instruction and group methods	Supportive services for specific groups of students
Indirect	Community organization and planning	Consultation with faculty members
	Protection of student rights	Working to make campus environment responsive to subgroups and changing student body
	Encouragement of community and student involvement in decision making and policy formation	

Raines organizes the activities of community service programs into the categories of (1) individual development functions, (2) community development functions, and (3) program development. In fact, these categorizations may be as appropriate for student services as they are for community services. The activities that focus on personal growth and development functions form the core of the extensive experiential programs offered to students and community members.

Direct Community Services

Individual development functions involve services to the community that help community members to develop greater competence and effectiveness. In many areas, the nature of the college or university makes it a particularly appropriate agency for meeting community needs.

Community Outreach   One particularly appropriate area of community outreach involves helping groups of community members to examine their vocational and educational goals and make decisions concerning their career plans. Many individuals who would not seek assistance from a community agency unless they were faced with employment crises might be comfortable participating in an ongoing, clearly developmental program connected with a local college or university. This is particularly true when they are considering the possibility of further education for themselves. Instead of simply recruiting new students, college counselors can help community members to examine the possible place of further education in their lives and make decisions based on their values, their strengths, and their concrete knowledge about the options that might be open to them. Programs like this have been particularly effective in opening new doors to women, to individuals seeking midcareer changes, to retirees searching for new vocations or avocations, and to low-income individuals who might not have perceived themselves as potential college graduates. Many colleges have been successful in reaching mature community members through centers designed for their needs and connected with the institution's division of continuing education or community education. It might be possible to bring such programs even closer to the people by offering workshops, short courses, and counseling opportunities through civic or neighborhood organizations with ongoing memberships and multipurpose functions.

Such brief courses or workshops might also be used to provide other kinds of educational experiences to community members. Counselors in college settings may actively seek to assess local educational needs or try to respond to needs that have been identified by community groups. Programs can be developed to assist individuals and groups to deal with practical problems in living or to enhance personal and community resources for growth. Such programs require coordinated efforts that a college or university is in a good position to make. When a community need or objective has been identified, the counselor can examine the resources of the college or university in order to determine how assistance can best be offered. The institution is likely to have much to offer, particularly in human resources.

Personal services and academic expertise can be brought together to work in concert when faculty members, for instance, are encouraged to offer services to the community at large. Thus, faculty in psychology, social work, or counseling can develop and teach courses in human development, mental hygiene, and human relations, or offer skill training in the helping relationship. Faculty in the health professions can offer educational programs dealing with preventive health care. Faculty in business or economics can provide assistance to individuals or groups desiring to become more efficient consumers or to handle family finances more effectively. Faculty in still other departments can develop programs in literacy training, basic mathematics, or English as a second language.

Just as important, in terms of human resources, are the students who form a pool of potential volunteers to reach out into the community. Students specializing in specific academic areas often value the opportunity to practice their skills by offering courses or workshops to community members. Students involved in human services or students receiving training as educators enjoy giving their time and energy to programs oriented toward children and youth, senior citizens, disabled individuals, or other populations in the local community. The chance to form helping relationships or to act as tutors to young people gives students a growth-producing experience while offering a community outreach service.

The college or university can also serve as a social, recreational, and cultural center for the community. Traditionally, this function of a university has been present, but has limited its appeal to small, highly educated segments of the community. Lectures, concerts, theater, and the arts have been attractions that drew attendance, at times, from neighbors outside the university. In isolated instances, there has been great community interest in athletic events on campus. Basically, however, the college was separate from the town, and students' leisure activities paralleled, but did not intermingle with, citizens' activities.

It is becoming more apparent that the college's contribution in this area can be broader and deeper. Some institutions, particularly community colleges, have been able to develop programs that appealed to the community at large by responding to the realities of local interests. Activities can appeal to people of varying ages, socioeconomic classes, and ethnic groups, and can provide the chance for very heterogeneous populations to come together. This can only happen when members of the college community both offer their services to local citizens and accept citizens' services in return. The resulting programs can do a great deal, not only to serve the community, but to enhance the education of the students themselves.

Community services are most effective when they form an integral part of the total college program. There is often little need to leave community involvement to the work of one office or one group of people who specialize in this aspect of institutional life. Instead, the campus can be open to shared experiences in which enrolled students and community members have the chance to learn and work together.

Student Services   Educational programs aimed primarily toward students are also meant to aid in the development of personal effectiveness. Providing meaningful programs that are accessible to all interested students means moving away from dependence on the traditional one-to-one counseling approach and utilizing a variety of techniques for encouraging individuals to help themselves. Great strides have been made at the college level in the creation of programs that use self-instruction, group methods, or a combination of both to aid in the development of personal skills, self-awareness, and interpersonal effectiveness. Such programs make developmental assistance relatively easy and convenient to obtain. They also lessen dependence on the professional counselor, relying instead on individual self-help or on the ability of students to provide help and support to one another. Programs revolving around the development of personal skills, such as educational and vocational decision making or effective study skills, are being joined by group work aimed toward the development of interpersonal skills or toward the orientation of new students to the college setting.

Group methods are becoming especially common for helping university students develop skills in decision making and career planning. Many counseling centers provide workshops to deal with career-related issues (Bartsch & Hackett, 1979; Heppner & Krouse, 1979). Often offering academic credit, seminars deal with such issues as self-assessment, decision-making processes, goal setting, utilization of resources, information gathering, work attitudes, and interviewing techniques.

Community counselors in higher education settings also attempt to develop workshops or seminars that focus on problems that are common among their own clients. For instance, both Frew (1980) and Meeks (1980) discuss the use of minicourses to deal with issues of loneliness, both as pressing concerns on a college campus and as universal life themes. Recognizing the existence of highly stressful situations in the campus environment, Barrow (1981) reports using intensive, structured workshops to deal with three general topics: (1) stress management and relaxation, (2) test anxiety management, and (3) how to feel more comfortable with others. Each topic is offered either as a one-time workshop to develop awareness of the issue or as a more extended, five-session course for people concerned about their own stress levels.

Self-instructional methods that can be used independently also seem particularly appropriate for helping students at the college level deal with vocational or personal issues. As the available technology improves, it is likely that more students will be exposed to such methods as computer interactions for decision making (Katz, 1980), self-help tapes by telephone (Thurman, Baron, & Klein, 1979), or use of television and other mass media (Warrington & Method-Walker, 1981).

Direct Client Services

Despite the number of developmental programs that can be offered, many students and community members will still desire the intensive experience of individualized counseling, and some will experience crisis situations that might require intensive interventions. In the past, when counseling centers were isolated from the mainstream of college and community life, only a small percentage of students were ever reached. Outreach counseling and crisis intervention programs make counseling more accessible and more likely to be used by a greater number of people before the onset of chronic problems.

Outreach Counseling Many college counselors offer their services to nonstudent community members. Sometimes the student counseling service is open to people from outside the university as a community service. Special counseling units often are set up to meet the needs of local citizens. Such units may offer a combination of personal and vocational counseling services, outreach educational programs, and dissemination of information concerning the college program. In most instances, the thrust is toward providing helping services to individuals who may be considering enrollment in the college program.

The methods of offering developmental counseling services to students are also changing rapidly. When counselors waited passively in their offices for clients to appear, they often saw only individuals who had serious problems or whose concerns were clearly related to academic adjustment. Now counselors in many colleges and universities are setting up satellite counseling locations to provide services in areas that are closer to the mainstream of campus life. Counseling is seen as a normal part of college living when counselors, themselves, are part of the scene in dormitories, classroom buildings, student recreational centers, and other high-traffic locations. These locations are more convenient. Even more important, however, the counselors' physical presence carries with it an implication that seeking the opportunity to participate in a counseling relationship is a natural, normal thing to do.

This implication is carried still further when counselors train others to develop helping relationships. Many students do desire assistance in dealing with normal developmental issues, and when they become aware of the counseling service, they use it. Professional counselors cannot meet the total demand for services alone. They can, however, train other people to provide effective help and thus expand the range of services offered. College campuses have provided much of the impetus for the peer counseling movement, with students in many institutions of higher education taking advantage of the chance to help others. In colleges and universities throughout the country, students have been trained to do the following.

1 *Provide counseling in walk-in counseling centers staffed by a combination of professionals, paraprofessionals, and peer counselors.*
2 *Provide counseling in centers designed, run, and staffed solely by students, with professionals acting as consultants.*
3 *Give helping services to students in specific settings, such as their own residence halls.*
4 *Develop helping relationships with new students as part of the orientation process.*
5 *Develop helping relationships with students who have been identified as needing extra support and personal involvement.*
6 *Create counseling and information centers devoted to specific issues, such as alternative vocational planning, decision making concerning the military, or women's concerns.*

In addition to training peer helpers, counselors in higher education settings often provide training to other members of the campus community so that they can recognize potential problems and make appropriate referrals to the counseling service. People such as residence hall supervisors, health service workers, student personnel workers, and faculty members are helped to understand the nature of the counseling service and to refer students who might benefit from the developmental counseling process.

Crisis Intervention   College students have been among the prime movers in the development of the twenty-four-hour "hotline" emergency counseling service. Such services are presently offered in hundreds of college communities, either as part of the college or university program of student services or as a community service closely linked with campus life. These services often are used by local citizens as well as by full-time students. Voluntary student participation will always be necessary to the provision of crisis intervention services, since professional counselors alone could never provide the human resources needed for around-the-clock service. Counselors can play an important part in responding to students' recognition of the need for crisis intervention; in providing support for their attempts to find facilities and financial resources; in helping with the planning stages; and in training volunteer counselors. Although professional counselors may recognize a need for a local hotline, most programs that have been successful have begun with a core of committed students who saw a need for services and were willing to work.

Services to Specific College Populations   Intensive experiential programs also include the provision of services to groups of students who might need assistance beyond that which is normally offered. On many campuses, the nature of the student population is rapidly changing. Students with experiences and interests unlike those of the traditional college attender are appearing in increasing numbers. New open admissions policies are bringing to the campus students whose academic backgrounds may be different than those of the traditional student body. Outreach admissions programs are encouraging the enrollment of mid-career adults, part-time students, and commuters. Minority group members are attending colleges and universities in greater numbers than in the past. The primary task of the counselor must involve working to make the campus environment more responsive to the needs of a heterogeneous group of students. Attention must also be paid, however, to providing intensive support for students who may see themselves as falling outside the mainstream of college life. Meaningful group experiences must be provided for instance, for commuting students in universities that are primarily oriented toward on-campus residents. Assistance in vocational planning must be provided for adult students attempting career changes. Academic tutoring and study skill programs must be available for those who need them. All of these programs should, of course, be available to any student. The counselor must, however, actively seek out those individuals who might need assistance in integrating the social and academic aspects of college life.

Indirect Community Services

Indirect community services are designed to make the environment more responsive to the needs of all community members. In the college setting, such programs are aimed toward both the locality in which the institution is located, as well as toward the environment created by the campus itself.

Community Outreach   One important aspect of the environmental program involves ensuring that the college or university itself is a positive factor instead of a negative force in community life. Particularly when large, sprawling universities are located in crowded urban areas, there are times when the growth of the institution and the well-being of the community at large come into conflict. Conflicts often arise around the issues of land use, congested traffic, or the destruction of parks or homes to make room for campus development. Some of these conflicts may be unavoidable. Often, however, they seem to be most severe when communication between civic and college leaders is poor and when the interests of the university are seen as entirely separate from the interests of local citizens. Often, severe conflict can be avoided by active efforts to involve citizens in the decision-making processes that can affect their environment and, therefore, their lives. There will always be dissatisfaction at some level unless community members feel that the institution belongs, at least in part, to them, and they are willing to face the problems in the locality and try to assist in their solution.

Colleges or universities may have an increasingly important role to play in community planning and development. The resources which the institution can offer may be of use to community members as they attempt to set priorities and to create agencies that meet their social, psychological, and economic needs. College resources may be utilized to assess community needs in systematic ways. This is of service to the community, however, only when the results of such surveys are utilized to plan for action—not when the local population is simply used as a subject for research. The college or university can also play a coordinating and training role, enhancing communication within the network of helping agencies and providing ongoing training and consultation for volunteer and paraprofessional workers.

The Campus Environment   Community counselors attempting to assist college students in the development of competency and effectiveness cannot overlook the powerful effects of the institutional environment. That environment can enhance human development or detract from it can complement the institution's stated goals or run counter to them.

> Statements of the objectives of higher education properly stress the acquisition of knowledge and the development of intellectual skills and abilities. In addition to these goals a concern is sometimes expressed for achieving growth in attitudes and values, personal and social development, citizenship, civic responsibility, aesthetic appreciation, and similar supracognitive attributes. In relation to such complex objectives, a college community must be viewed as more than classrooms, professors, libraries, and laboratories. It is also a network of interpersonal relationships, of social and public events, of student government and publications, of religious activities, of housing and eating, of counseling, and of curricular choices (Stern, 1970, pp. 3–4).

Particularly when students are in full-time residence, the climate of the institution may be the most powerful current influence on their development. The college is their community. It is the place where their needs are met, where their interactions with others take place, and where they express their competence and individuality. If the institution is to be a responsive community, it must allow — and, in fact, encourage — students to find ways to express their competence and to influence their world. It must, at the same time, eliminate unnecessary restrictions that serve to block individual expression.

A primary task of the counselor must involve acting as an advocate for the student body in general, ensuring that in all institutional policies and practices, their rights are protected. The Joint Statement on Rights and Freedoms, endorsed by the United States National Student Association, the Council of the American Association of University Professors, and the Association of American Colleges, enumerates some of the most essential, including (Richardson, 1972, pp. 61–63):

1 Freedom in the classroom. . . .
2 Confidentiality of student records. . . .
3 Freedom of association. . . .
4 Freedom of inquiry and expression. . . .
5 Freedom of expression in student publications. . . .
6 Freedom to exercise the rights of citizenship. . . .
7 Guarantee of procedural due process in disciplinary proceedings. . . .

With these basic rights as an initial guideline, the counselor must confront institutional policies that limit the freedom of the general student body as well as practices that impinge on the rights of individuals.

To these rights must be added the right of each student to participate as a full-fledged member of the college community. Such membership implies the opportunity to have an effect on the environment and to play a part in the creation of policies and decisions that affect students' lives. This means that officially sanctioned student government bodies must have real power to implement their decisions, and that students must be involved in all policy-making groups. They must be able to influence not just decisions related to extracurricular activities (the traditional area of student autonomy), but policy relating to all aspects of campus life, including curriculum, administrative structures, and staff appointments.

Institutions of higher education—particularly very large ones—can be impersonal and depersonalizing. They can allow students to go through their college years feeling both isolated and powerless. Counselors, of all people, must recognize and act on the responsibility to build a sense of community and find ways to make use of the vast human resources that the campus has to offer.

Indirect Client Services

In many colleges and universities, faculty members as well as students may feel isolated. Counselors seem to be the appropriate individuals to take the initiative in breaking through the barriers that separate people, if for no other reason than to bring to the surface the helping skills that many members of the college community possess.

Because many psychological counselors have cultivated an image as "specialists," some faculty have felt that they need not, and perhaps should not, involve themselves in the personal problems of students; counseling requires an expertise possessed only by the professional. Faculty members thus avoid counseling and quickly refer troubled students to specialists. Moreover, the typical university structure isolates professional counselors from the teaching faculty both physically and organizationally. This isolation discourages contact, communication, and mutual consultation with teaching faculty. . . .

Indeed, specialization appears to promote isolation, competitiveness, and a reluctance to assume nonacademic responsibilities to students. . . . Mental health consultation can increase the sensitivity and ease with which teachers relate to those in need of help (Kopplin & Rice, 1975, p. 368).

In colleges and universities even more than in elementary and secondary schools, the academic and nonacademic aspects of the educational process have traditionally been separate and distinct. Consultation between counselors and instructors has been rare. But individual development does not occur in separate and distinct segments; the student's academic and personal growth are interlinked and inseparable. Faculty members, as well as other workers in the college setting, engage in constant interaction with students. That interaction can be helpful to students as whole persons if faculty and staff are encouraged to view themselves as helpers and to view students as total beings. Consultation with faculty members can make them part of the college's helping network, able to recognize situations that require specialized assistance and to relate more effectively with all students. The growth of this kind of sensitivity and awareness can make the campus setting more responsive to the special needs of individual students as these needs surface.

Counselors can also help to prevent many individual problems by recognizing and pointing out the need to make the campus environment more responsive to the needs of particular subgroups of students. Many colleges and universities are organized to meet the needs of a population of students that is homogeneous in terms of age, culture, and academic background. Student populations are changing, however, and many campuses have failed to keep pace. Every college and university must make adaptations in cirriculum, in student services, in housing, and in regulations so that college life is relevant to a rapidly changing student body.

Institutions of higher education are often very complex communities. It is difficult for those who have the power to act to respond to the needs of all students, as well as the needs of the local community. The counselor can be the link, acting to enhance communication among diverse groups and individuals and advocating in behalf of those who lack the voices to be heard.

SUMMARY

Community counselors in educational settings actually deal with two communities: the institution itself and the larger community in which the school or college is located. The multifaceted approach involves:

1 *Developing educational programs through which students can gain awareness of themselves and others and develop personal and interpersonal skills. Integrating such programs into the school curriculum when possible.*
2 *Creating educational programs as outreach services to the community at large.*
3 *Providing accessible developmental counseling services, using community volunteers and peer counselors as well as professionals.*
4 *Ensuring that the needs of special student populations are met.*
5 *Advocating in behalf of the rights of students.*
6 *Assisting in the development of flexible, democratic, and responsive decision-making processes within the institution.*
7 *Consulting with teachers and other workers in the educational setting in order to improve the learning climate and to meet the special needs of individuals.*
8 *Providing a link between school and community.*

ACTIVITIES TO ENHANCE UNDERSTANDING OF CHAPTER 6

1 Identify a specific educational setting in which you might work as a counselor. Specifying the age group of the population you would be serving, sketch out the nature of the counseling program you would develop. Consider the developmental level of the students in designing your direct interventions, and be sure to take into account the influences of the educational setting itself as an environment.
2 Many people, when they first hear the term "community counseling," assume that it refers to the work of counselors in community agencies. We know that, in fact, counselors in educational settings can also share a community perspective. If you worked in an educational setting, to what degree would you feel a responsibility to deal with the locality in which your institution was located? Try to list the components of the local community that you would try to affect and that would, in turn, affect your clients.

CHAPTER
7

COMMUNITY COUNSELING IN AGENCY AND BUSINESS SETTINGS

T he four major facets of the community counseling approach are appropriate to any setting in which a helper might work. Regardless of the nature of the agency concerned, effective counseling should include both services to individuals and attempts to affect the environment. Regardless of the immediate problems being faced, community counseling's major thrust is still toward the development of personal competency and the prevention of difficulties.

The community counselor intervenes in a number of ways. The precise nature of these interventions—the actual content of the programs developed—depends on the setting in which the counselor works and the needs of his or her particular group of clients. Since community counseling is an approach, rather than a job title, the community counselor can be found almost anywhere—in any one of a multitude of agencies and institutions. In order to make the approach more concrete and understandable, we have selected several types of settings to use as examples, indicating the specific kinds of programs that might be developed there. These settings were selected as examples because they tend to employ many kinds of helpers with differing specializations and training backgrounds. In no way is community counseling limited to these types of agencies.

In the long run, each community counselor must find the most appropriate adaptations to fit his or her own setting.

EMPLOYMENT AND VOCATIONAL SETTINGS

Many agencies—particularly government-administered employment services—see the vocational development of their clients as a primary task. The agency is considered successful when clients find work that is appropriate to their abilities, their interests, their career goals.

Yet such agencies must go far beyond their traditional images as places where nothing more happens than that an individual is "fitted" with—or even trained for—a new job. Blocher (1973, p. 76) describes far-reaching goals for the "new vocational guidance," including:[1]

1 Helping all individuals become more aware of the vocational alternatives available to them at particular stages of their development and to understand the probable consequences of those alternatives.

2   Helping all individuals to achieve a satisfying vocational identity that allows them to relate a productive work life to an acceptable life-style.

3   Helping all individuals to acquire a set of work-relevant coping and mastery behaviors that enable them to engage the world with dignity, self-esteem, independence, and effectiveness.

4   Helping the total society to conceive of and organize the institution of work in ways that satisfy legitimate human needs in fully human ways.

5   Helping the total society to build an opportunity structure that is devoid of racial, ethnic, sexual and social prejudice and that is based upon recognition of the talent and potential inherent in all its members.

If these are the goals of vocational guidance, then it is vocational guidance that must be offered in the effective employment setting. Attention must be paid, not just to immediate job needs, but to long-range career goals in the context of the individual's total life-style. Concern must exist, not just for the economic needs that a job can fulfill, but for the dignity of the worker as a person. And the goals of the agency must include not just helping the individual to adapt to the world of work, but helping the world of work to adapt to the needs of the individual.

The work of the community counselor in such an agency must, in fact, be multifaceted. Table 1 illustrates possible adaptations of the multi-faceted community counseling approach to the employment or rehabilitation setting.

Table 7.1
Community Counseling in Employment and Vocational Settings

	COMMUNITY SERVICES	CLIENT SERVICES
DIRECT	Workshops and educational programs for vocational planning, job-seeking skills.	Counseling, evaluation, and placement services for individuals. Programs for newly employed workers.
INDIRECT	Action against discriminatory hiring practices. Support of groups attempting to increase job safety and to humanize work settings.	Consultation with employers. Linkage of clients with other needed services. Advocacy on behalf of individual clients, particularly in instances of discrimination.

Direct Community Services

Agencies that are oriented toward vocational decision making should provide developmental programs that allow individuals to consider their values, their goals, and their occupational options *before* a crisis of unemployment is reached. Workshops for groups of clients are obviously helpful and can provide for much of the learning that might otherwise have to take place in repetitive, one-to-one counseling relationships. It would also be appropriate, however, for agencies to provide the opportunity for participation to any community members who might be interested, regardless of their present job status. A number of workshop approaches have been developed for use with adult populations. Community counselors can select among them or develop comparable experiences that would be particularly appropriate in their own communities.

VECTOR "Vocational Exploratory Counseling to Optimize Role-Relationships," was developed by Burck as a career-oriented course involving multimedia presentations and group discussion. VECTOR, as described by Sauber (1973, p. 47), helps individuals to:

1 *Become more skilled in learning how to generate alternatives.*
2 *Become more cognitively flexible, giving up rigid categorical notions of work and common occupational stereotypes.*
3 *Deal intimately with their belief systems and personal constructs about society, work, and themselves.*

The course, which is completed in 12 sessions, includes discussion of topics such as the changing world of work, values and commitments about work, work as a life-style, personal expectations, work as a set of role relationships, the authority structure, the social system, and mobility within and between jobs. Instead of examining vocations alone, VECTOR provides for an integration of information about the world of work, the place of work in the society as a whole, and the place of work in the individual's own life.

Vocational Exploration Groups Developed and implemented by Daane and Studies for Urban Man, Inc., the Vocational Exploration Group (V.E.G.) provides a short-term program for helping individuals to develop vocational planning skills. The program, as described by Hansen and Borow (1973, pp. 216 217), uses a step-by-step group process, including the following phases.

1 Inclusion activities (aimed at reducing fear of job exploration).
2 Job inventory (clarifies the person-job relations of the individual's preferred occupation by examining the world of work . . .).
3 Job personalization (group sharing of job information).
4 Expansion (each group member expands his vocational choice by relating one job to several others).
5 Next step (group focus on the specific plan of each member).

The V.E.G. was first developed for public employment service applicants and participants in other government-sponsored programs. It is meant to increase knowledge and motivation, as well as to provide an opportunity for group members to share their experiences and learn from one another. Studies for Urban Man, Inc., now trains V.E.G. leaders who may, in turn, train other leaders. The leaders, many of whom are paraprofessionals, utilize kits developed by the center.

Life Work Planning Life Work Planning Workshops (Kirn & Kirn, 1979) can also be offered both to clients of the agency and to the community at large. These workshops, which are appropriate for small groups, can be completed in about 25 hours. They can be offered in long, intensive sessions of several days' duration or through a format of brief weekly seminars. Delivery systems can be adapted to the needs of the population being served. However, the structured approach allows all participants to move from self-discovery to concrete planning and decision making.

Job-seeking Skills Prazak (1969) describes a program designed to assist unemployed clients in developing the skills needed to represent themselves effectively in job interviews. Clients, meeting in groups, observe model interviews on videotape, discuss what they have seen, and then participate in mock interviews that are also videotaped and discussed. Participants try to increase their effectiveness in describing their own work skills, in answering difficult questions, in presenting an appropriate appearance, and in displaying their enthusiasm about work. Instead of simply being "placed" in a job situation that may or may not last, clients learn the skills needed to seek and obtain their own employment—skills that will be useful to them throughout their careers.

Direct Client Services

Obviously, a high priority must still be placed on meeting the immediate needs of the unemployed person who needs a job. Counselors will always be involved with individualized counseling. They will always help counselees to evaluate their own interests and abilities, to consider the alternatives open to them, and to plan for education and training. They will always seek appropriate job placements. Even then, however, attention must be paid to the long-term goals of independence and effectiveness. As Prazak points out in discussing clients seeking job placement:

> Other counselors have placed them on jobs—jobs which they promptly lost—and they have come to expect direct job placement as an established service of every agency that works with unemployed people. They look surprised and very skeptical when they are told, "We will help you find out what your skills are, and help you to decide what kind of work to look for; but, instead of placing you directly on a job, we will teach you how to look for work on your own." The center subscribes to the philosophy that providing a temporary solution to alleviate a chronic problem is not good rehabilitation. Instead, the client must be taught more effective ways of solving his own problems so that he can be independent in the future (Prazak, 1969, p. 414).

Direct services to individuals and groups must take into account the strong personal impact that unemployment has on anyone affected by it. Brenner (1973) has found longstanding correlations between economic changes and hospital admissions for emotional disturbances. Individuals seem to find sudden unemployment most stressful when they cannot point to broad economic trends as the reason for their problem. "The more an individual feels that he is among a minority of the economically disadvantaged, or the closest he comes to feeling singled out by economic loss, the more likely he is to see the economic failure as a personal failure, one due to his own incompetence" (Brenner, 1973, p. 236).

When economic downturns do affect a community, the counselor working in a career-related setting has a role to play in attempting to prevent adverse effects.

> When a social stressor cannot be prevented, the role of mental health professionals lies in mitigating the adverse effects of social stress. Monitoring the economic changes in a region should . . . allow the development of primary prevention programs. . . . These programs would aim at preparing the population to deal with the psychological ramifications of an economic downturn. . . . Techniques such as anticipatory guidance . . . could be used

to persuade the about to be unemployed that their situation is not of their own doing. . . . They should not view themselves, nor be seen by family and friends, as failures (Monahan & Vaux, 1980, pp. 22–23).

In vocational and employment settings, programs involve direct services to people in immediate need. This aspect of the agency's work is, of course, important, but it is not the only one that is important. Traditionally, many agencies have concentrated on this one facet of their work at the expense of all of the other necessary programs. In fact, counselors can be more effective in their work with individual clients when they combine this service with others. Many vocationally centered problems can be prevented if community members have the chance to participate in educational workshops before the onset of employment crises.

Indirect Community Services

In vocational settings, the "world of work" constitutes an environment that affects every actual or potential counselee. Extensive environmental programs must be adapted so that the work world can be made more responsive to the needs of all community members.

A primary concern must be the examination of hiring, training, and promotion practices of businesses in the community. Vocational counselors are in a unique position to know, through the experiences of their counselees, when equal employment opportunity is a myth and when it is a reality. Thus, they are also in a unique position to confront discrimination when it occurs and to fight for fair and equitable policies. Combatting sexism and racism in employment practices is an obvious and necessary part of any attempt to affect the work environment. It is also important to be aware of unnecessary obstacles that may be placed in the paths of job seekers. These may involve the use of screening tests that are culturally biased or that measure aptitudes that are not relevant to the job. They may involve unnecessary or inappropriate educational requirements. They may involve the denial of opportunities to ex-offenders, ex-mental patients, or handicapped individuals whose disabilities do not really interfere with their job performance. In any case, effective community counselors do not turn their backs, but actively face and confront practices that are unhealthy for human beings.

Awareness must extend, not just through the hiring process, but through what happens to clients once they have begun working. Counselors may not have the power to change the work environments of large corporations and bureaucracies. They can, however, lend their active support to groups seeking to improve industrial safety, to increase workers' roles in decision making, and to make workplaces more satisfying settings for the human beings who spend so much of their time there.

Indirect Client Services

Community counselors may act as advocates for workers in general; there are also times when they must go to the support of individual clients. Where vocational matters are concerned, this is most likely to occur in instances of employment discrimination or other unfair treatment—at any time, in fact, that a powerful policy or person stands in the way of the individual's optimal vocational development.

In vocational agencies, as in any other setting, the counselor's concern is with the counselee as a whole person. It is impossible to separate vocational development from human development or one's work from the rest of one's existence. The counselor whose primary mandate is in the employment sphere is, like any other community counselor, aware of the interchange between the individual and the environment. In the employment setting, the counselor is particularly aware of the aspects of the individual's immediate surroundings that affect vocational decisions and dictate the likelihood of job success. Because it is so impossible to isolate vocational development from other factors, the community counselor often acts as a link, helping the client to find assistance with non-employment matters that might, in turn, affect the individual's vocational development. In many instances, the community counselor may act as a consultant, helping others to serve the client more effectively. Just as often, he or she may seek the opportunity to be a consultee, so that social, psychological, or physical factors affecting vocational development can be more fully understood.

COMMUNITY MENTAL HEALTH SETTINGS

A community mental health agency is responsible for dealing with the mental health needs of the general population residing within given geographical boundaries. Those community mental health centers receiving federal funds in accordance with National Institute of Mental Health regulations must serve populations of 75,000 to 200,000, and offer inpatient and outpatient services; partial hospitalization; 24-hour emergency services; and education and consultation. The Community Mental Health Act of 1963, which authorized seed money for centers developed according to N.I.M.H. guidelines, was meant to provide for community-based services with heavy emphasis on the prevention of mental health problems. In fact, however, the guidelines are subject to interpretation, and some agencies more than others have attempted to make major inroads in dealing with community problems.

The community mental health concept has great potential, because agencies dealing with specific "catchment areas" have the opportunity to develop well-coordinated human services and, at the same time, to recognize environmental situations and assist in organizing the local population to deal with them. This can occur in a small agency dedicated to outpatient care, or in a major mental health center providing comprehensive services to meet a variety of mental health needs.

A multifaceted approach that such agencies might attempt to implement is illustrated in Table 7.2.

Table 7.2
Community Counseling in Community Mental Health Agencies

	Community Services	Client Services
DIRECT	Educational programs concerning the nature of mental health	Ongoing counseling and rehabilitation programs
	Educational programs encouraging community involvement in planning and evaluating services	Walk-in assistance with problems of living
		Crisis intervention
	Educational programs to enhance effective mental health development and prevent psychological problems	
INDIRECT	Assistance in organizing local community to bring about needed environmental change	Linkage with support systems and helping network
	Class advocacy in behalf of individuals such as former or present mental patients	Advocacy in behalf of individual clients
	Organizing and planning for alternatives to hospitalization	Attempts to secure placements more appropriate than hospitalization
		Consultation with helping network

Direct Community Services

Educational programs should be made available to the entire community being served. These programs can involve two distinct thrusts: (1) educating community members *about* mental health, and (2) providing experiences that can enhance community members' own development and prevent the occurrence of serious problems.

Programs dealing with mental health itself as a subject matter should help to clarify what is presently known about the positive factors that encourage health and effectiveness in everyday living. They should attempt to eliminate the lay person's assumption that mental problems always involve some kind of illness that comes from within the individual. They should, instead, encourage recognition of the notion that mental health cannot really be understood without an understanding of the relationships between individuals and their environments. This kind of program might help to erase the stigma that is all too often placed on people who have needed intensive assistance with psychological problems in the past.

Educational programs should attempt to increase understanding of the dynamics of mental health and mental illness and should also define the kind of contribution that the mental health agency is trying to make. This can help community members to set their own mental health goals and to become more actively involved in the planning and evaluation of the services that are offered.

Extensive experiential programs also include attempts to help community members develop skills and awarenesses that can make a difference in their own development as effective human beings trying to create heathful environments for themselves. Community mental health agencies deal with relatively large, heterogeneous populations, and have a mandate to help with *all* of their mental health needs instead of a specialized few. Offerings that might be particularly appropriate to the thrust of such agencies are those that help community members and the community as a whole to become more self-sufficient in dealing with personal and interpersonal needs as they arise, for example,

1   *Training programs for the development of helping skills among community members. Such programs might be offered on an open basis to individuals who wish to become more skillful helpers. This approach can mean that effective help is readily available to community members when they need it, and might prevent the development of problems into serious discomforts requiring very intensive care. It can also increase the sense of community within a given locality, since mutual help becomes everyone's responsibility instead of the special province of professionals.*

2   *Provision of group experiences to help community members develop more effective interpersonal relationships. Workshops or ongoing groups can help community members to deal with one another more effectively, and also to give and receive assistance in dealing with specific concerns. The thrust of such groups would be toward development and education instead of toward the remediation of existing problems.*

3   *Provision of skill-building programs that can help individuals to live more effectively and to develop competence in ap , oaching the major issues of their lives. Many community members can be reached through educational programs when such programs are designed for implementation through large-group workshops or through individualized programmed learning kits. Learning experiences can be designed to help individuals develop skills in the use of behavior change techniques applied to themselves (self-modification) or in the area of decision making and problem solving. The thrust of these programs is to help individuals enhance the personal resources that can help them to face problems and issues occurring throughout their lives.*

4   *Education for everyday living. Programs may be most effective if they assist individuals to develop competence in meeting the issues they face every day as workers, as citizens, and as family members. Educational programs can deal with the development of effectiveness in areas such as family relationships, consumerism, or nutrition. In fact, they can deal with the development of whatever skills community members see as important. The effectiveness of such programs is enhanced when community members gain experiences that they can then share with their neighbors and associates.*

5   *Encouragement of self-help programs. Although community counselors may feel a responsibility to confront all aspects of community mental health, they know that the most important resources for developing competency and preventing problems are in the community itself. Mental health workers can play a part in the organization of neighborhood groups that can provide support and assistance to all of their members, while decreasing the isolation which many individuals feel in an urban, industrialized, and overspecialized society.*

Direct Client Services

Client counseling programs, meant for those individuals who need or desire more active interventions in their lives, must provide for highly accessible services. It is important that "mental health" be interpreted broadly, so that assistance related to any problems in everyday living can be offered, and so that counselees can be helped to relate more effectively to all aspects of their environment. Ideally, a community mental health agency should have walk-in facilities that allow community members to get whatever short-term services they may need as quickly as possible.

An essential part of this service should, of course, be counseling for individuals who desire to interact with a counselor in order to increase their understanding of themselves and their environment and to set long- and short-range goals for themselves. Such counseling services must be readily accessible, and that means having a large enough pool of helpers available so that needs can be met immediately. This can only be accomplished when counseling is provided by a number of helpers with differing levels of training instead of depending on the services of a highly trained professional.

When dealing with very troubled individuals, community counselors try to recognize and build on the strengths of their counselees and to do all that they can to prevent the need for inpatient care in a mental health facility. This kind of prevention can take place when interventions are made as early as possible in crisis situations and when arrangements are made so that very active help is provided in the context of the individual's normal living situation. When an individual's problems have been so severe as to interfere with self-sufficiency or require hospitalization, the thrust of counseling must be toward rehabilitation in accordance with the counselee's own goals. The community counselor has a particular responsibility to help former inpatients become effectively integrated into jobs and living situations in the mainstream community.

Thus, programs should include opportunities for the following.

1 *Assistance with any human needs that are interfering with an individual's growth and well-being.*
2 *Individual, group, and family counseling.*
3 *Rehabilitation and reintegration into the community.*

Indirect Community Services

Because of their close association with the people of their community, counselors in commuity mental health settings are in a particularly strong position to recognize the factors in the environment that are interfering with human development and, at the same time, to be aware of the great strengths and resources available within the locality.

When the mental health agency is an integral part of the community, it can play a role in helping community members to organize in support of their own goals. Citizens can, with the agency as a central coordinator and supporter,

1 *Organize to plan for services that can best meet the needs they themselves have defined.*

2 *Confront political and economic forces to ensure that policies are responsive to community needs and that decision making is open to citizen participation.*

3 *Act to confront immediate needs such as adequate housing, sanitation, transportation, employment, and medical care.*

While mental health workers can act as initiators, supporters, and encouragers of this process, leadership must ultimately come from the community itself.

Actual leadership on the part of community counselors might be important to bring about needed changes in the mental health system and the helping network itself. Pressure from within may be necessary to ensure that the system is responsive to those it is meant to serve, and community counselors may find themselves acting as advocates for the consumers of mental health services. Mental health workers should participate actively in the movements to:

1 *Ensure that inpatient mental health facilities offer treatment instead of just incarceration and recognize the civil rights of patients.*

2 *Search for and implement programs that can provide alternatives to institutionalization for any citizen.*

3 *Fight against any policies that discriminate against peole who have been institutionalized in the past.*

4 *Ensure that helping agencies treat all consumers with respect and actively confront policies or actions that fail to recognize human dignity.*

Indirect Client Services

A counselor working in a comprehensive community mental health agency is in a particularly good position to forge links with the total human care service network. Dealing with the mental health needs of a local population means dealing with a broad range of agencies and services. It also means dealing with the client as a total human being.

Counselors in community mental health settings provide links between their clients and the services that those clients may need at any time. Good "mental health" requires that practical needs are met, and a client may need any one of a number of services to meet those practical needs. The counselor can serve as a first contact and coordinator, ensuring that the maze of services and facilities becomes reasonably clear and accessible to the consumer.

It must also be recognized that the mental health of an individual is dependent, to a great degree, on the interaction between that individual and the other people who make up part of his or her environment. The counselor, in working with the needs of any one individual, is also working with that individual's family and associates—in fact, with any community members who might make up part of the counselee's problem or part of the potential solution.

In approaching the counselee's environment, the community counselor may act, not solely as a link, but also as an advocate. Often, the counselor is able to get action, particularly from community agencies or governmental bureaus, that the counselee is powerless to obtain alone.

Finally, the community counselor may act as a consultant, helping members of the total helping network to be aware of their own role in community mental health and to work more effectively with the people whose lives they touch.

AGENCIES FOR COMMON-BOND POPULATIONS

Many community agencies provide comprehensive services for the members of a specific group, or a population of individuals with something in common. Examples of this include agencies that meet the needs of women, of youth, of homosexuals, of the aged, or of members of racial or ethnic minority groups. In most instances, such agencies have a multifaceted, human service approach. They provide whatever services may be needed to deal with a variety of problems and to increase the strength of individuals and of the group as a whole. An illustration of the kinds of programs such agencies might develop is provided in Table 7.3.

Perhaps the most effective of the agencies serving specific populations are those that were originated by members of the group themselves—or at least by individuals who identified closely with their needs—as alternatives to existing institutions. Often, such agencies arise out of a perception that traditional social service agencies fail to fully understand or aequately respect members of the group in question. Thus, women may create alternative agencies to serve themselves; homosexuals may develop gay counseling centers; people who share the new cultural norms being generated by young people may create agencies meant to serve youth; members of minority groups, seeing established agencies as distant from the people, may create alternatives with closer ties to the immediate community.

These "alternative human care services" are usually characterized by the fact that they are community owned and controlled; that they are nonprofit; that decision making is democratic; and that responsibility is

Table 7.3

Community Counseling in Agencies for Common-Bond Populations

	Community Services	Client Services
DIRECT	Peer counseling training Encouragement of self-help Courses appropriate to the needs of the specific group	Accessible counseling services, using professionals, paraprofessionals, and/or volunteers or peers Crisis intervention
INDIRECT	Attack social, legal, economic, governmental policies discriminating against members of the population being served (class advocacy)	Advocacy in behalf of individuals (case advocacy) Consultation concerning special needs or interests of specific population Linkage with specialized agencies

collective, not centered in the hands of a "leader" or "expert." Just as there is little differentiation among workers in terms of roles or status, there is often no attempt to make a sharp distinction between workers and community members, between those being helped and those offering help. In many cases, an individual does both, and this orientation toward helping has a great effect on the programs developed and implemented.

Direct Community Services

In agencies that encourage very active participation by community members, programs usually include the building of helping skills. People who wish to help others as well as themselves can receive training in basic counseling approaches or group dynamics, so that they are then able to help their "peers," or people with whom they share something in common. This kind of training is especially appropriate in agencies dealing with common-bond populations. People seeking assistance are likely to enjoy the opportunity to interact with someone from their own age group, for instance, as in the case of a young person seeking help from a youthful "peer counselor." They know that they might be able to find real understanding much more quickly with a peer than they would with someone who had not shared their experiences. At the same time, people learning to help others can increase their own knowledge and develop the feeling that they are very useful members of the group with which they identify most strongly. Encouragement of this kind of "self-help" means that individuals can find help from someone like themselves and also that the group, in turn, can be strengthened.

Community services also involve courses or workshops to provide knowledge or skills that have been identified as important by the particular populations being served. Women's centers, for instance, often provide courses dealing with women and their bodies; with economic issues, such as equal employment opportunity, financial credit, or free day care; with personal skills, such as assertiveness; with self-defense; or with women's art, literature, and film. Youth agencies often provide courses dealing with drug education or other topics. Senior citizens' centers create opportunities for seniors to learn how to obtain health care, social security, or other benefits, or even provide training in second careers. Gay counseling centers provide informational seminars dealing with legal, employment, or housing problems. Agencies planned and implemented by minorities provide information on practical concerns of everyday living, as well as courses in ethnic or racial history, literature, and art. Any of the agencies for common-bond populations may provide training in organization for change.

These agencies are—or should be—very close to the people they serve. They may become community centers, with a strong social-recreational component. The agency is not just a place to go for help; it is a place to go for leisure activities and human contact.

Direct Client Services

Some people will use a community-based agency simply as a recreational or social center; other individuals will need much more. The fact that an agency is centered around the needs of a specific population means that it can be particularly responsive to those needs. Workers are aware of particular problems that are common to group members and are ready to deal with them.

When such agencies are effective, members of the population being served feel a sense of ownership. They may expect to be able to drop in and get help with immediate problems—whether minor or severe—and to have the chance to obtain counseling as it is needed. It is important that these expectations be met. Counseling services should be easily accessible, whether they are provided by professionals or by trained community members.

Agencies that are oriented toward common-bond populations often include among their services some kind of mechanism for helping people in crisis situations. One reason for this is that an agency that is close to the community may be the first place to which an individual might turn in a time of severe stress. Another important factor is the agency's unique awareness of the kinds of crises most common among group members. Thus, many youth agencies have "hot lines" to deal with drug-related crises, or short-term housing for transient young people with no place to stay. Women's centers have developed crisis intervention services for women who have been the victims of rape. Many gay counseling centers offer general crisis services through 24-hour switchboards; some can provide immediate, on-the-scene help for individuals who have been arrested.

Whether or not they are in immediate crisis situations, people tend to turn for help to an agency that belongs to them.

Indirect Community Services

Community counselors in such agencies are accountable to the populations they serve. There is no question of objectivity. They work actively to support the group's striving for social justice and act as *advocates* in behalf of their clients as a total group.

> The concept of advocate has different meanings to almost every person who uses the term. It means legal counselor, spokesman, supporter, pleader, defender, protagonist, intercessor, proponent, mediator, monitor, petitioner, activator, coordinator, ombudsman, expediter, enabler, promoter, protector, instigator, investigator, and exposer. There are two important common elements in these meanings; first—all are activist terms, and secondly—all imply that the activity is in behalf of another person or cause (Hiett, 1973, p. 39).

Advocacy in behalf of an individual client is generally termed "case advocacy," while advocacy in behalf of a cause or of the rights of an entire group is termed "class advocacy." Programs dealing with common-bond groups have class advocacy at their core. The community counselor is responsible to a given population and serves as an advocate for its rights. The community counselor speaks up in behalf of the group but, even more importantly, acts to support the group's own efforts in self-advocacy.

Thus, community counselors in youth agencies may be active in support of students' rights or may work to bring about change in juvenile court and corrections systems. Workers in gay counseling centers may seek an end to employment or housing practices that discriminate on the basis of sexual orientation; they may also deal with such issues as police harassment. People working in senior citizens' centers may find it necessary to take active stands to help bring about policies that can solve urgent problems of economics, health care, and physical mobility; their work with seniors will also have made them aware of unethical practices in institutions such as nursing homes. Community counselors in women's centers form part of the women's movement, striving to end sexism in our society and its institutions and to bring about an end to discrimination in all areas of life. They may work for passage of the equal rights amendment, for stronger sanctions against discriminatory practices in employment or lending, for the provision of day care and other services that women need, and for women's rights to own and control their own bodies—in short, for whatever changes are needed to bring women into full and equal citizenship. This parallels the activities of community counselors on behalf of all minority groups. A major thrust must involve enhancing the power of the total group and helping it to become a major force in political, economic, social, and educational policy making.

Workers in human service agencies must play a part in broad-based efforts for social change. At the same time, the agencies themselves may act as centers of activity for dealing with immediate, local issues. They may be the places in which local groups can come together, learn to organize, and begin to implement active approaches to the solution of common problems.

Indirect Client Services

Until the ideal of complete social justice becomes a reality, there will be a continuing need for "case advocacy," a continuing need to stand up for the rights of individuals. Case advocacy can take the form of ensuring that individuals receive the services to which they are entitled. It can also require taking action to defend the rights of individuals who may not have the power to defend those rights alone.

Community counselors working with youth, for instance, are likely to face occasions when they must confront school or juvenile court officials, who have tremendous power over young people's lives. When decisions concerning a youth's immediate future are being made, the individual—and even his or her parents—may lack the power to affect those decisions. The input of the community counselor may be desperately needed. Counselees, regardless of their ages, may sometimes need advocacy in their behalf, particularly with governmental and social agencies that were designed to help people, but that can sometimes overlook the intricate needs of particular individuals when large numbers of cases must be handled.

Counselees may also need help in locating and making use of specialized services to meet their needs. An agency cannot—and should not—try to be completely self-sufficient. Many services are more specialized than what one agency could hope to offer, and it is part of the community counselor's responsibility to maintain close, cooperative contact with other helpers. These efforts mean that counselees can be quickly and effectively linked with legal aid, medical facilities, specialists in vocational development, and agencies equipped to deal with severe psychological difficulties—whatever resources are needed to fill the gaps in service delivery.

At the same time, counselors in agencies serving common-bond populations are often called on to act as consultants to other helpers, filling them in on the special needs, values, and characteristics of the populations they serve, and helping them to be more responsive.

SPECIALIZED AGENCIES

A specialized agency is one that has been created to deal with a specific concern. Examples of such agencies would include centers designed to provide services to the victims of drug or alcohol abuse, mental retardation, and physical disabilities. It is recognized that the individual clients of such agencies need a variety of direct services. It is also important to remember, however, that the agency must deal with the environment, which impinges on the group of counselees being served, and must recognize a responsibility to the community as a whole. The kinds of services that might be implemented by a specialized agency are indicated in Table 7.4.

Table 7.4

Community Counseling in Specialized Agencies

	Community Services	Client Services
DIRECT	Educational programs for community at large, including preventive programs and attempts to increase understanding of the problem area	Rehabilitation programs, including counseling, training, vocational and educational placement Encouragement of self-help group programs Recruitment and training of volunteers
INDIRECT	Class advocacy: attempts to change legislation and social environment so that opportunities for group's integration are enhanced	Linkage with helpers in generalized agencies and with informal support systems Advocacy in behalf of individuals Consultation concerning specific problem area

Direct Community Services

Community counselors in specialized agencies deal, on an everyday basis, with a specific area of human concern. If they work with individuals affected by a particular disability, for instance, they are very much aware of the effect of the problem, and just as aware of the strengths exhibited by their clients. They are able to place the problem or disability in perspective, and they are in a position to know how small the differences really are between their own clients and the rest of the community.

Extensive experiential programs in such settings can serve a twofold purpose: preventing the occurrence of a problem with which the agency is concerned and increasing public awareness of the situation of its victims.

Workers in drug or alcohol abuse settings, for instance, often provide their services to the community at large for educational programs dealing with substance abuse. Informational lectures and workshops are offered for students at many educational levels, for parent groups, and for civic or church-related organizations. When such programs are effective in preventing widespread drug or alcohol abuse, they avoid "scare tactics," concentrating instead on presenting accurate information, as far as it is presently known; on dealing with drug or alcohol use as a question related to decision making and personal values; on correcting misinformation; and on attempting to eliminate stereotyped images of addicts.

Breaking through "stereotypes," or fixed notions about what a particular group of persons "must be like," is also of urgent importance when the counselor provides information concerning physical or mental disabilities. Educational programs must not generate pity, since that only increases the separation between the disabled and the rest of the community. Instead, they must generate understanding of the people in question as having needs, desires, and rights that are not really distinguishable from those held by anyone else. While educational programs can deal with the causes and effects of particular disabilities, and with the special needs that disabled individuals might have, emphasis should be placed on the community's responsibility to integrate all of its members into normal community life. Such programs can, while providing information to the public, also enlarge the pool of volunteers ready to devote time and energy to building the necessary bridges and helping to create and provide needed services.

Direct Client Services

The individual most able to define the kinds of services needed is the one who will be making use of them. The experiences provided for individuals using specialized agencies must depend, to the degree possible, on the goals that they have developed for themselves.

Direct services include rehabilitation for individuals. Rehabilitation services involve those efforts, including counseling and vocational training, that can help the individual to become more self-sufficient. The term "rehabilitation" has sometimes been associated with vocational development; effective rehabilitation was thought to involve preparing an individual for the greatest possible degree of economic self-sufficiency, through vocational counseling, training, and job placement. In reality, however, it is impossible to separate vocational development from total human development. Effective rehabilitation must be concerned with the whole person—in many cases, with a whole family—and with the immediate environment. An initial step must be the development of an agreement between the counselor and the counselee concerning the ultimate

goals of the rehabilitation process and the kinds of services that can help
to make those goals attainable. The process may then include services
such as:

1   *Personal and vocational counseling.*
2   *Assistance in locating appropriate living or work settings.*
3   *Help in ensuring that basic physical needs are met.*
4   *Locating appropriate medical or legal services.*
5   *Locating appropriate resources for financial aid.*
6   *Providing for necessary equipment to maintain economic and personal self-
    reliance.*
7   *Assistance in selecting training or educational programs.*
8   *Placement in training programs or jobs.*

The rehabilitation program developed for each individual must be adapted to that individual's particular goals and needs, and the thrust of a
particular agency will, of course, affect the kinds of programs developed.
In an agency dealing with substance abuse, a major thrust of rehabilitation might involve detoxification, methadone maintenance, or withdrawal from alcohol. An agency serving retarded adults might emphasize
placement in group homes and work settings providing optimal opportunities for learning, self-care, recreation, and normal living. An agency
dealing primarily with physically disabled individuals might concentrate
on services helping clients to maintain the great possible mobility, independence, and work satisfaction. These services vary greatly, just as the
problems being faced vary among individuals and among agencies. What
the programs have in common is their attempt to deal with whole individuals, helping them to make the most of all of their strengths and to live
as fully and as independently as possible.

A major factor in the struggle for independence involves independence
from professional helpers themselves. Part of the counselor's job must, in
fact, be to encourage the formation of self-help groups that allow individuals with common problems to help one another and, at the same
time, help themselves. Such groups provide opportunities for individuals to receive the assistance they need, to participate in the growth-
producing process of assisting others, and to develop relationships with
effective and productive people. For example, a social worker who himself contracted polio 18 years ago, writes:

Just as with disabled children, the lack of role models, and isolation based on not being like (or acceptable to) able-bodied people, also have significant impact on newly disabled adults. Since it is impossible for them ever to be "like" the able bodied in the ways that are generally held to be valuable, contact with other, effectively functioning people with disabilities is crucial in order to provide the foundation for the redevelopment of a positive self-image, *inclusive* of the physically disabled body image (Leach, 1974, p. 12).

Just as this experience may be helpful for the physically disabled, it is also important to the development of others who feel themselves cut off from the mainstream of society or devalued for whatever reason.

At the same time, it is important to tackle this isolation by providing opportunities for interaction with people who neither work as professional helpers nor share the individual's problem or disability. In addition to the concrete help that can be provided, volunteers can increase contact between the community that they represent and the individuals they seek to assist.

Indirect Community Services

Awareness of the interaction between individuals and their community brings with it the realization that, in many instances, it is the environment not the individual, that must be changed.

Community counselors working in specialized agencies providing services to handicapped individuals must become aware of—and, in fact, involved with—the movement to gain civil rights for the handicapped. Their contact with such individuals makes them highly aware of the problems being faced every day; their responsibility as counselors must include attacking the sources of those problems instead of just making life a little more comfortable for society's victims.

Both class advocacy through the courts and political action planned and implemented by the handicapped themselves are coming to the fore as effective civil rights activities.

Handicapped persons are in court. . . . Developmentally disabled and multi-handicapped children have won significant victories on the right to a free publicly supported education. Mentally disabled persons have established constitutional standards for adequate treatment and habilitation. Physically handicapped persons have secured judicial enforcement of their right to access to public transportation and public buildings.

Favorable decisions have been rendered in regard to entitlement to minimum wage and classification and placement procedures for specialized education. Litigation on employment discrimination and rights to community services are on the horizon (Laski, 1974, p. 15).

While strides are being made through the courts, political action to raise the consciousness of legislators, business leaders, and the public is still needed. Presidential veto of the Rehabilitation Act of 1972 was protested by a Washington, D.C., demonstration by the handicapped. The demonstration, which was initially organized by the New York-based Disabled in Action, was attended by deaf, blind, and disabled people from all over the country.

What we have seen so far is only the beginning. All individuals, regardless of disability, have rights to education; to treatment, when needed; to free access to public buildings and transportation; and to equal employment opportunity. They have a right to expect the creation of any possible alternative to large, dehumanizing institutions. The disabled and their families must continue their leadership positions in this struggle, but there is room for active support, especially from community counselors who see the results of discrimination every day.

When counselors work in agencies dealing with substance abuse, the rights of their clients are further complicated by the impingement of criminal law. Fellows of the Drug Abuse Council (1974, p. 45) write:

The policy of criminalizing drug users has gravely threatened civil liberties by fostering an attitude among some law enforcement personnel that encourages and justifies the use of illegal means to control drug traffic and experimentation. We are in agreement with many criminal justice leaders who deplore such practices as entrapment, the use of unreliable informants, illegal wiretapping, employment of undercover provocateurs, illegal searches and seizures by overzealous law enforcement officers, and the setting of high bails where no indication exists that defendants will abscond. . . .

The second mechanism for controlling addiction—the healthy system— has been granted special trust and authority in the United States. It can impose its demands on citizens in the name of health, often bypassing the established safeguards of due process that are inherent in criminal justice procedures. We believe that there are many traditional benefits the health professions can provide in the treatment of addiction, such as those functions specific to restoring persons to a state of physical and mental health. But when physicians act as agents of social control, we fear that those traditional functions are seriously compromised.

Community counselors must confront the erosion of human rights whenever they see it occurring. They must also engage in a continual examination and reexamination of their own part in the process. Community counselors have to find their own role in the national civil rights movements that are quickly developing. They may be particularly useful in helping to highlight problems and potential solutions in their own localities.

Indirect Client Services

Just as counselors must see themselves as advocates for the total populations with which they work, they must also recognize and act on opportunities for case advocacy. In the final analysis, legislation and judicial action can only make a difference when individuals are aware of their rights and can act to safeguard them. Counselors often face situations in which individual clients are denied rights to education, to needed services, or to equal employment opportunity. When clients receive anything less than equality under the law, their rights must be protected. Community counselors can act in their clients' behalf, but only by knowing what their rights are and by being willing to confront inequities when they occur. Good resources that can help in this area include the Policy and Action Conference for the Handicapped, and the National Center for Law and the Handicapped, a South Bend, Indiana, center that collects and disseminates information and also provides legal referrals. Advocacy can be even more effective when community members have the opportunity to act as "citizen advocates," safeguarding the rights of an individual or group of individuals, and acting to ensure that all of their service needs are met. Citizen advocacy centers can be administered and coordinated by community members themselves. Counselors, however, can encourage their formation and continue to support them.

The community counselor working with the whole person must also be able to link counselees with other needed services. Close ties must be maintained with other agencies, so that the counselor is aware of all types of helping resourcs available in the community. Then clients can be assisted in contacting appropriate government agencies, such as social security and welfare departments, and community facilities providing specific services to the general population.

Community counselors in specialized agencies have also gained expertise in dealing with a specific area of human concern. Thus, they are often called on to act as consultants to other helpers, sharing their knowledge of the specific problems and special needs of the populations they serve. As these populations become more integrated, particularly into educational institutions, requests for consultation are likely to increase.

COMMUNITY COUNSELING IN BUSINESS AND INDUSTRY

Counseling for employees in their work settings has become more and more prevalent, with the number of consultants involved in such programming increasing from about 125 in 1972 to about 1250 in1981 (Roman, 1981). Counseling programs in industrial settings are normally termed *employee assistance programs* (EAPs), and they focus on helping troubled workers to return to their former levels of productivity. In fact, it is because of their positive effects on employee performance that corporations fund and support employee assistance programs.

Yet the traditional approach to employee counseling programs tends to be oriented to treatment, rather than prevention.

> EAPs tend to be treatment-oriented. By stressing referral to professional assistance, an EAP is focusing on activity designed to get the employee's performance back to an acceptable level. While there certainly is nothing wrong with improving the employee's performance, this approach neglects to initiate any activity to reduce or eliminate factors causing or contributing to the problem. The employee's *"problem"* (e.g., stress, marital, family, drug abuse) may actually be a *symptom* of the real problem or combination of problems, such as a boring job, improper placement . . . insufficient or too much job responsibility, undue pressure to achieve results, or lack of recognition for superior performance (Hollmann, 1982, p. 38).

Employee assistance programs can utilize a community counseling approach, especially through contracting with external counseling providers who can ensure confidentiality, objectivity, and the ability to provide services to companies that are too small to be able to support in-house programs. For instance, P.A.C.E. (Professional Assistance for

Table 7.5
Community Counseling in Business Settings

	Community Services	Client Services
DIRECT	Educational programs provided on site in working settings	Counseling services for workers desiring assistance
INDIRECT	Consultation in reducing stressors affecting total organization	Consultation in recognizing, referring, and advocating for troubled employees

Corporations & Employees, Inc.) provides multifaceted services to companies attempting to enhance employee performance while providing positive benefits for workers and their families. The multifaceted approach to employee assistance programming is illustrated in Table 7.5. Effective programs attempt to increase employees' coping skills while concurrently trying to decrease stressors in the work environment.

Direct Community Services

Programs based on community education models are very appropriate for business and industry. Such programs may relate specifically to stress management. For instance, Murphy (1982) reports the successful delivery of programs teaching such stress-reducing techniques as biofeedback, muscle relaxation, and meditation. But any program that might normally be delivered in a workshop, seminar, or self-teaching format can be delivered at the work site, making educational efforts accessible for people who might not otherwise attend mental health-related programs. Examples of workshops that have been provided for workers during lunchtime or after work include communication skills, parenting, alcohol and drug information, time management, assertiveness training, and preparing for retirement—some only indirectly related to job performance.

The employee assistance program can also form part of a company's total approach to employee health and wellness. "Increasingly, corporations are seeing themselves in the role of health care service providers for their employees" (Manuso, 1981, p. 137). When this corporate responsibility takes the form of health promotion, rather than merely treatment and rehabilitation, the employee assistance program can join forces with fitness thrusts to provide for physical and psychological well-being.

Direct Client Services

Counseling services form a major part of the employee assistance effort in any company. Normally, counseling that is provided through a business-related program is limited to short-term assistance in problem solving, decision making, or coping with situational stressors. If more assistance is needed, employees are linked with community agencies. The EAP serves as "a method for disentangling employee problems from routine personnel concerns" (Sonnenstuhl & O'Donnell, 1980, p. 35).

The counseling process may relate to such concerns as alcohol or drug abuse, family conflicts, stress, interpersonal difficulties, or legal/financial crises. When such problems are handled in the employment context, help is timely. Employees are more likely to seek assistance through an accessible service provided free of charge by their employers than through an agency that they assume is meant for people with serious problems, as long as they know that their use of the service will be held in confidence.

Indirect Community Services

The work organization itself may contribute to the development of stress-related problems troubling employees. The counselor is in a particularly good position to recognize the existence of environmental stressors affecting counselees, and can therefore consult with management "in an ongoing effort to develop the kind of work environment that provides employees with opportunities for satisfaction, self-esteem, and dignity, enabling them to work at their best" (Leeman, 1974, p. 154).

Jobs and organizations can be made less stressful through purposeful design. Kahn (1981), for instance, suggests that stress can be lessened if attempts are made to do the following.

1 Minimize unpredictability and ambiguity at work . . .
2 Minimize uncontrollable events at the individual level . . .
3 Eliminate avoidance learning, that is, performance or punishment . . .
4 Minimize physical stressors . . .
5 Avoid recurring (daily) stresses . . .
6 Watch for negative affect . . . (p. 30).

Employee assistance counselors, like other community counselors, can attempt to make the organization as a whole less stressful to all employees, while assessing the effects of major temporary stressors associated with sudden organizational changes.

Indirect Client Services

Community counselors in industrial settings provide effective linkages with internal and external resources for help.

A counseling program in a work setting serves as an alternative to disciplinary measures, but it is workable only if supervisors know how to use it. A major thrust of indirect service delivery involves supervisory training. Counselors in virtually all employee assistance programs provide training for managers and line supervisors, helping them to recognize incipient employee problems, to confront issues directly and facilitatively, and to make appropriate referrals. An effective supervisory training program makes the organization more responsive to the needs of employees who may be facing either personal or work-related problems.

The counselor also provides linkage between the troubled employee and the helping network available in the community. When an individual needs social, psychological, medical, or other services, the counselor identifies and contacts appropriate service systems, and even provides individual advocacy when it is needed. The counselor who is familiar with issues affecting individual employees and also knowledgable about the organization and the outside community can provide the kind of consultation needed to ensure that systems work in favor of troubled employees, rather than against them.

SUMMARY

Community counselors can be found in a number of business and agency settings. Regardless of the particular situation, programs should be multifaceted, should aim toward effective human development and the prevention of difficulties, and should deal with the environment as well as with the individual. Multifaceted community counseling programs can be implemented effectively in employment and vocational settings, in agencies serving common-bond populations, in specialized community agencies, in community mental health centers, or in business and industry. In each instance, community counselors can adapt the basic model to meet the unique needs of the community they seek to serve.

ACTIVITIES TO ENHANCE UNDERSTANDING OF CHAPTER 7

1 Now that you are very familiar with the application of community counseling concepts, you will find it helpful to visit another community agency. Using the community counseling model as a guide, try to evaluate the effectiveness of this agency in meeting its goals. You might find that there is a conflict between the stated goals of the agency and the kinds of activities or services that seem to be prioritized. Could there be implicit objectives that are not written down but that really direct the agency's work?

2 Take this opportunity to reexamine your own hypothetical program. If someone unfamiliar with your unique agency examined the nature of the services to be delivered, what would he or she assume to be the goals of your work? Do you have a good fit between your program's goals and the methods you have designed for reaching them?

CHAPTER
8

MANAGING THE COMMUNITY COUNSELING PROGRAM

The effectiveness of community counseling programs depends on thoughtful planning, deliberate organization, rigorous evaluation, and responsive leadership. In human service settings, management involves the process of making a plan to achieve a desired outcome, organizing the people and resources needed to carry out the plan, encouraging the human service workers who need to perform the component functions, and evaluating the results. It is clear that community counselors must be aware of and competent in these managerial functions if they are to maintain control of the directions their programs take. Like other human service workers, they are "forced to choose either to participate actively in the administration of their own programs or to leave leadership in the hands of others who may have little understanding of the helping process. Many are being forced to manage their programs or lose them altogether" (Lewis & Lewis, 1983, p. 2).

Because community counseling programs are innovative and multifaceted, their management is challenging. Because such programs are based on clear philosophical assumptions, their directions must be controlled by people who understand their goals. Community counselors have little choice but to gain expertise in the functions of management: planning, budgeting, organizing, supervising, and evaluating.

PLANNING

Community counselors base their work on the assumption that they should identify and choose among many kinds of services in the interests of meeting mental health-related goals. As Krumboltz and Peltier (1977, p. 58) point out,

> The interview is only one tool in our kit. We need to begin looking at ourselves as change agents, concerned with discovering and applying the best means to help the largest number of people effectively, efficiently, and inexpensively.

For community counselors, this process involves the development of multifaceted programs. These programs, or sets of related services, are designed to be responsive to community needs. Thus, the goals of each program must be based on the results of careful needs assessment.

Needs Assessment

The planning process in any human service setting must begin with a careful evaluation of the needs and desires of community members. Through this needs assessment, the community counselor attempts to determine what local problems are troubling citizens, what resources are available to solve the problems, and what services could help to fill the gaps in the current delivery system.

Although the main thrust of this process is toward the identification of problems or unmet goals, the perceptions of community members concerning the seriousness of any situation must also be taken into account.

> Many conditions in society are not perceived as social problems. Only a few conditions become social (or community) problems for which policy is developed. For conditions to become recognized as problems, there must be a process of perceived, collective definition in which a given condition is selected and identified as a social problem" (Barton, 1978, p. 38).

Thus, counselors cannot identify problem situations in isolation. They must also assess the perceptions and values of the communities they seek to serve. If a need is defined as "the lack of a positive condition or the presence of a negative condition which affects the health, social, or economic well-being of the community" (Barton, 1978, p. 40), the community itself must define the *negative* or *positive* in each situation or condition.

A comprehensive needs assessment can use any one or a combination of available tools, or instruments, including the following:

1 *Surveys.* Community members may be asked, through questionnaires or interviews, to provide information concerning characteristics or needs. Such surveys can be administered to all members of a target population or to a sample of community members. Community counselors might utilize this method to develop new programs, to update needs assessment data or to reevaluate current services.

2 *Community meetings.* The perceptions of community members can also be assessed through community forums. Meetings perform two dual purposes: assessing local priorities and increasing community involvement in the service system. This approach can be based on

formal hearings or informal get togethers. It sheds light on strategies that would not be determined through other assessment methods.

3 *Social indicators.* The community counselor can use existing quantitative information concerning aspects of the community that might, indirectly, relate to service needs. Social indicators might include demographic characteristics, health and education statistics, socioeconomic variables, employment patterns, family patterns, and other data. Statistics concerning such problems as delinquency, suicide rate, school dropout rate, divorce figures, or other problem-related data can help to shed light on possible service priorities.

4 *Surveys of local agencies.* Survey approaches can be used to determine what services are currently being offered in the community. Questionnaires dealing with services and types of consumers served can help to identify service gaps and to avoid needless duplication.

5 *Interviews with key informants.* Local leaders or informal care givers might be able to provide information concerning unmet service needs or community opinion. This information can provide the basis for the development of other approaches, such as survey questionnaires.

Needs assessment tools provide the means for identifying the priorities that, in turn, lead to the development of goals and objectives.

Assessment provides one important informational input to a much broader planning process that leads to (a) the selection of and priority setting among problems and target populations to be addressed; (b) the selection and operationalization of specific community program activities; and (c) the evaluation of these program activities (Siegel, Attkisson, & Carson, 1978, p. 221).

Once initial needs assessment has taken place, community counselors turn their attention to the identification of program goals.

Goal Setting

Identifying clear goals may be the single most important underpinning of the community counseling management process. The counselor is ready to provide the services that meet program goals and to eliminate activities that do not relate to the objectives that have been set. Providing a coherent set of services thus depends on the existence of clear goals, reached through a consensus among policy makers, service deliverers, and consumers.

The goals of community counseling programs should relate to the outcomes that are desired for the community or for clients. They should be systematically related to objectives that are measurable, realistic, and acceptable to the groups holding any stake in the success of the program. The desired outcomes provide the basis for all subsequent decisions concerning the nature of services to be delivered.

Decision Making

The difference between community counselors and human service workers having a narrower focus on services is the community orientation's avoidance of what Odiorne (1974) calls the "activity trap." When human service professionals become caught in the activity trap, the activity becomes an end in itself. "Having spent years mastering one class of activities, called a profession, (they) persist in practicing those activities, as learned, even when the objectives practically cry out for some other kind of behavior" (Odiorne, 1974, p. 7).

The community counseling approach, in contrast, depends on the use of a number of differing activities, all leading toward goal accomplishment. Decisions concerning program development depend on canvassing a wide range of alternatives for service delivery, weighing the negative and positive implications of each, and finally making a choice based on a reasonable search of available data. The key to this decision making process is openness, with counselors considering innovative activities as freely as they consider accustomed services, such as one-to-one counseling.

The following questions should be asked about each alternative.

1 *Does this kind of service fit our program goals?*
2 *What resources are available for delivering this service?*
3 *Are community members and consumers interested in this service?*
4 *Do the potential benefits of this service outweigh the projected costs?*
5 *How can we measure the effectiveness of this service?*

Once services have been selected, a plan for implementation and evaluation can be developed.

Planning for Implementation

Once the set of services to be delivered has been selected, planners can lay out an action plan for delivery. Each service brings with it the need to perform a series of specific activities to get the program into motion. Young (1978, p. 16) suggests that the following questions be answered at this point.

1 *What are the major activities necessary to implement the methods selected?*
2 *Who will be responsible for performing each activity?*
3 *What are the starting and completion dates for major activities?*
4 *What are the basic resources needed to perform each activity?*

A time line can be utilized to ensure that plans are carried out on schedule. At the same time that this initial plan is developed, methods for evaluation should also be devised. This careful planning process brings with it the ability to carry out other management processes, from budgeting through evaluation, more efficiently.

BUDGETING

Developing a budget translates planning into financial terms. Community counselors must be involved in, or at least understand, the budgeting process, since it brings plans into reality.

> A budget is a "plan of action." It represents the organization's blueprint for the coming months, or years, expressed in monetary terms. This means the organization must know what its goals are before it can prepare a budget. . . . All too often, the process is reversed and it is in the process of preparing the budget that the goals are determined (Gross & Jablonsky, 1979, p. 359).

The budget is, and should always remain, the servant of the agency's previously determined goals and objectives, especially when resources are severely limited.

> During a period of growth, the absence of any clear understanding of purposes, plans, and resources may not threaten the survival of the organization—at least not immediately. Resources are growing. There is no need to deny support to anyone. . . . Next year there will be an additional increment of resources, which can be used to expand those activities that proved worthwhile without having to eliminate the ones that failed (Behn, 1980, pp. 616 ' 617).

When resources are dwindling, rather than expanding, the budget must be based on a clear understanding of the agency's mission.

The traditional budgeting process has always been based on the assumption of growing resources. Human service agencies have most commonly used a "line-item budget," with expenditures categorized by functions, such as personnel, consultant costs, supplies, travel, telecommunications, capital outlay, and others. Normally, a budget request is made each year, with estimations of necessary resources based on a slight "increment" over the current year's budget. In this process, attention is usually placed on expenditures, rather than on specific programs. Accountability is based more on limiting expenditures than on accomplishing program goals, and current levels of spending are often accepted as a "given" to which the agency is entitled.

Reforms in the budgeting process have focused attention on tying the budget more consciously to programs. Program budgeting involves categorizing expenditures by program area, rather than by line item, and holds the programs accountable for goal accomplishment. Zero-based budgeting, a related budgetary reform, emphasizes the need for each program to justify its existence in order to obtain funding. Decision makers consider each program in terms of its success in meeting agency goals, and existing programs are in equal competition with new sets of services. These budget reforms use cost-benefit or cost-effectiveness analysis to relate costs to program accomplishments.

Using complex rational analyses may be beyond the funds and technical expertise available to small community counseling programs. The idea of relating budgets to program priorities can be adapted, however, even without highly sophisticated analyses. A yearly budget may be tied to the line-item approach but can still be built on the implementation plans developed as part of the planning process. Budget makers can determine the costs of each of the activities to be carried out, using these figures to make an accurate estimate of the costs of a program. These costs can then be integrated into the line-item budget of the agency or institution. If plans have been reasonably detailed, the creation of a budget involves simply a translation from activities to dollar amounts.

The creation of an annual budget depends both on estimates of expenditures and on expected revenues. Community counseling programs receive revenues most frequently through appropriations, grants and contracts, fees, contributions, or a combination of sources.

Appropriations, made by the legislative branch of government, affect the support of mandated public services. Often, programs are affected indirectly, through contracts received from public agencies that depend on appropriations each year. Dependence on legislative appropriations means that an agency is subject to variation in funding depending on economic stress or political changes. Planners need to develop a high degree of sensitivity to economic and political forces, so that forecasts can be accurate.

Grants and contracts can be either from private foundations or from public fundors. A grant is awarded to the agency receiving it in order to meet certain goals and objectives. A contract usually specifies the activities to be carried out in meeting goals and objectives even before a recipient is chosen. Whether funding is in the form of a grant or a contract, the funds are allocated to specific projects that meet the priorities of the funding source. Thus, if a proposal is made to a funding agency or foundation, the project will not be considered unless it meets the priorities and guidelines set by the fundor. If proposals meet funding guidelines, they are usually considered on the basis of the completeness of the needs assessment, the clarity and attainability of the project's objectives, the suitability of the plan of action, the appropriateness of the budget, the stringency of the evaluation plan, and the "track record" of the agency seeking funds. An agency that uses effective planning processes can put those same procedures to good use in applying for earmarked funding.

Community counseling programs may also charge fees, either directly to clients or through third parties, such as insurance companies, Medicare, or public agencies. It is important for counselors in programs depending on fees to recognize that the fee structure tends to encourage direct, rehabilitative services and to discourage the kinds of indirect, preventive programs that form the heart of the community counseling concept. Fees tend to be paid for direct services to individuals, so counselors must seek other methods of support for innovative modalities.

Contributions also add significantly to the operating budgets of most agencies. Sometimes, such contributions may be restricted to use for specific purposes, which means that agencies need to educate contributors concerning the kinds of programs that can best meet clients' needs. People making contributions to programs may be unfamiliar with innovative approaches to human services, so public relations efforts need to bring communitywide organizational or educational efforts to the public's consciousness.

Regardless of the kind of funding involved, community counselors need to be careful to maintain a clear awareness of their primary mission. When funds become available, it is tempting to take on projects, even if they do not fit overall goals and objectives. Yet continual implementation of projects that are tangential to the agency's mission or clients' assessed needs can move an organization away from its programmatic thrust. Getting funding from a variety of sources can help to sustain autonomy. Eliminating one source of funding should not throw a program into crisis.

ORGANIZING

The way a program or agency is organized should also be based on its mission and approach to helping. When planning has been completed, an organizational structure is needed to carry out the activities that have been chosen. There are tremendous variations in organizational design, and the kind of structure that is built can have major implications for the work of the community counselor. The organizational design indicates how activities are divided among individuals or groups, who makes decisions, how specialized roles and jobs should be, and how coordination and communication take place.

Many agencies are structured along traditional, bureaucratic lines because their organizational designers are unaware of the alternatives that are available. A traditional bureaucracy is based on a hierarchical chain of command. Each member of the organization has a clear, specialized function to perform: each individual reports to one direct supervisor; and each manager is responsible for the activities of his or her subordinates. In the bureaucracy, routine is important. Each employee depends on written regulations and procedures to provide guidelines for action.

If a human service agency is organized along bureaucratic lines, the tasks to be performed tend to be specialized, with one employee or department doing individual counseling, another doing community outreach work, another performing managerial functions, another doing consultation, and still another doing group work. Members of the organization tend to become highly involved in their own specialty, and only the executive-level managers have a picture of the workings of the whole agency.

Organizational structures based on human relations approaches are in direct contrast to the traditional hierarchy. In these more organic structures, freedom of action and widespread participation in decision making are encouraged. Instead of departmentalizing by function, designers tend to divide activities according to purpose or population being served, so that each individual works as part of a team to determine what activities can best serve common goals. Control and power are shared, rather than centralized, and motivation is based on responsibility and participation, rather than just on economic rewards.

Human service agencies based on human relations approaches tend to make use of task forces or teams to work out the problems of helping a particular population. Both agency employees and consumers are involved in policy making, and staff members participate in planning and evaluating their programs. Work is divided along project lines, rather than along lines of specialization. An individual service deliverer maintains an awareness of all of the needs of a client group, rather than identifying solely with a professional specialization. This approach to organization is more in keeping with the community counseling model, since it brings about consistency in the way both clients and employees are treated. Yet it is a difficult task to manage an organic agency, and people have to be encouraged and trained to adapt to a structure that is less familiar to them.

Many organizational designers find it useful to consider making use of parts of each approach. No one type of design is always appropriate. "Contingency theorists" (Burns & Stalker, 1961; Lawrence & Lorsch, 1967; Woodward, 1965) have indicated that the most effective type of structure for a specific organization depends on the contingencies being faced by that organization. Mechanistic, or traditional, forms of organization are appropriate when conditions are stable and efficiency is a high priority. Organic, less formal methods are needed when the organization must be ready to deal with rapid change or solve new problems. If the environment is in a state of rapid change, the organization has to have many points of contact with the external world, a good information flow, and the flexibility to adapt quickly.

In human service settings, contingency theories offer a conceptualization that helps in the determination of the most appropriate form of organization. If counselors view themselves primarily as specialists who offer consistency in their services to a large number of clients, they can consider the use of mechanistic organizational structures, with their emphasis on stability. Yet this approach would be less useful for counselors attempting to deliver multifaceted services based on the needs and goals of the community. If counselors deal with stable environments and steady funding, they can use hierarchical forms of decision making. This approach, however, would be too slow and unwieldy for dealing with sudden changes in populations served, funding patterns, or community priorities.

At best, human service settings are complex and difficult to manage. Many programs are in not-for-profit organizations, which means that they tend to have intangible objectives and that rewards, punishments, and funding are not thoroughly under internal control (Newman & Wallender, 1978). Even more difficult is the factor of professional commitment. Most human service agencies employ a number of professional helpers, whose training makes close supervision unnecessary but whose commitment to their professional identity may override their concern for agency goals. When professionals adhere to their traditional role, they sometimes fail to change with shifting consumer needs. Yet it is inappropriate and wasteful to attempt to force professional helpers into a role of placing organizational priorities above what they interpret client needs to be. Kouzes and Mico (1979) identify three domains in human service organizations: the policy domain, the management domain, and the service domain. Each of these domains, or subgroups, has differing goals and interests. No method of organization can be workable unless the people with a stake in the agency's success can find some commonality in their goals and commitments.

SUPERVISION

Community counseling programs depend on the cooperative efforts of a number of people, including service deliverers, support personnel, community members, and other participants in the helping network. The community counselor who wishes to have impact on the quality of service delivery must, at times, act as a leader, influencing others in the interest of achieving goals. The most direct and common form of leadership required of community counselors is supervision of less experienced service deliverers. The form that such supervision takes depends on the supervisor's leadership style, the supervisee's motivation, and the nature of the supervisory relationship.

Leadership Style

Many approaches to the study of leadership involve making distinctions between opposing forms of relating to others. McGregor (1960) described one of the most commonly used distinctions: the contrast between a Theory X and a Theory Y leadership style. McGregor's "Theory X" leader is one who assumes that people lack interest in work, lack intrinsic motivation, and try to avoid responsibility. The Theory Y manager assumes that people desire responsibility and enjoy having the opportunity to work, to create, and to work toward organizational objectives. The differing assumptions of the two types of leaders bring differences in their approaches to supervision. The Theory X leader supervises closely, controls carefully, and uses reward and punishment to keep employees in line. The Theory Y manager is more likely to delegate decision making and responsibility, and to encourage natural creativity.

Many students of leadership style believe that there are no pure types. Instead, leadership behavior may form a continuum, with the authoritarian, Type X, boss-centered leader at one pole and the employee-centered, Theory Y, process-oriented leader at the other. The "managerial Grid" of Blake and Mouton (1978) uses a two-axis model, making a distinction between "concern for people" and "concern for production." An individual leader may have a high degree of concern for one factor, for both, or for neither. The most effective manager is considered to be the team management leader who combines a high degree of concern for production with a high degree of concern for people. The two concerns are seen as complementary, with concern for people potentially enhancing their productivity.

Hersey and Blanchard (1982) also use a two-axis model, but add the component of appropriateness to the situation. Hersey and Blanchard's "situational" model recognizes that differing leadership styles may be appropriate in dissimilar situations. They distinguish between leaders who are oriented toward concern with the relationship they have with their followers and leaders who are more oriented toward the task that has to be accomplished. The appropriateness of each kind of leadership behavior depends on the maturity level of the follower. Thus, a supervisor should use a high-task orientation with people who have not yet developed expertise and internal motivation, a high-task and high-relationship approach with supervisees who need help in performing the job, a high-relationship and low-task approach with people who lack motivation, and a low-relationship and low-task approach (delegation) with supervisees who are willing and able to accomplish their tasks without assistance.

As Hersey and Blanchard make clear, the nature of the supervisor is only one of the components of the supervisory process. The motivation of the supervisee must also be considered in the development of an appropriate leadership style.

Motivation

Supervision of human service workers, like counseling of clients, depends on an understanding of the complex needs that affect individual behavior. The needs and drives that determine how actively an individual will work toward job-related goals have been examined from a number of perspectives.

Many managers, for instance, find it useful to think of motivation in terms of Maslow's hierarchy of needs (Maslow, 1954). Maslow's hierarchy includes, from lowest to highest: (1) physiological needs, (2) needs for safety and security, (3) needs for belonging, love, and social interaction, (4) esteem and status needs, and (5) self-actualization needs. The individual becomes motivated to satisfy higher needs only when the lower needs have been met. This construct becomes relevant to the consideration of work-related motivation when one considers that lower needs are limited in the degree to which they serve as motivators. When economic security has been achieved, workers can best be motivated through attention to the higher need. At some point, workers can only be motivated if their jobs give them the opportunity to work toward self-actualization.

Herzberg (1975) also distinguished between differing sets of motivating needs. Herzberg terms *maintenance factors* the aspects of the work environment that relate to job dissatisfaction. *Motivator factors* relate to the job itself and can bring about job satisfaction and motivation. Qualities like salary, job security, and working conditions can affect job dissatisfaction, but cannot serve as motivators. The opportunity to demonstrate competence, to accomplish things, and to grow and develop serve as motivators that will encourage hard work and dedication.

Another motivator is the degree of fit between the person and the task to be accomplished. Individuals vary in terms of the things that motivate them. Thus, some individuals are motivated by the need for achievement (McClelland, 1965), while others are more interested in having a chance to express themselves in the work setting (Johnson & Stinson, 1980). The effectiveness of the supervisory process depends on the goodness of fit between the supervisor's leadership style, the supervisee's motivation, and the work to be accomplished.

The Supervisory Relationship

Most community counselors act as supervisors, at least on occasion, whether they are directing the work of volunteers, of paraprofessionals, or of less experienced professionals. The purpose of such supervision normally involves the following elements (Lewis & Lewis, 1983, p. 135).

- Providing encouragement and support for the supervisee.
- Building motivation.
- Increasing the mutuality of individual and organizational goals.
- Enhancing the supervisee's competence in service delivery.

All of these responsibilities are complementary in meeting the general goal of helping supervisees to help clients more effectively.

The supervisory relationship itself must vary, not only between one supervisee and another, but also at different times in working with the same person. The supervisory process changes because its nature depends on the supervisee's needs and developmental level, as well as on the supervisor's methods. More mature and competent supervisees need different approaches than beginners who are unsure of their own skill levels. As an individual grows in competence and self-esteem, he or she is likely to grow in independence as well.

Boyd (1978) describes three stages in the supervision of counselors: (1) the initial stage, during which a working relationship is established, (2) an intermediate stage, designed to serve the purposes of appraisal and goal setting, and (3) a terminal stage, when the now-competent supervisee learns to work autonomously. As supervision proceeds through different stages, the nature of the supervisory relationship also changes. Littrell, Lee-Borden, and Lorenz (1979) point out that the early stages require a high degree of activity by the supervisor, who acts as a counselor or teacher and manages the process. Later, the supervisee takes increasing responsibility for setting goals, while the supervisor acts as a consultant. In the final stage, "self-supervision," supervisory activity is no longer needed.

When community counselors act as supervisors, they need to take into account the maturity level of their supervisees. This can, at times, be difficult, since a supervisee may be highly mature and competent in delivering accustomed services, but unsure and inexpert in using innovative methods. Effective supervision requires sensitivity to the difficulty that service deliverers may face in adapting their work to changing client needs. Supervisor and supervisee can work together to determine what services should be provided and how much supervision and training the counselor needs in order to provide them. Most human service workers are motivated by higher needs, and seek self-actualization and feelings of accomplishment through their work. Good supervision builds on this factor, and provides the kind of supportiveness that people need if they are going to use themselves as instruments for helping others.

EVALUATION

Evaluating community counseling programs is a decision-making aid, allowing counselors to plan new projects or adjust current services on the basis of useful data. Attkisson and Broskowski (1978, p. 24) define program evaluation as being:

1 A process of making reasonable judgments about program effort, effectiveness, efficiency, and adequacy.
2 Based on systematic data collection and analysis.
3 Designed for use in program management, external accountability, and future planning.
4 Focused especially on accessibility, acceptability, awareness, availability, comprehensiveness, continuity, integration, and cost of services.

Although evaluation uses many of the same methods and techniques as research, its central purpose is to be put to practical use in program planning. Evaluation serves as part of the cycle of management, from planning, to implementation, to evaluation, and then to replanning. Thus, evaluation helps in managerial decision making, brings about improvement in current programs, makes services accountable, and can even build increased public support. It can only accomplish these purposes, of course, if results are widely disseminated to policy makers, managers, service deliverers, consumers, and the public at large.

Comprehensive program evaluation deals with both process and outcome. Process evaluation seeks to determine whether services are actually being carried out in accordance with plans. Outcome evaluation attempts to assess whether services have had the expected impact on the target population.

Process Evaluation

Process evaluation assesses whether members of target populations were served in the numbers expected and whether the services provided were in accordance with the quality and quantity expected. The process evaluation depends on the presence of clear, measurable program objectives. Evaluators attempting to implement process evaluations begin by specifying clear, quantifiable objectives and developing management information systems that provide the data required for evaluation. When programs are being planned, decision makers should specify the kind of information that will be needed for the purposes of process evaluation. Then, appropriate data can be gathered routinely, through direct observation, use of service records, data from service providers, and information from program participants. The information system should include demographic information about the community, data about clients, information about services and staff, and information about resources available. Services can then be monitored, so that progress toward meeting objectives can be easily assessed at any time.

These procedures cannot be carried out just by professional evaluators. They obviously require the active involvement of all human service workers, since appropriate objectives must be set and data must be gathered on a continual basis. If service providers are involved from the beginning, they can play a useful role in making sure that objectives are appropriate and that monitoring procedures are workable. Service consumers, too, can be very helpful in planning and evaluation, since they are often well aware of any problems in the service delivery system.

Outcome Evaluation

Outcome evaluation assesses the impact of services, attempting to discern the degree to which clients and the community have been affected by the program. Community outcomes might be measured by changes in the incidence of a targeted problem, while client change is normally evaluated in terms of functioning levels before and after services.

The real goals of community counseling programs, which tend to be oriented toward prevention, are difficult to assess, since only a combination of many programs can lead to measurable differences in the prevalence of dysfunction in a community.

> Prevention research is faced with two separate problems. The first is to determine the effects on behavior of specific intervention programs. The second is to link proximal objectives such as effective behavior change (if the program was successful) with the ultimate reduction in rates for the end-state goals in question. . . . When the data are in on how separate risk factors can be modifed, we would be in a better position to mount intervention programs that combine a number of interventions which would be likely to impact on the distal goal (Heller, Price, & Sher, 1980, p. 292).

Thus, evaluating preventive programs might best be oriented toward evaluating the effectiveness of interventions in bringing about client changes that can reasonably be expected to affect risk factors and, ultimately, the incidence of a disorder. For instance, programs that demonstrate effectiveness in enhancing developmental levels and competency can be assumed to affect "real-world functioning" (Sprinthall, 1981). A combination of many evaluation studies, dealing with a number of measures of client competencies, can lead to clearer knowledge of the types of interventions that have the greatest preventive potential.

At the programmatic level, outcome evaluation, like process evaluation, depends on the existence of clear objectives. Routine outcome measurements can be used to provide ongoing assessments of the impact of services. Criteria and standards can be developed to make any real objectives measurable. For many objectives, standardized instruments for assessing client functioning are available. In addition, measures of client satisfaction can also be used, not as a sole measure of program effectiveness, but in combination with other factors.

Of course, routine measures of outcome do not indicate whether the program or service was responsible for change in the client. Community counselors can also expect to use experimental or quasi-experimental designs to gain more useful information about the efficacy of specific programs.

The most important aspect of any evaluation effort—whether oriented toward process or toward outcome—is the need to measure objectives that suit the real goals of service providers and consumers. It is always necessary to search for ways of measuring the real goals of stakeholders in a program's effectiveness, rather than to settle for objectives that are easily measured but less central to the agency's mission. As Carver (1979, p. 6) pointed out, "A crude measure of the right concept is far more effective in directing organizational activity than a precise measure of the wrong one."

UNIQUE MANAGERIAL CHALLENGES

The special nature of the community counseling concept brings unique managerial challenges. Each aspect of the model has implications for the approaches that management should use.

Community counseling programs use a number of services to reach their goals. As community needs change, the focus of services also change, and service deliverers are forced to adapt their efforts. The multifaceted nature of the community counseling program places a major burden on the planning and evaluation process. Goals and objectives must be clear in order that the services selected are the ones that are most appropriate. At the same time, service providers must continually retrain themselves to perform innovative activities as they are needed. This requires broad participation in planning, as well as highly supportive supervision. Professionals cannot be asked to deal with constant risk and change unless they have been closely involved with decision making at every possible point and unless they receive encouragement in their efforts to develop new skills. Community counseling programs virtually require a participative approach to management.

The community counseling model also works under the assumption that resources in the community should be discovered and heavily used. Because of this emphasis on self-help and volunteerism, programs should also be planned by combined task forces of service deliverers and consumers. Efforts need to be made to provide effective supervision for volunteers and paraprofessionals, as well as for professionals, and to make all of these role groups feel part of the planning, implementing, and evaluating processes.

Because community counselors are delivering highly innovative services, they need to maintain vigilance concerning the central missions of their programs. Often, funding methods and reward structures support traditional methods. Managing community counseling programs often requires developing support bases for innovation and working doubly hard at evaluation and accountability.

SUMMARY

Community counseling programs require effective management, and counselors should expect to perform a number of managerial tasks. The functions of management in human service settings include planning, organizing, budgeting, supervising, and evaluating.

Effective planning begins with careful assessment of the needs and desires of community members. Using surveys, meetings, social indicators, and interviews, community counselors can begin to lay the groundwork for setting appropriate goals. Once goals and objectives have been specified, decisions can be made concerning the most appropriate services or activities to be used in meeting identified needs.

The program budget translates plans into reality by allocating financial resources for carrying out activities. Although the traditional budgeting process has been based on the line-item budget, reforms in the process have focused attention on tying the budget more consciously to program accomplishments. Even without using highly sophisticated analyses, budget makers can build financial documents on the activities designated as part of the planning process.

Community counselors should be careful to keep the agency's central mission in mind, both in seeking funds and in building an organizational structure. Many agencies are structured along traditional, hierarchical lines, with each member of the organization specializing in a particular function. An alternative is to organize agencies or programs more organically, encouraging widespread participation in decision making. Departmentalization can be designed either by function or by population served, and the design that is chosen has major implications for the kinds of services that are provided.

Since community counseling programs depend on the cooperative efforts of many people, supervision is particularly important. Supervision—whether of professionals, paraprofessionals, or volunteers—involves providing encouragement, building motivation, and enhancing competence in service delivery. The nature of the supervisory relationship depends on the supervisor's leadership style, the supervisee's motivation, and the specific situation.

Finally, the cycle of management also includes evaluation. Comprehensive program evaluations attempt to aid in decision making by assessing the success of services delivered. Process evaluation attempts to measure whether services were provided in the amount and quality expected. Outcome evaluation assesses the impact of the services on clients and the community.

Although all human service programs depend for their effectiveness on good planning, budgeting, organizing, supervising, and evaluating, community counseling programs present unique challenges. Because programs are multi-faceted, community based, and innovative, they depend on widespread involvement in decision making and on vigilance concerning their central missions.

ACTIVITIES TO ENHANCE UNDERSTANDING OF CHAPTER 8

1. Try to describe the behavior of the best manager you have known (preferably someone in an administrative capacity in a place where you, yourself, have worked). What was it about this manager that made him or her effective? Would the approaches used in that setting

be effective in a community counseling program, or would special adaptations have to be made?

2. Suppose that you had the immediate opportunity to implement the community counseling program that you have been designing. What skills do you have now that would help you manage your agency? What skills would you need to develop? Lay out a plan of action that would help you to develop your managerial effectiveness.

CHAPTER
9
TRAINING THE
COMMUNITY
COUNSELOR

C ommunity counseling represents a distinctive approach to helping. Because community counselors must develop new roles and
perform tasks that have not traditionally been associated with
the helping professions, their training must also be distinctive. Community counselors must be trained, not just to fit into existing systems or
perform traditional tasks, but to create roles and functions in response to
community needs. The performance of nontraditional functions requires
the background of nontraditional training.

NEW DIRECTIONS IN TRAINING

Community counselors take a human service approach. They adapt their
roles to the needs of the consumers being served instead of to the limiting
job descriptions of the traditional helping professions. Their approach is
multifaceted, which means that they are able to deal not just with individuals, but with total communities; not just with direct services to
consumers, but with attempts to change the total environments in which
consumers live and work.

If the multifaceted, human services approach to helping is to become a
reality, it must have its base in training that takes new directions. Each
innovative aspect of community counseling practice has clear implications for the training process.

1   Community Counselors Must Be Responsive to the Populations They Serve. Therefore, Community Counseling Should Be Open to Community-based Volunteers and Paraprofessionals

Implementation of the "new careers" concept gives community members
the opportunity to embark on careers as human service workers, assisting
other individuals within their own communities. This concept assumes
that people within a given community do have the potential to help
themselves and to help others. It assumes that the new professionals
have an awareness of their own needs and those of their neighbors, and
that they can gain helping skills and expertise through training and
experience.

One of the most important achievements of the paraprofessional movement in general and of New Careers in particular has been its facilitating the
widespread acceptance of the fact that poor people—many of them living on

> welfare for a long time and lacking education, training and credentials—
> could very quickly be trained to provide useful service. . . . We have also
> seen increased acceptance and utilization of peers, or "indigenous per-
> sons," in colleges, public schools, and other human service agencies. As a
> society, we are becoming more convinced that many people can provide
> services to those who need them and that the service providers do not have to
> possess credentials and advanced degrees. (Gartner & Riessman, 1974, p.
> 255).

"New careers" has provided many with the opportunity to be trained
for valuable work. Ideally, this concept can also help human service
agencies and institutions to become more responsive to the communities
they seek to serve. In the past, agencies were operated in such a way that
there appeared to be an assumption that only specialized professionals
knew what services were needed and how they should be provided. The
growth of the "new careers" concept might provide some inroads into
established practices, helping agencies to become more aware of and
responsive to the real needs of community members as those community
members see them.

The creation of training programs for these new professionals requires
a close association between training institutions and in-the-field agencies, so that workers are trained to meet existing needs and so that job
placement and advancement are realities.

2 Community Counselors Recognize That Workers at Many Levels Are Needed to Serve the Community and That Experience—Not Just Credentials—Helps Them to Become More Effective. Therefore Training Must Involve an Effective Career Ladder

Community counselors do not enter a community with a fully developed,
preconceived plan for the provision of services. Instead, they learn
through their participation with other community members and develop
programs that are appropriate to the community's goals. They become
more effective as they work.

A "career ladder" concept means that workers can progress to higher,
more responsible, and more highly paid positions as they gain more
competence in their field. Still more effective is a "career lattice," which
allows workers to move horizontally, adapting their work to differing
types of agencies and populations. Individuals can enter an agency at the
paraprofessional level and progress to the highest professional and
administrative levels through work experience, demonstrations of com-

petency, and continuing education and training. Training programs that involve a career lattice allow training and experience to complement one another. Those who reach the professional level possess a core of practical experience, not just a core of theoretical knowledge. As more individuals enter the human services field and progress through stages of skill development, agencies are strengthened by the existence of workers with varying competencies and approaches.

3   Community Counselors Attempt to Develop Programs That Meet Unique Community Needs. Therefore, Training at All Levels Should Help Potential Counselors to Gain Skill in Assessment of Needs and Program Development and Evaluation

If counselors were trained only to provide the services that have traditionally been offered in agencies and institutions, there would be no possibility of change, no chance of developing creative programs in response to the needs of specific communities. Human service agencies can become more effective and can fill the gaps in service delivery only if workers in these agencies have the ability to assess community needs, to work with community members in setting goals, and to develop programs that efficiently meet the priorities that have been set.

It is very difficult for counselors to perform these functions on the job if their training has not prepared them for it. If their training has provided them with a narrow view of the tasks they will be required to perform, they fail to see all of the possible options from which they and their clients can choose. Community counselors should not only be aware of the need for developing and evaluating new programs, they should also have practice in applying this skill. Training programs must involve field work that gives trainees the chance to work creatively with others. This is as true at the preprofessional level as it is at the graduate school professional level. The creation of innovative programs must be seen as a responsibility of all workers in an agency—not just a select few.

4   Community Counselors Work with Their Clients as Whole Persons and Try to Ensure That All of Their Service Needs Are Met. Therefore, Training Should Provide an Overview of How Human Service Agencies Work

If training programs concentrate on educating potential counselors only for the performance of specifically delineated activites, services continue to be fragmented. Community counselors, in their attempts to work with people as whole individuals, need to be aware of the kinds of services that are offered in varying types of agencies and the ways in which those services are delivered. Only then can they help consumers to obtain coordinated, holistic assistance when they need it.

Community counselors' training absolutely must involve placement in the field from beginning to end. Such placements can be inadequate, however, if they give trainees the chance to see only one aspect of the agency's operation. Training must include opportunities for students to examine all aspects of service delivery; to participate in decision-making processes; to observe the work of many kinds of agencies and many kinds of workers; and to learn to evaluate services. Community counselors must have a broad view of human service agencies and institutions, and they can obtain such a vantage point through training that combines information and experience.

5 Community Counselors Must Work as Team Members if They Are to Implement a Flexible and Comprehensive Program. Therefore, Their Training Should Give Them the Opportunity to Work Cooperatively with a Group

A community counselor working alone and independently, could not provide a multi-faceted program. Community counselors on the job must work cooperatively with others, ensuring that a varied program is offered by a closely knit team of helpers with complementary skills.

The ability to work with such a team requires training and experience. These experiences can be offered as part of the training process, either by training agency workers together, as a group, or by creating teams in an educational setting and giving them the chance to plan and work as a unit. Through this experience, potential community counselors can learn how to work as team members. They can also become more concretely aware of the unique contributions that they, as individuals, can make.

6 Community Counselors, in Their Work, Attempt to Bring About Change, Not Just in Individuals, but in Their Environments. Therefore, Their Training Must Provide Them with Knowledge Concerning Social Systems and the Nature of Social Change

Community counselors must, of course, possess a core of helping skills to assist them in providing direct services to individuals. Additionally, however, they must possess the skills needed to intervene in the community as a total environment. Often, counselors become aware of the need for action, but lack the knowledge and the expertise that can make them effective.

> Practicing counselors are being increasingly urged—by counselor educators, by writers in the field, and sometimes by their own clientele—to leave their offices behind and to place a high priority on dealing with, and even changing, their counselees' environment. Many have tried, and more are trying. But viewing the institution itself as a client is a far cry from knowing how to plan a course of treatment. . . . Too often . . . with our training consisting only of what we have given ourselves on the job, we find ourselves plying our budding "change agent" skills . . . (without benefit of theory). Too often we find ourselves shooting in the dark. (Lewis & Lewis, 1974, p. 320).

Training programs must help community counselors to become as comfortable in dealing with the environment as they are in helping individuals. Counselors like all human service workers, need a solid core of knowledge concerning the nature of social systems and the ways in which change is most likely to occur. They should know not just how to encourage and facilitate, but how to organize.

These practical skills require a training program that is interdisciplinary. Many fields of study can offer knowledge that is truly relevant to the work that community counselors must learn to do. While the fields of counseling and psychology have must to offer, so do philosophy, anthropology, economics, sociology, political science, and history. Individual students should be able to develop educational programs that include course work in a number of disciplines. At the same time, interdisciplinary seminars should bring varying fields of knowledge together so that students, as a group, can draw implications for their own work.

7   Community Counselors Attempt to Draw On and Develop the Helping Resources Available in Their Communities. Therefore, Training Programs Should Assist Them to Become Trainers and Consultants, as Well as Helpers

The work of the community counselor goes well beyond the provision of direct helping services. Community counselors must also be able to train community members in the helping process, so that the helping resources of the community are enhanced. When many community members are able to develop helping relationships, assistance to individuals becomes easily accessible and the new helpers, themselves, benefit from the experience. The ability to train others depends on the ability to be a helper oneself. It is, however, a separate skill in which one must be trained.

This kind of training is particularly important at the professional levels. As individuals climb the career ladder, they need not become more specialized. Instead, ever greater emphasis should be placed on the skills of training and consultation. It is possible that, in time, professionals will no longer provide many direct services, but will, instead, act as educators, consultants, and evaluators.

> Counselors must become the developers, designers, and trainers who will allow others to offer direct services to helpees. . . . The first step is for professionals themselves to become effective helpers. Only in this way can they serve as models and trainers for helpers. The second step is to train others in the helping process. Training is thus mandatory for counselors who are either ineffective helpers or unskilled trainers (Delworth & Moore, 1974, p. 429).

Community counselors must be trained as trainers. They must also be trained as consultants, so that they can assist other members of the helping network to enhance their skills. When professionals know their own field, it does not automatically follow that they are able to impart their knowledge to others. The sharing of expertise requires a degree of skill, and that skill can be developed in effective training programs.

8 Community Counselors Offer Educative, Developmental Programs to the Community at Large. Therefore, They Must be Trained, Not Just as Helpers of Individuals, but as Educators of Large Groups

Training programs must give community counselors the opportunity to practice the skills that they will actually be needing in their jobs. It is difficult for them to develop educative programs that are meant to help community members live more effectively if they have been trained only in the techniques needed for remediation of difficulties. The creation of community education programs requires that community counselors have the ability to work with community members in setting goals and to construct experiences that can best meet those goals. Effective training helps community counselors to recognize their responsibility for working developmentally with the total community. Opportunities should be presented so that the skills needed for these endeavors can actually be practiced and evaluated.

9 The Community Counseling Approach Is Applicable to Many Settings and to Work with Many Kinds of Populations. Therefore, Community Counselors Should be Trained as Generalists Rather Than as Specialists

The competencies that community counselors must possess are applicable to many settings. This common core of skills also crosses the boundaries of traditional professions and job titles. Training community counselors as generalists means that the existence of these common skills and areas of knowledge is recognized, and that students are trained so that they can apply their skills in a number of settings and with a variety of clients. Specialized skills needed to deal with specific populations can be obtained through work experience and through extra training as needed. What specialization that does occur should be in terms of the population to be served instead of in terms of any assumption that particular knowledge can be categorized as "belonging to" a specific profession.

Many "career ladder" training programs allow students to begin as human service generalists, but then encourage increased specialization as more education is received. Instead, it is possible to create a career lattice that allows generalists to be trained at every level of expertise. The highest levels allow not for increased specialization, but for increased responsibility. The "career cone," as pictured in Figure 9.1 allows for an ever-broadening focus, instead of for a narrowing focus.

An examination of the career cone makes it apparent that the competencies to be attained at each level are general in nature and apply to a number of settings. (Those who reach the ice cream at the top do so not because of the number of college credits they have accumulated, but because they now have the ability to implement a truly broad and multifaceted program.) From the earliest stages of the program, attention is paid to allowing students to study not just the tasks that they will be expected to perform, but the social context in which they will be working. Individuals can only progress in their ability to have an impact on service delivery if they possess, from the start, a broad view of community counseling goals.

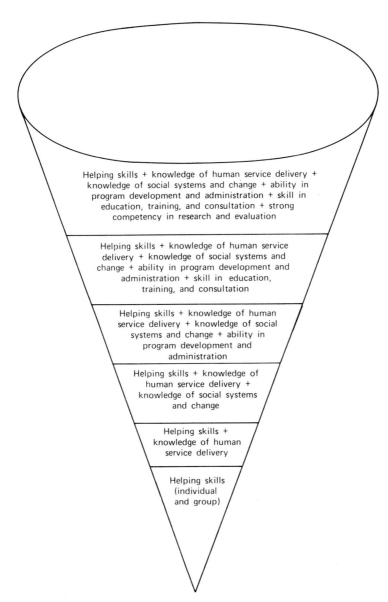

Figure 9.1   The career cone.

10 Community Counselors, if They Are to Bring About Creative Change, Must Have a Strong Sense of Identity and a Willingness to Move in New Directions. Therefore, Training Programs Should Provide Students with the Opportunity to Examine Their Values, Attitudes, and Goals

Community counselors must enter the field with a strong sense of their identity as helpers and with a clear awareness of their own goals. Without this self-awareness, counselors would be content to fit into existing systems and to accept the values on which the helping network has traditionally been based. It takes a great deal of inner strength to face the pressures that mediate against change and to develop fresh programs based on new ideas about helping. Community counselors can find this strength only to the degree that they have clarified their own values and attitudes and know where they, personally, are headed.

Community counselors, then, should be trained as generalists, with the understanding that a basic core of skills is applicable to a number of settings and a variety of job titles. There should be a truly effective career ladder, allowing counselors to develop ever-broadening expertise through both training and experience. Throughout the training program, emphasis must be placed on practical experience and an awareness of the social context in which human service delivery takes place. Community counselors must be trained not solely in the techniques needed to remediate individual problems, but in the creation of programs to meet the developmental needs of total communities. Most important, if community counselors are to be responsive to consumer's needs, they cannot be trained in institutions that stand apart from the real world. Instead, the educational institution, the employing agency, and the community must be closely linked as training goals are generated.

Only then can training play an appropriate role in the attempt to:

- Integrate the present helping services into one humane service based on generic knowledge and on performance.
- Identify the significant performance behaviors—the competencies—necessary for human service professional work.
- Educate for these performance results through a blend of theory and practice, and place persons who best evidence these competencies in professional positions.
- Work with human service agencies on retraining and reassessing the personnel most responsible for the quality of service delivery.

- Involve the citizen/client in the performance based assessment process and continue this assessment process throughout professional life (Cohen, 1974, p. 4).

These goals—and the 10 "new directions in training"—represent an attempt to bring training into line with fresh developments in human service role definitions and delivery systems. They represent a break with the past insofar as they attempt to resolve some of the major problems that have plagued traditional training programs.

PROBLEMS IN TRADITIONAL TRAINING

Basically, traditional training programs have fallen short because too little has been done to blend theory and practice and because students have not been encouraged to use their training as a base for creating new thrusts in helping. Training has tended to bring about the continuation of existing practices, both at the preprofessional and at the professional levels.

The Preprofessional Level

One of the many problems involved in traditional, short-term training at the preprofessional level is that students are often trained for delimiting roles.

> Existing professional jobs are broken down into separate tasks and activities and the pieces assigned to various levels of workers. The pieces assigned to a new level worker are likely to be the more boresome, choresome, and least challenging aspects of the work. This worker will function as an aide or assistant to an existing professional and will be perceived as a "nonprofessional" or "sub-professional" by the "professional." Such jobs are quickly developed and are acceptable to the established professionals, but they are dead-end and frustrating to the job holder because they allow him no opportunity to use his own initiative, creativity, or judgement. With this approach, new dimensions to traditional practices are seldom conceived (McPheeters & King, 1971, p. 4).

This approach, unfortunately, closes off many options for the individual students. Instead of gaining the overview of human services that would provide an appropriate beginning step up the career ladder, they learn to perform specific, assigned tasks without connections to the broader goals of the agency or institution. They are not encouraged to see themselves as new professionals or beginning professionals with unique contributions to make. This is particularly sad when community members are brought into an agency under the impression that their sensitivity to community needs is appreciated. When these workers are trained only to perform traditional, routine tasks, that unique sensitivity is wasted and their expectations for a true "new career" are doomed.

Beyond the limitations that are placed on those being trained, this approach also places limitation on the growth of human services and the creativity of service delivery. When new workers are trained only to perform specific, well-defined tasks, the traditional roles of professionals remain unchanged and the services available stay within traditional limits. While it is true that more people can be served because human resources have been increased, it is also true that few innovative approaches are likely to be tried. The roles and functions of traditional workers remain unchanged.

Overcoming the basic problems involved in preprofessional training implies that communities, service agencies, and training institutions must work closely together. Only then can new and more responsive roles be developed and people be trained to implement them. This kind of coordination has been, if anything, even more difficult to obtain in training at the professional level.

The Professional Level

At the professional level, training is often too far removed from reality. Professionals in university-based programs are trained to perform the functions that have traditionally been performed by members of their own professional specialty. Seldom are these professional identities redefined to take into account changing communnity needs or altered agency structures. Students must become affiliated with one profession, even when it is apparent that several helping professions share a common core of skills and approaches. What this boils down to is that students are trained in isolation, and their potential to bring about change in the helping services is blunted. In practice:

1 *Students are trained to carry on the practices with which their profession has traditionally been identified.* In traditional training programs, specialists are trained by other specialists. They become aware of what their own

specialty can offer, but remain unaware of the thrusts of other professions and other disciplines. When they do become practitioners, they have no choice but to try to impose their helping techniques on a community that may have totally unrecognized needs. They develop their programs on the basis of what they know how to do instead of on the basis of what must be done to meet the needs and goals of the communities they seek to serve.

2 *Students are trained for idealized roles.* Students are encouraged to believe that, as professionals, they are prepared to perform specific functions and act in particular roles. Often, they find that the agencies that employ them are not organized in such a way that those roles and functions are practical. Sometimes, they attempt to work in isolation, plying their profession without concern for the total thrust of the agency or institution. Sometimes they give up their self-identification as professionals and attempt to fit their functions to those outlined by agency leadership. In neither case have they been trained to assess community needs and adapt their skills to programs that are responsive to the consumers of their services.

3 *Students lack practical field experience.* In professional programs even more than in programs which train preprofessionals, students fail to get enough practical experience to blend theory and practice. Often students obtain field placements only at the end of their programs, after years of classroom instruction. This limits the effectiveness of didactic classroom training, since students lack the reality of the work world that can help them to integrate knowledge, to ask meaningful questions, and to try out the ideas being generated. It also limits the effectiveness of the field experience, since students are already approaching their work with an established (and traditional) point of view. If field experience continued throughout the training program, students could be trying out new ideas and establishing their identities of themselves as professionals within a realistic setting. The real environmental problems and try to rectify them. Students are trained to bring about change in individuals. They are discouraged in their attempts to bring about change in agencies or communities, especially when they do not see their instructors acting as change agents themselves.

At All Levels

At all levels of training, the basic problem is that practitioners are taught to fit into existing roles and to continue traditional methods of helping.

New ground can be broken, but only if community members, training institutions, and agencies work together to define appropriate goals and ensure that workers are trained to meet those goals. This kind of teamwork can occur whether the training programs are actually based in the agencies themselves or whether they exist primarily in college or university settings.

In the future, it may be that the strongest students at the professional level will be those who have been recruited from among human service generalists. Such students might come into master's and doctoral level programs with strong experiental backgrounds that have helped them to make some clear decisions about where they are headed as professionals. They might enter into graduate programs with a core of helping skills and with an overview of the kinds of directions that helping can take.

Work experience and additional course work can prepare such students to function in specific settings, such as educational institutions, community agencies, or institutions for special populations. It is important, however, that counselors at the professional level remain generalists, able to work in many ways with many types of clientele. In fact, as counselors become more secure in their knowledge and skills, the thrust of their training should be toward having broader influence in the human services. Instead of increased specialization, graduate education should bring about increased breadth. Instead of narrowing their focus to specific helping skills or particular populations, professionals should broaden their outlook to consider the general applications of their expertise.

It can be hoped that students come into a professional level program with many skills and awarenesses already developed. In a true career ladder program, this is the case. At present, of course, many students enter graduate level programs without prior experience as helpers and often without prior course work in the field. In that case, preparation at this level must be particularly intensive and allow for a great deal of practical experience throughout the program. The professional must be prepared to work with others both to plan and to implement a truly multifaceted program. That preparation involves not just intellectual awareness, but a great deal of practice in applying the necessary skills.

TRAINING FOR MULTIFACETED SERVICES

Community Education

It cannot be assumed that counselors who have skill in helping individuals necessarily know equally well how to aid large groups of people in their development toward effectiveness. Professional training programs should provide opportunities for students to set concrete goals and to implement and evaluate educational programs for meeting them. This might involve planning workshops or courses on campus, developing community experiences in an agency setting, or creating structured self-teaching materials. Every student cannot participate in every kind of experience or deal with every conceivable topic. What is important is that all students have the opportunity to experience themselves as educators, to be aware of the role that they can play in helping effective community members to live even more effectively.

Client Counseling

Counselors must, even by definition, be trained to provide helping relationships to individuals. Their training must prepare them to work effectively in developmental counseling and in crisis intervention.

Counselors must also be prepared to work effectively with paraprofessionals, volunteers, peer counselors, and others who also help to bring about accessible services to individuals. Training programs should give professionals an awareness of the contributions made by many helpers, and this can best be accomplished if they have the chance to work in settings where many levels of service are being offered. It must also be recognized that, in practice, professionals will be called on to train and supervise a number of other helpers. Although one must be an effective helper in order to train others, it does not necessarily follow that an effective helper does, in fact, posses the skill to be a trainer or supervisor. That skill, too, must be developed in professional-level programs of preparation. Many traditional programs give this opportunity to doctoral students by utilizing them in the training of master's level students. These opportunities should be expanded to involve all of those preparing to act as professional counselors in the planning and implementation of short-term training programs for others.

Community Organization

If one area of training is often neglected, it is the development of the knowledge and skill needed to deal with the community as an environment. One significant problem in this area is that those who are preparing to be counselors are often unaware of the need to deal with environmental change. Their career fantasy is that they will be direct helpers of people, and it is only experience that moves counselors to experience the frustration of knowing that that, alone, is not enough. *Information* about social systems and change is not easily integrated until students feel that they have a need for knowledge in this area.

It is the responsibility of those who train professional-level counselors to ensure that their trainees gain the kinds of experiences that can involve them in the process of environmental change. Often overlooked as resources are the variety of community organizations that might be willing to allow counseling students to act as interns, gaining experience in the practical problems of community-based planning and social action.

Client Advocacy

Counselors, in practice, will face the need to intervene in the environments of their individual counselees and to act as advocates on their behalf. They will also be called on as consultants, assisting other members of the helping network to work effectively.

The willingness to act as advocates requires that counselors come into the field with a strong awareness of their own values as helpers and their own responsibility to counselees. That kind of value clarification must occur as part of the training program itself. The need to act as a consultant is more widely recognized as part of the counseling role. This skill must be developed in the same way that counseling skills are developed, with students being given the opportunity to study alternative approaches, to role-play consultative situations, and to act as consultants under supervision.

The Counselor as Leader

Professional counselors will need to take leadership in bringing about change in the way in which human services are delivered. They will only have the chance to implement responsive, multifaceted programs if they are able to influence the policies of their own agencies and institutions. If they are to create new programs and move the field into new directions, they must leave their training programs with confidence in their ability to use research methods to evaluate community needs and measure the effectivness of traditional and innovative programs. Effective research tends to fall by the wayside in practice, unless counselors enter the field with some feeling of comfort in dealing with it. That expertise must come from training.

EFFECTIVE TRAINING IN ACTION

It is possible for training programs in college and university settings to prepare creative human service workers who will lead their agencies and institutions in new directions. At the preprofessional level, this can happen most effectively if students are helped to develop broad conceptualizations, rather than narrow views of their skills as helpers. At the graduate level, a key to effectiveness is the encouragement of active involvement with varying communities and cultures.

Cuyahoga Community College

A number of community colleges provide two-year training programs in mental health technology. At Cleveland's Cuyahoga Community College, the program is especially congruent with the community counseling model.

A major strength of the Cuyahoga program—and one that differentiates it from many others—is the fact that it is built on a clearly stated point of view. The approach to mental health upon which the curriculum is based is the "ecological model" (Bailis, 1981), described as an approach to problem solving that concentrates on,

a. enabling people to respond to community-based needs with community-based services;

b. enabling people to develop and implement behavioral interventions based on observations made in one's natural environment;

c. enabling people to pursue a holistic model for dealing with individuals that provides opportunities to build up and reinforce potentials while at the same time enhancing natural support systems and preventing problems from occurring;

d. and . . . enabling people to get involved with others as participant/observers in the natural systems that affect people's lives and to develop interventions that take into account the real world circumstances that brought them about (p. 2).

Workers trained to implement this model of helping must develop skills to intervene with individuals, with natural support systems, with agencies, and with communities. They must learn to approach problems from a systematic point of view. As Bailis points out,

We readily confess that this approach represents a Herculean task for a single worker with a cluttered caseload. This approach has to involve teams working together. It has to involve innovative approaches to community resources. It has to involve the building of cooperative networks not only between agencies, but also among the ecological units that will support the well-being of an individual. It has to result in the building of stronger communities through the cumulative effect of building supportive, growth producing networks of relationships (p. 4).

Courses designed specifically for the Community Mental Health Technology (CMHT) program and completed by all students help to provide broad and consistent views of mental health and the role of the mental health worker. Courses like Social Ecology, Community Resources, Service Strategies, Roles in Community Mental Health, Legal Issues in Mental Health, Prevention of Psychopathology, and Alternatives to Institutional Care help to familiarize each student with social ecology as a theoretical underpinning of future practice. At the same time, each student is actively involved in a field of placement through five quarters of the training program, with coursework and reading enhancing the individual's development "from self to system, from learner to teacher." At this point, the student is ready to write a developmental or preventive proposal that applies ecological principles. At this point, the student is ready to take his or her place as an innovator and leader in a human service setting.

University of Massachusetts

At the graduate level, professionals can be prepared to recognize changing community needs and respond with innovative methodologies. If students have opportunities to work with widely varying client groups, to deliver training and consultation services, and to develop community-based programs, they are unlikely to join the ranks of helpers who limit their activities solely on the basis of narrow professional traditions. Curricula can meet accreditation, registration, or certification requirements and still maintain openness to creativity and change.

At the University of Massachusetts, for instance, graduate students can either tailor programs to meet their specific career goals or follow the more structured counseling psychology curriculum. Even within the structured program, however, course work and practicum experiences are oriented toward theoretical breadth and practical project development (Ivey, 1983).

Students must, of course, develop competencies in individual counseling and assessment, but required courses in cross-cultural counseling and multicultural assessment help to overcome the cultural biases that so often permeate these customary activities. In individual and family therapy courses, students participate in treatment teams, allowing for valuable experience in working cooperatively with other helpers. A "training of trainers" course helps students gain experience and expertise in planning and leading workshops, but such opportunities are also built in throughout the curriculum. In a microcounseling course, for example, students are required to run workshops in which they teach the counseling skills they have learned to someone else.

The fact that students also learn to develop responsive programs and to implement effective change projects is proven best by the hundreds of community action projects that have been completed over the years. Among the accomplishments of students in the program have been—

- Founding of one of the nation's first women's centers.
- Creation of the Amherst Community Resource Center.
- Development of drug and alcohol treatment and education programs.
- Delivery of work skills training for unemployed individuals.
- Facilitation of peer counseling programs at local high schools.
- Planning and implementation of a training program for Eskimoes in the Arctic, as well as for other ethnic and cultural groups.

The ability of these graduate students to recognize and meet varied human service needs can, in part, be attributed to the selection process. Both master's and doctoral level programs have been developed specifically for in-service community mental health workers and delivered at the work settings. Even for the on-campus program, however, students with previous experience in human service delivery are actively sought. There is a recognition that training and experience can no longer be considered separate entitities but must, instead, be seen to form part of the same unified whole.

SUMMARY

Because the community counseling role represents a new direction in practice, training of the community counselor must also move in new directions. Needed changes in training practices include the following elements.

1 *Community counseling should be open to community-based volunteers and paraprofessionals.*
2 *Training should involve an effective "career lattice" so that individuals can move to higher or related positions through experience, competency, and continuing education.*
3 *Training should help potential counselors to gain skill in needs assessment and program development and evaluation.*
4 *Training should provide an overview of how human service agencies work.*
5 *Training should give community counselors the opportunity to work cooperatively in team efforts.*
6 *Training must provide community counselors with knowledge concerning social systems and the nature of social change.*

7   Training programs should assist community counselors to become trainers
    and consultants as well as helpers.

8   Community counselors must be trained not just as helpers of individuals, but
    as educators of large groups.

9   Community counselors should be trained as generalists, rather than as
    specialists, at all levels.

10 Training programs should provide students with the opportunity to examine
    their values, attitudes, and goals.

These new directions are an attempt to resolve the major problems
existing in traditional training programs. At all levels, training tends to
allow for too little blending of theory and practice and new workers are
often encouraged to continue existing practices. Instead, community
counselors should be trained to broaden their awareness of community
needs and to create new roles and new functions that can respond more
effectively to those needs. This is happening at a number of institutions,
including Cuyahoga Community College and the University of Massachusetts.

ACTIVITIES TO ENHANCE UNDERSTANDING OF CHAPTER 9

1. Consider once more the agency you have designed. Suppose you
    were ready to hire personnel who would work in your agency. What
    previous training or skills would you hope these workers would
    bring to the job? (Be as specific as possible.) What kinds of in-service
    training programs would you want to provide to make sure that
    service delivery was consistent, effective, and valuable to your
    clients?

2. Design for yourself the ideal training program that would take you
    from where you are now to effectiveness as a community counselor.
    Take into account the fact that you already possess many of the skills
    and much of the knowledge you would need. How would you fill in
    the gaps? What kinds of learning approaches would work best for
    you? If you were developing a training program for other people,
    would it be similar to the one you would want for yourself?

CHAPTER
10
LOOKING
TO THE FUTURE

No matter where community counselors work—no matter where and how they have been trained—they are bound together by their shared assumptions. They are linked to one another:

- By their belief that human problems, as well as their solutions, lie in the interaction between individuals and the environment.
- By their awareness that an approach to helping must involve many facets.
- By their desire to aid in the development of human effectiveness.
- By their knowledge that they are accountable to the communities in which they work.

Community counseling is a multifaceted human services approach. This approach combines direct and indirect services in order to:

1 Help community members to live more effectively.

2 Prevent the problems most frequently faced by counselees.

Community counselors are human service workers. They try to give practical assistance to their clients as whole persons with many needs and just as many strengths. They know that they can accomplish this only by being part of a network of helpers. They know that they can accomplish it only by responding to the realities of community needs.

None of this can happen if individual workers function in isolation. The degree to which agencies and institutions can respond to the consumers of their services depends on their ability to devise new organizational methods, new policies, and new programs.

The human care service network is faced with a challenge. All human service workers are being asked to deal with a new set of questions. Whether effective service delivery systems can be created and implemented depends on the answers that can be found.

1 How Can Coordinated Services Be Offered to Individual Consumers?

The orientation of the community counseling approach is toward treatment of the individual as a whole person, interacting with the immediate environment in many ways. Service systems have been poorly coordinated in the past because segmented services tried to deal with separate pieces of the "whole person" when those separate pieces did not, in fact, exist. Human service concepts are being developed to bring agency practices into alignment with the reality of total human development.

The community counselor may well develop into a generalist, who maintains continuity in service to clients and brings in specialists as needed. Ideally, such a human service generalist would be accountable to a number of individuals and families, attempting to see that all of their various service needs are met.

Right now, it seems as though specialization is still overly valued. Workers tend to specialize in terms of populations served, in terms of problem areas addressed, and in terms of skills practiced. Rather than identifying a specific group of workers as "generalists," it would seem even more appropriate to try to encourage all workers—at whatever level of training—to take a more holistic approach to the provision of services.

If coordinated services are to be offered to consumers, there can be no room for "procedure-oriented" workers. Instead, each helper must be trained to take responsibility for dealing with clients in terms of the totality of their lives. Each agency must be part of a network that can provide common training programs, interagency consultation, and effective linkage. Independent agencies must be linked to one another to avoid duplication of services and to strengthen the helping network. This linkage must, however, meet the additional criterion of being visible to the individual consumer.

2 How Can Accessible Services Be Offered to Individual Consumers?

Attempts to make services more accessible to consumers have tended, in recent years, to involve decentralization. Placing small centers in a number of neighborhoods makes services more physically accessible than they would be if they were offered only in large, centralized agencies.

This type of organization has added benefits. Outreach services into the community are more easily accomplished than they might be otherwise. Additionally, the agency becomes identified with the neighborhood in which it is located. The agency *belongs* to the people of that neighborhood and can respond to community influence in a way that highly complex, centralized agencies cannot. When the agency is also staffed by people living in the immediate area, physical accessibility is joined by psychological accessibility. People feel comfortable coming to the agency for help. They know that they will be understood.

Accessibility also involves time. When local agencies utilize the skills of paraprofessionals and volunteer workers, they avoid the long waiting lists that, at one time, characterized services dependent on a small number of professionals.

Decentralized, neighborhood-based agencies that utilize the skills of local people provide accessibility. This accessibility may be obtained, however, at the expense of coordination and efficiency. When services are centralized, one decision-making body sets policies, allocates resources, and evaluates services. Coordinated functions can be maintained, resources can be allocated according to need, and duplication of services can be avoided. When services are truly decentralized, there may be a large number of agencies, all acting independently of one another. At worst, they may duplicate services unnecessarily and compete against one another for scarce resources, particularly funding. While an agency may be highly responsive to the needs of the immediate locality, it also lacks the power and the resources needed to bring about major environmental changes.

It should not be necessary to choose between accessibility and efficiency. Both can be maintained if agencies, while remaining autonomous, also attempt to coordinate their services. When independent agencies are linked together through a network approach to human service delivery, they can:

a *Decide which services should be duplicated in each locality and which could be offered in a more centralized setting.* A number of youth agencies, for instance, could decide that each should provide walk-in counseling services and crisis intervention. However, one might also offer a runaway center, another a group home for disturbed adolescents, and still another a family education program.

b *Decide which programs should be offered independently and which would be more effective if planned and implemented jointly.* Independent agencies could adapt direct services to the needs of the small populations they served. Joint action would be more appropriate, however, when large-scale community action projects required greater resources and the mobilization of a large number of people.

c *Identify gaps in service delivery.* If communication among agencies is adequate, workers know what services are being offered and at what locations. When a demand for a particular service is not being met, the agencies can work together to encourage the creation of a new facility or to work out plans to use existing resources more effectively.

d *Work together to obtain funds and other resources.* When helping agencies compete against one another, the consumer of services is ultimately shortchanged. Scarce resources are allocated more efficiently through cooperative endeavors among agencies.

e *Improve the quality of services.* Although independent agencies may differ a great deal, there are some needs that they all share. Agencies can join together to provide ongoing training programs, to consult with one another, and to share ideas concerning services and their evaluation.

Such coordinated efforts can involve a very complex network. A youth agency, for instance, might have close contacts with other, similar agencies throughout the city or state. Workers in the agency would, at the same time, need links with other types of service settings within the immediate locality, including crisis intervention agencies, drug clinics, and schools. This requires a great deal of effort. It means, however, that the efficiency of a centralized agency can be duplicated, while the accessibility and responsiveness of a decentralized system is not sacrificed.

3   How Can a Full Range of Services Be Offered?

A full range of service must include programs dealing with the environment, as well as those designed to provide growth experiences for individuals and groups. Services should also include both programs, offered to the community at large, and services for individuals needing extra help.

Agencies have, in the past, tended to concentrate on direct services, such as one-to-one counseling, at the expense of other services that may be just as important. Part of the reason for this seems to involve the nature of the workers themselves. Most have been trained to provide specialized direct services, while few feel adequate to deal with the immense tasks involved in environmental change. Another aspect contributing to the emphasis on programs involves the reality of immediate individual needs. Counselors and other human service workers tend to feel unable to devote their time to long-term preventive programs when their offices are filled with individuals in desperate need of immediate attention. The presence of these troubled individuals reveals the great need for preventive programs. At the same time, it complicates the setting of agency priorities for use of time and human resources.

Part of the solution to this dilemma is now being implemented. Training programs at many levels are beginning to emphasize the importance of preventive and developmental services, so that workers begin their careers with somewhat broader perceptions of their roles. Certainly training programs, particularly at professional levels, have a long way to go in this area. Many continue to emphasize traditional services, and those dealing with innovative approaches often treat them generally and theoretically, so that concrete organizational skills are still lacking. In the long run, however, new workers with fresh orientations toward helping will continue to be integrated into the service agencies, and some of them might be able to make a difference. The trend toward staffing agencies with people from the immediate locality may also have some effect, since these workers may provide greater sensitivity to problems in the environment. Unfortunately, those workers with the greatest orientation toward dealing with community factors are often those who lack the power to implement changes in agency priorities. No drastic changes can be expected to take place until individuals in positions of leadership become committed to multifaceted approaches. They will have to be convinced of the efficiency of these new directions.

The actual implementation of new priorities, of course, requires more than changed attitudes and interests. Reallocation of resources calls for basic organizational and administrative changes.

Workers providing direct services to individuals are in a particularly good position to spot negative aspects of the community's environment. They see the victims of the community's ills and become highly conscious of the kinds of individual-environmental interactions that are taking place. It would be difficult, however, for one worker to be able to do justice to the tasks of planning and implementing both experiential and environmental programs. This can be accomplished by a close-knit team, working together to identify problem areas, to set concrete goals, and to plan for effective use of resources to meet those goals. A team approach within an agency would mean that individual workers could share their awareness and expertise, and that programs could be developed in the most efficient possible way. Each worker deals, of course, with individuals and with their environment. Long-range, time-consuming programs could, however, be implemented by part of the team, with ongoing support from the remaining members.

It must be remembered, too, that the community counselor need not do everything alone. It is not necessary that every possible service be provided under the auspices of the agency itself. What is important is that the counselor make sure that all needed services are being offered somewhere and that counselees are aware of them. The agency can play an important role in locating community resources to provide experiential programs and in assisting local readers to emerge in response to issues. Once a new program or community action project is underway, community members should replace human service workers as the prime movers. Thus, a small expenditure of time at the beginning stages of a new project brings major impact in the long run.

4 How Can People with Differing Levels of Training and Experience Work Together Most Effectively?

It is becoming a well-accepted fact that meeting community needs requires a pool of helpers beyond the limited number of credentialed professionals. When agencies began hiring paraprofessionals, whose training was of briefer duration, there was an assumption that they would be limited in the kinds of tasks they would perform. Now, however, people with varying levels of education and training are performing many tasks and delivering many services that once were considered part of the professionals' territory. "To a considerable extent, it is now taken for granted that persons without formal preparation and traditional credentials can do significant human service work—not just relieve the professional of scut work" (Gartner & Riessman, 1974, p.254).

In many agencies, professionals, paraprofessionals, and volunteers work side by side, utilizing similar skills and performing comparable jobs. Often, however, workers without traditional graduate training are closed out of the decision-making process and denied the opportunity to advance to the levels where real power lies.

> Many years ago I categorized three types of paraprofessional arrangements: the "plantation system," the "medical model," and "true New Careers." In the plantation system, paraprofessionals toil for miserable wages without promise of mobility; without power to control hours, wages, or conditions; and without meaningful training, because if trained they might become "uppity." The medical model allows for some training, some organization, and some mobility, but no path is open to upper echelons of professional status—where true power reigns—other than the traditional and basically flawed professional education. A true New Careers program attempts to be open-ended; here persons can attain the highest positions while remaining on the job and receiving credits for work experience, life experience, and an academic experience that is provided to the paraprofessionals in their work or community settings.
>
> The concerns of a decade ago remain. Too many paraprofessionals are locked into plantations. . . . (Pearl, 1974, p. 265)

The creation of authentic career ladders can do much to revitalize community agencies. Paraprofessionals can work more effectively if their expectations are met and if they know that all doors are open to them. Just as importantly, a "true New Careers program" makes it clear that *compe-*

tency—not just professional title or years of schooling—is really valued. Ongoing training and evaluation becomes part of *everyone's* work life, so that education and job experience are continuously interrelated.

It is not enough, however, to give workers the chance to *rise* to positions of influence and power. If agencies are to be effective, influence and power must be shared among workers at all levels as well as among community members. The "new professional" has a great deal to offer in terms of creativity, skills, and awareness of community needs. If professionals and administrators cannot respond to the workers in their own agencies, chances are slim that they will be able to respond to the voices raised in the community at large. Workers at all levels are trying to devise new methods of relating to the community. They must also work out effective methods of relating among themselves.

5 How Can Agencies Become Accountable to the Communities They Serve?

Agencies must begin to perceive themselves as being responsible to the consumers they were created to serve. If they are to be accountable to those consumers, they must:

1 *Involve community members in the process of setting goals.*
2 *Devise new methods of evaluation in order to determine the degree to which those goals have been met.*

This process must be implemented in terms of the total thrust of the agency and all of its workers. It must also be duplicated as each individual counselor works with each individual counselee. The service provider and the consumer must work together to set goals, to identify the kinds of services that might be effective in meeting those goals, and to evaluate the end result when the services have been provided. *Evaluation must take place in terms of objectives that are as specific and measurable as possible and that have been derived from the general goals set by workers and consumers in concert.*

There has been a tendency in the past for agency effectiveness to be evaluated in terms of the number of helping activities taking place. Whether the service being offered is individual or group counseling, consultation, or development of an educational program, that service is only a means to an end—not an end in itself. Attempts to be accountable on this basis cloud the issue and disguise the need to examine the *results* of activities that are only assumed to be helpful. Evaluations based on factors such as "number of clients seen in individual counseling" may, in fact, even *interfere* with effectiveness by encouraging emphasis on direct services at the expense of such difficult-to-measure activities as participation in community action projects.

It is difficult to translate long-range goals into immediate, specific objectives. It is doubly difficult when new values bring with them the emergence of goals that are unlike any that community agencies have worked toward in the past. The effort must be made, however, because agencies can only consider themselves accountable to the community if they can demonstrate that they are striving toward ends that community members themselves value. The success of workers hoping to be responsive to community needs will, in the long run, depend on their success in evaluating their efforts.

6 What Role Can Human Service Workers Play in Action for Social Change?

As community counselors and other human service workers attempt to respond to the needs of their communities, the urgent need for change becomes obvious. Their work brings them face to face with the victims of poverty; of racism, sexism, and stigmatization; of political, economic, and social systems that allow individuals to feel powerless and helpless; of governing structures that cut off communication and deny the need for responsiveness; of social norms that stifle individuality; and of communities that let their members live in isolation from one another. In the face of these realities, human service workers have no choice but to blame those victims or to seek ways to change the environment.

> . . . Blaming the victim means application of a psychological intervention aimed at fitting an individual into existing social conditions, which are presumed to have victimized him or her in the first place. Implied is the notion that the individual has some sort of deficit or emotional difficulty that is the basis of his or her problems in living. . . . It matters little whether one applies the medical model or any other if the interventions are victim blaming while the problems are social systemic in nature (Rappaport, Davidson, Wilson, & Mitchell, 1975, p. 525).

It is now becoming well accepted that human service workers must have some involvement with social action, some identity as "change agents." Yet the nature of their participation is still in the process of being defined. *The question is not whether human service workers should become involved in social action, but what they have to offer.*

Human service workers certainly do not have the power to bring about political or social change single-handedly. They do not even have the power to set goals in other people's behalf. They can, however, act as equal partners with other community members—all struggling for change and all having unique attributes to share. Several functions seem to be emerging as possible avenues for human service involvement.

a   *The needs assessment function.* Because of their close involvement with community members as individuals, human service workers may have a unique perspective on environmental problems. They might be able to identify situations that are hazardous to human growth and seek allies with common interests dealing with those areas.

b   *The coordinating function.* Human service workers are in a good position to develop an awareness of the resources available in their communities. Just as they link consumers with other helping services, they can also facilitate linkage among individuals and groups working toward enivronmental change. Human service agencies could, conceivably, act as coordinating centers.

c   *The skill-building function.* Human service workers can share whatever organizational and helping skills they might have with groups attempting to develop unified efforts in their own behalf. They can offer their services to groups that lack power in an attempt to build their strength and cohesiveness and to assist in the development of strategies for change.

d   *The advocacy function.* Human service workers might need to defend the rights of individuals or groups who are, at present, powerless to defend themselves. They may have a certain degree of credibility in dealing with the helping network, in particular, when offices and agencies that were developed to provide services overlook the need for consumers to be treated with dignity.

e   *The leadership-building function.* There can often be a natural transition from experiential programs to environmental programs. Groups of people participating in educational experiences may evolve into groups ready to deal more actively with community problems. Human service workers can provide active support and allow local leadership to emerge.

In general, human service workers do not have the power to bring about vast change. They can, however, form part of a power base, adding their skills and awarenesses to those of other participants.

On the other hand, human service workers may be able to develop the power to bring about significant change in the helping network of which they are a part. It seems unrealistic to perceive the need for change in the community at large without, at the same time, being aware of the role played by helping agencies and institutions. Human service workers themselves are the appropriate leaders in the struggle to help their colleagues provide responsive and responsible human care.

7   How Can Service Providers Be Trained to Respond to Community Needs?

A new kind of worker is needed to staff a new kind of agency. If human service agencies are to develop into truly responsive centers for human development, they must create new worker roles and new methods of responding to community needs. The people who will create the new agency are those being trained now.

In many traditional training programs, workers learn how to deliver a particular brand of service or how to function in a specific, delineated role. When people trained in this manner are ready to serve their communities, those communities have no choice but to use what is offered or to avoid the agency. When workers are comfortable with only one kind of role, a "take it or leave it" philosophy is a natural consequence.

One way that training programs are dealing with this recognized problem is to add new areas of concentration. This sometimes serves, however, to do nothing but pile one specialization onto another. Workers may know how to do group work as well as individual work. They may be able to do consultation as well as counseling. Their flexibility is still limited, unless they also know how to assess community needs and forge a role that helps them to deliver whatever services are best able to meet those needs.

Training programs are also attempting to provide more meaningful preparation by making on-the-scene field work in local agencies a required part of every student's learning experience. Again, this provides only part of the solution. Experience in traditionally organized agencies enhances the trainee's ability to work with people, but it fails to make clear the vast possibilities for the development of fresh options in human service delivery.

Workers for the future will have to develop new identities based on new approaches. It might prove necessary for them to give up the security of professional specializations and established functions and titles. While established titles may serve to give workers some kind of respectability, they may also provide undue limits on the development of new roles. Too much is assumed about what a "psychologist" does, what a "social worker" does, or what another specialist does—not only by the public, but by the workers themselves.

Training programs, instead of simply providing entrees into established professions, must prepare students to develop unforeseen practices to deal with future needs that are, at best, vague. Trainees need practical experience, not just in delivering tried-and-true services, but in entering communities, seeking the strengths of community members, and entering into planning partnerships with others. They will need training, not in well-honed specializations, but in a common core of competencies that all helpers and organizers need.

Agencies, as they have developed up to the present time, have not been coordinated, accessible, accountable, or devoted to social change. They have not offered a full range of experiential and environmental services. If agencies are to change, their workers must change. Preservice and inservice training will need to pave the way.

8 How Can We Create a Real Commitment to Preventive Efforts Among Human Service Policy Makers and Providers?

The focus of community counseling is preventing conditions and behaviors that our clients find dysfunctional. These conditions may involve either states that are traditionally termed "mental illnesses" or simply the existence of behaviors, feelings, or relationships that are upsetting. In any single agency, preventive efforts are oriented toward the problems faced by the consumers of that agency's services.

As Albee points out, "No mass disorder affecting large numbers of human beings has ever been controlled or eliminated by attempts at treating each affected individual or by training enough professionals as interventionists" (1982, p. 1045). Yet the focus among most helping professionals still tends to be placed on direct services to clients already troubled or disturbed. Part of this problem can be attributed to professionals' discomfort in leaving their accustomed areas of expertise. Another related issue is the fact that people with the power to change the emphases of service delivery feel distress at the idea of addressing mental health problems by confronting the need for social, political, and economic change. Still other professionals doubt that we have sufficient "proof" of the efficacy of preventive programs.

We do know, however, that a number of preventive efforts have been successful. We cannot point to single causes of single mental health-related problems, but we do not need to.

> Just as a single disorder may come about as a consequence of a variety of stressful life events, any specific stress event may precipitate a variety of disorders, as a result of differing life histories and patterns of strengths and weaknesses in individuals. . . . Many disorders can come about as a consequence of any of a variety of causes. With this acceptance come the realization that successful efforts at the prevention of a vast array of disorders (particularly emotional disorders) can take place without a theory of disorder-specific causative mechanisms (President's Commission on Mental Health, 1978, p. 1847).

The Task Force on Prevention of the President's Commission on Mental Health (1978) points out that there is a sufficient research base to move ahead on such strategies as competence training, modification of social systems, and management of naturally occurring life development stresses. Community counselors, like other human service professionals, face the choice of continuing "business as usual" or making a commitment to deliver and defend innovative preventive efforts.

> Efforts at prevention require the ideological decision to line up with those humanists who believe in social change, in the effectiveness of counsultation, in education, in the primary prevention of human physical and emotional misery, and in the maximization of individual competence (Albee, 1982, p. 1050).

9 Can Community Counseling Become a Reality in the Face of Increased Service Demands and Decreased Resources?

It is unlikely that the human services will see again the steady growth in services and resources that characterized the mid twentieth century. Instead, the allocation of funding for services seems to shrink as rapidly as the need for them expands. Social, political, economic, and psychological problems show no signs of abating, leaving human service workers little choice but to learn how to meet more needs with fewer dollars. We cannot afford the luxury of insisting on traditional, one-to-one methods. If anything, we are forced to move in the direction of providing the more efficient, multifaceted services that characterize the community counseling model.

The early 1980s brought both a deepening of economic woes and a lessened financial commitment to human services. As one hard-hit city found,

> Detroit's human service agencies, their own staffs and budgets gored by the financial pressures crippling Michigan's economy, are struggling to tend to the thousands of emotional casualties felled by more than two years of double-digit unemployment. . . . Confronted by the meager resources of the mental health system, professionals are particularly emphasizing self-help support groups and retraining for those whose old jobs are gone forever to new technology or robotics (Cordes, 1983, p. 3).

Realism forms the heart of community counseling. This approach is not a Utopian dream. It is a phenomenon that is beginning to happen, as individuals, groups, and communities make it happen. Whether a community counseling point of view begins to permeate all helping networks depends on the combined efforts of trainers, human service managers, workers at all levels, and consumers. The questions facing us today are answerable. The nature of the answers we find will shape the future.

ACTIVITIES TO ENHANCE UNDERSTANDING OF CHAPTER 10

1. Find out all you can about the human services offered in your own community. (You will find that no one source has all the information you need.) Once you feel you know your community's human service network pretty well, think about the local needs of which you are aware. To what degreed are these needs being met by existing agencies? To what degree do the agencies seem to be aware of and cooperating with one another? How can this human service network be more effective?

2. Identify two trends or social issues that you think will be especially important in your community in the next 10 years. Is your community's human service network ready to meet the new needs that these trends will bring? How can community counselors make sure that they are ready to deliver services that meet, not just today's needs, but tomorrow's?

REFERENCES

Albee, G. W. Preventing psychopathology and promoting human potential. *American Psychologist.* 1982, *37,* 1043–1050.

Adler, P.T. An analysis of the concept of competence in individuals and social systems. *Community Mental Health Journal,* 1982, *18* (2), 34–45.

Alinsky, S. D. *Reveille for radicals.* New York: Vintage Books, 1969.

Almond, R. *The healing community: Dynamics of the therapeutic milieu.* New York: Jason Aronson, 1974.

Alpert, J. L., & Rosenfield, S. Consultation and the introduction of problem solving groups in schools. *Personnel and Guidance Journal,* 1981, *60,* 37–40.

Ardell, D.B. *High level wellness: An alternative to doctors, drugs, and disease.* Emmaus, Pa.: Rodale Press, 1977.

Attkisson, C. C., & Broskowski, A. Evaluation and the emerging human service concept. In C. C. Attkisson, W. A. Hargreaves, M. J. Horowitz, & J. E. Sorensen (Eds.), *Evaluation of human service programs.* New York: Academic Press, 1978.

Aubrey, R. Power bases: The consultant's vehicle for change. *Elementary School Guidance and Counseling,* 1972, *7,* 90–97.

Bailis, M. Community mental health technology: An ecological model. Unpublished manuscript, 1981.

Bandura, A. Self-efficacy mechanism in human agency. *American Psychologist,* 1982, *37,* 122–147.

Barber, T. X. Foreword to R. G. Straus, *Strategic self-hypnosis.* Englewood Cliffs, N.J.: Prentice-Hall, 1982.

Barrow, J. C. Educational programming in stress management. *Journal of College Student Personnel,* 1981, *22,* 17–22.

Barton, A. K. A problem, policy, program model for planning community mental health services. *Journal of Community Psychology*, 1978, 6, 37−41.

Bartsch, K., & Hackett, G. Effect of a decision making course on locus of control, conceptualization, and career planning. *Journal of College Student Personnel*, 1979, 20, 230−235.

Behn, R. Leadership for cut-back management. *Public Administration Review*, 1980, 40, 613−620.

Benson, H. *The relaxation response.* New York: William Morrow, 1975.

Blake, R.R., & Mouton, J. S. *The new managerial grid.* Houston: Gulf Publishing Company, 1978.

Blocher, D.H. Social change and the future of vocational guidance. In H. Borow (Ed.), *Career guidance for a new age.* Boston: Houghton Mifflin, 1973.

Bloom, B. L. Strategies for the prevention of mental disorders. In G. Rosenblum (Ed.), *Issues in community psychology and preventive mental health.* New York: Behavioral Publications, 1971.

Boston Women's Health Collective. *Our bodies, our selves.* Boston: New England Free Press, 1971.

Boyd, J. D. Integrative approaches to counselor supervision. In J. D. Boyd (Ed.), *Counselor supervision.* Muncie, Ind.: Accelerated Development, Inc.,1978.

Brammer, L. M. *The helping relationship: Process and skills,* (2nd ed.).Englewood Cliffs, N.J.: Prentice-Hall, 1979.

Brenner, M. H. *Mental illness and the economy.* Cambridge: Harvard University Press, 1973.

Brickman, P., Rabinowitz, V. C., Karuza, J., Coates, D., Cohn, E., & Kidder, L. Four models of helping and coping. *American Psychologist*, 1982, 37, 368−384.

Buckner, D. R. Developing coed residence hall programs for sex role exploration. *Journal of College Student Personnel*, 1981, 22,52−54.

Burns, T., & Stalker, G. M. *The management of innovation.* London: Tavistock Publications, 1961.

Caplan, G. *The theory and practice of mental health consultation.* New York: Basic Books, 1970.

Caplan, G. *Support systems and community mental health.* New York: Behavioral Publications, 1974.

Carlson, J. Health, wellness, and transpersonal approaches to helping. *Elementary School Guidance and Counseling*, 1979, 14, 85−90.

Carver, J. Mental health administration: A management perversion. Address to the Association of Mental Health Administrators Annual Meeting, September 8, 1979.

Chesler, M. A., & Lohman, J. E. Changing schools through student advocacy. In R. A. Schmuck & M. B. Miles (Eds.), *Organizational development in schools.* Palo Alto: National Press Books, 1971.

Cohen, A. C. New model for professional education defined. *The College for Human Services Journal.* 1974, *1*(1), 4.

Cohen, R. E. Interface teams as an integrating agent in mental health services. *International Journal of Mental Health,* 1974, *3,* 65–76.

Community Congress of San Diego, Inc. *Training trainers grant proposal.* Submitted to: Division of Experimental and Special Training. National Institute of Mental Health, 1975.

Cordes, C. Detroit: A ravaged city copes with the human toll. *APA Monitor,* 1983, *14*(1), 3, 17.

Cowen, E. L., Gesten, E. L., Borke, M., Norton, P., Wilson, A. B., & De Stefano, M. A. Hairdressers as caregivers. I. A descriptive profile of interpersonal help-giving involvements. *American Journal of Community Psychology.* 1971, *7,* 633–648.

Cowen, E. L., McKim, B. J., & Weissberg, R. P. Bartenders as informal interpersonal help-agents. *American Journal of Community Psychology,* 1981, *9,* 715–729.

Cull, J. G. & Hardy, R. E. *Volunteerism: An emerging profession.* Springfield, Ill.: Charles C Thomas, 1974.

Danish, S. J. Human development and human services: A marriage proposal. In I. Iscoe, B. Bloom, & C. D. Spielberger (Eds.), *Community psychology in transition.* New York: Wiley, 1977.

Delworth, U. Paraprofessionals as guerrillas: Recommendations for system change. *Personnel and Guidance Journal,* 1974, *53,* 335–338.

Delworth, U., & Moore, M. Helper plus trainer: A two-phase program for the counselor. *Personnel and Guidance Journal,* 1974, *52,* 428–433.

Developmental disabilities planning council of Washington: *State plan: Fiscal year 1981.* Olympia, Wash.: Developmental Disabilities Planning Council and Division of Developmental Disabilities, 1981.

Dinkmeyer, D., & Dinkmeyer, D., Jr. Working with teachers: In-service and C groups. *Counseling and Human Development, 1979, 11*(10), 1–16.

Dinkmeyer, D., & Dinkmeyer, D., Jr. An alternative: Affective education. *The Humanist Educator.* 1980, *19,* 51–58.

Dinkmeyer, D., & McKay, G. *Raising a responsible child: Practical steps to successful family relationships.* New York: Simon and Schuster, 1973.

Dixon, M. C. & Burns, J. L. Crisis theory, active learning, and the training of telephone crisis volunteers. *Journal of Community Psychology*, 1974, *2*, 120−125.

Doane, J. A. & Cowen, E. L. Interpersonal help-giving of family practice lawyers. *American Journal of community psychology*, 1981, *9*, 547−558.

Dohrenwend, B. S. Social stress and community psychology. *American Journal of Community Psychology*, 1978, *6*, 1−14.

Dreikurs, R., & Soltz, V. *Children the challenge.* New York: Duell, Sloan and Pearce, 1964.

Drum, D., & Figler, H. *Outreach in counseling.* New York: Intext, 1973.

Dye, L. L., & Sansouci, J. P. Toward a new era in corrections. *Personnel and Guidance Journal*, 1974, *53*, 130−135.

Federal Register. Developmental disabilities program, 1980, *45*. 31006-31026.

Fellows of the Drug Abuse Council. Disabusing drug abuse. *Social Policy*, 1974, *4* (5), 43−45.

Foster, C. *Developing self-control.* Kalamazoo, Mich.: Behaviordelia, Inc., 1974.

Frederickson, C. Coalition organizing: Our crack at revenue sharing. *C/O: The Journal of Alternative Human Services.* 1974, *1* (4), 20−29.

Frew, J. E. A group model with a loneliness theme for the first year college student. *Journal of College Student Personnel*, 1980, *21*, 459−460.

Frisch, M. B., & Gerrard, M. Natural helping systems: A survey of Red Cross volunteers. *American Journal of Community Psychology*, 1981, *9*, 467−579.

Gartner, A. Self-help/Self-care: A cost effective health strategy. *Social Policy.* 1982, *12*(4), 64.

Gartner, A., & Riessman, F. The paraprofessional movement in perspective. *Personnel and Guidance Journal*, 1974, *53* 253−256.

Girdano, D. A., & Everly, G. S. *Controlling stress and tension: A holistic approach.* Englewood Cliffs, N.J.: Prentice-Hall, 1979.

Goffman, E. *Stigma: Notes on the management of spoiled identity.* Englewood Cliffs, N.J.: Prentice-Hall, 1963.

Goodman, G. *Companionship therapy.* San Francisco: Jossey-Bass, 1972.

Gordon, T. *A new model for humanizing families and schools.* Pasadena: Effectiveness Training Associates, 1971.

Goshko, R. Self-determined behavior change. *Personnel and Guidance Journal*, 1973, *51*, 629–632.

Gottlieb, B. H. *Social networks and social support.* Beverly Hills: Sage Publications, 1981.

Gross, M. J., & Jablonsky, S. F. *Principles of accounting and financial reporting for nonprofit organizations.* New York: Wiley, 1979.

Hallowitz, E., & Riessman, F. The role of the indigenous nonprofessional in a community mental health neighborhood service center program. *American Journal of Orthopsychiatry*, 1967, *37*, 766–778.

Hansen, L. S., & Borow, H. Toward effective practice: Emerging models and programs. In H. Borow (Ed.), *Career guidance for a new age.* Boston: Houghton Mifflin, 1973.

Hawkinshire, F. B. S. Training procedures for offenders working in community treatment programs. In B. G. Guerney (Ed.), *Psychotherapeutic agents: New roles for nonprofessionals, parents, and teachers.* New York: Holt, Rinehart and Winston, 1969.

Hayes, R. D. Democratic schools for a democratic society. *The Humanist Educator*, 1982, *20*, 101–108.

Heller, K., Price, R. H. & Sher, K. J. Research and evaluation in primary prevention: Issues and guidelines. In R. H. Price, R. F.Ketterer, B. C. Bader, & J. Monahan (Eds.), *Prevention in mental health: Research, policy, and practice.* Bevery Hills: Sage Publications, 1980.

Hepner, P. P., & Krouse, J. B. A career seminar course. *Journal of College Student Personnel*, 1979, *20*, 300–309.

Hersey, P., & Blanchard, K. H. *Management of organizational behavior: Utilizing human resources* (4th ed.). Englewood Cliffs, N.J.: Prentice-Hall, 1982.

Herzberg, F. One more time: How do you motivate employees? In Harvard Business Review. *On management.* New York: Harper & Row, 1975.

Hiett, N. Quoted in A. J. Kahn, S. B. Kamerman, & B. G. McGowan. *Child advocacy: Report of a national baseline study.* Washington: U. S. Dept. of Health, Education and Welfare, 1973.

Holahan, C. J., & Moos, R. H. Social support and adjustment. *American Journal of Community Psychology*, 1982, *10*, 403–413.

Hollmann, R. W. Beyond contemporary employee assistance programs. *Personnel Administrator*, 1981, 26, 37–41.

Holmes, T., and Rahe, R. The social readjustment rating scale. *Journal of Psychosomatic Research*. 1967, 11, 213–218.

Ivey, A. Media therapy: Educational change planning for   psychiatric patients. *Journal of Counseling Psychology*, 1973, 20, 338–343.

Ivey, A. University of Massachusetts program in counseling and consulting psychology. Personal communication, 1983.

Jean-Grant, D. S. Assertiveness training: A program for high school students. *The School Counselor*, 1980, 27, 230–237.

Johnson, J. H., & Sarason, I. G. Moderator variables in life stress research. In I. G. Sarason & C. D. Spielberger (Eds.), *Stress and anxiety*. Washington: Hemisphere Publication Corporation, 1979.

Johnson, T. W., & Stinson, J. Person-task fit and leadership strategies. In P. Hersen & J. Stinson (Eds.), *Perspectives in leader effectiveness*. Athens: Ohio University, The Center for Leadership Studies, 1980.

Kahn, R. L. Work, stress, and individual well-being. *Monthly Labor Review*, 1981, 104(5), 28–30.

Katz, M. R. SIGI: An interactive aid to career decision making. *Journal of College Student Personnel*, 1980, 21, 34–40.

Ketterer, R. F., Bader, B. C., & Levy, M. R. Strategies for promoting mental health. In R. H. Price, R. F. Ketterer, B. C. Bader, & J. Monahan (Eds.), *Prevention in mental health: Research, policy, and practice*. Beverly Hills: Sage Publications, 1980.

Kirn, A. G., & Kirn, M. O. *Life work planning* (4th ed.). New York: McGraw-Hill, 1979.

Kobasa, S. C. Stressful life events, personality and health: An inquiry into hardiness. *Journal of Personality and Social Psychology*, 1979, 37, 1–11.

Kohlberg, L. *Essays on moral development*. San Francisco: Harper & Row, 1981.

Kolton, M., Dwarshuis, L., Gorodezky, M., & Dosher, A. *Innovative approaches to youth services*. Madison, Wisc.: STASH Press, 1973.

Kopplin, D. A., & Rice, L. C. Consulting with faculty: Necessary and possible. *Personnel and Guidance Journal*, 1975, 53, 367–372.

Kouzes, J. M., & Mico, P. R. Domain theory: An introduction to organizational behavior in human service organizations. *The Journal of Applied Behavioral Science*, 1979, 15, 449–469.

Krumboltz, J. D. An accountability model for counselors. *Personnel and Guidance Journal,* 1974, *52,* 639–646.

Krumboltz, J. D., & Peltier, B. What identifies a counseling psychologist: Method or results? *Counseling Psychologist,* 1977, *7*(2), 57–60.

Krumboltz, J. D., & Sheppard, L. Vocational problem-solving experiences. In J. D. Krumboltz & C. Thoresen (Eds.), *Behavioral counseling: Cases and techniques.* New York: Holt, Rinehart and Winston, 1969.

Laski, F. Civil rights victories for the handicapped. *The Social and Rehabilitation Record,* 1974, *1*(5), 15–22.

Lawrence, P. R., & Lorsch, J. J. *Organization and environment.* Boston: Harvard University Press, 1967.

Leach, P. The newly disabled adult. *The Independent,* 1974, *2*(1), 6, 12.

Leeman, C. P. Contracting for employee counseling service. *Harvard Business Review,*1974 (March–April), 20–24, 152–154.

Leofanti, C. G. The organization of community-based youth services: Direct service versus community action. Unpublished manuscript, 1981.

Lerner, B. *Therapy in the ghetto: Political impotence and personal disintegration.* Baltimore: The Johns Hopkins University Press, 1972.

Levine, M. Some postulates of practice in community psychology and their implications for training. In I. Iscoe & C. D. Speilberger (Eds.), *Commmunity psychology: Perspectives in training and research.* New York: Appleton-Century-Crofts, 1970.

Lewis, J., & Lewis, M. Educating counselors for primary prevention. *Counselor Education and Supervision,* 1981, *20,* 172–181.

Lewis, J., & Lewis, M. *Management of human service programs.* Monterey, Cal.: Brooks/Cole, 1983.

Lewis, M., & Lewis, J. A schematic for change. *Personnel and Guidance Journal,* 1974, *52,* 320–323.

Lewis, M., & Lewis, J. *The Woodlawn experience: Community organization and mental health.* Chicago: Governors State University and The Woodlawn Organization, 1978.

Littrell, J. M., Lee-Borden, N., & Lorenz, J. A developmental framework for counseling supervision. *Counselor Education and Supervision,* 1979, *19,* 129–136.

Manuso, J. S. F. Psychological services and health enhancement: A corporate model. In A. Broskowski, E. Marks, & S. H. Budman (Eds.),

Linking health and mental health. Beverly Hills: Sage Publications, 1981.

Martin, D., Gawinski, B., Medler, B., & Eddy, J. A group premarital counseling workshop for high school couples. *The School Counselor*, 1981, *28*, 223–226.

Martin, D., & Martin, M. Nutritional counseling: A humanistic approach to psychological and physical health. *Personnel and Guidance Journal*, 1982, *61*, 21–24.

Maslow, A. H. *Motivation and personality*. New York: Harper & Row, 1954.

Matarazzo, J. D. Behavioral health and behavioral medicine: Frontiers for a new health psychology. *American Psychologist*, 1980, *35*, 807–817.

Matthes, W. A., & Dustin, D. The counselor as a trainer: Principles of workshop design. *The School Counselor*, 1980, *27*, 310–314.

Mazer, E., & Leofanti, C. G. *You've got a friend*. Park Forest, Aunt Martha's Youth Service Center, Inc., 1980.

McClelland, D. Achievement motivation can be developed. *Harvard Business Review*, 1965, *43*, 6–8, 10, 12, 14, 16, 20, 22, 24.

McCord, J. B., & Packwood, W. T. Crisis centers and hotlines: A survey. *Personnel and Guidance Journal*, 1973, *51*, 723–728.

McGee, R. K. *Crisis intervention in the community*. Baltimore: University Park Press, 1974.

McGregor, D. M. *The human side of enterprise*. New York: McGraw-Hill, 1960.

McPheeters, H. L., & King, J. B. *Plans for teaching mental health workers*. Atlanta: The Southern Regional Education Board, 1971.

Meeks, C. On loneliness seminar. *Journal of College Student Personnel*, 1980, *21*, 470–471.

Menke, R. Teaching self-modification in an adjustment course. *Personnel and Guidance Journal*, 1973, *52*, 97–101.

Midwest Academy. *Building the community: Modes of personal growth*. Chicago: Midwest Academy, 1973.

Monahan, J., & Vaux, A. The macroenvironment and community mental health. *Community Mental Health Journal*, 1980, *16*, 14–26.

Mosher, R. L. *Moral education: A first generation of research*. New York: Praeger, 1980.

Murphy, L. R. Worksite stress management programs. *EAP Digest*. 1982, *2*(3), 22–25.

Neleigh, J. R., Newman, F. L., Madore, C. E., & Seard, W. F. *Training nonprofessional community project leaders.* Community Mental Health Journal Monograph Series, Monograph 6. New York: Behavioral Publications, 1971.

Newman, W. H. & Wallender, H. W. Managing not-for-profit enterprises. *Academy of Management Review,* 1978, 3, 24–31.

Odiorne, G. S. *Management and the activity trap.* New York: Harper & Row, 1974.

Options for Women. Brochure. Philadelphia, 1972.

Pearl, A. Paraprofessionals and social change. *Personnel and Guidance Journal.* 1974, 53, 264–268.

Prazak, J. A. Learning job-seeking interview skills. In J. D. Krumboltz & C. E. Thoresen (Eds.), *Behavioral counseling: Cases and techniques.* New York: Holt, Rinehart and Winston, 1969.

President's Commission on Mental Health. *Report of the task panel on prevention.* Washington: U. S. Government Printing Office, 1978.

Price, R. H., Bader, B. C., & Ketterer, R. F. Prevention in community mental health: The state of the art. In R. H. Price, R. F. Ketterer, B. C. Bader, & J. Monahan (Eds.), *Prevention in mental health: Research, policy, and practice.* Beverly Hills: Sage Publications, 1980.

Project C.A.N. *Summary of services: April, 1982.* Atlanta: Central Fulton Community Mental Health Center, 1982.

Raines, M. R. Community services. In T. O'Banion & A. Thurston (Eds.), *Student development programs in the community junior college.* Englewood Cliffs, N.J.: Prentice-Hall, 1972.

Rappaport, J., Davidson, W. S., Wilson, M. N., & Mitchell, A. Alternatives to blaming the victim or the environment. *American Psychologist,* 1975, 30, 525–528.

Recovery, Inc. *Recovery, Inc.: What it is and how it developed.* Chicago: Recovery, Inc., 1973.

Reed, M. Mother study groups. In R. Dreikurs, R. Corsini, R. Lowe, & M. Sonstegard (Eds.), *Adlerian family counseling: A manual for counseling centers.* Eugene: University of Oregon Press, 1959.

Richardson, R. C. The student's role in the affairs of the college. In T. O'Banion & A. Thurston (Eds.), *Student development programs in the community junior college.* Englewood Cliffs, N.J.: Prentice-Hall, 1972.

Rioch, M., Elkes, C., Flint, A. A., Usdansky, B. S., Newman, R. G., & Silber, E. National Institute of Mental Health pilot study in training of mental health counselors. *American Journal of Orthopsychiatry*, 1963, 33, 678−689.

Roman, P. M. Prevention and health promotion programming for work organizations: Employee assistance program experience. DeKalb, Ill.: Northern Illinois University, Office of Health Promotion, 1981.

Romano, J. L. Biofeedback training and therapeutic gains. Clinical impressions. *Personnel and Guidance Journal*, 1982, 60, 473−475.

Rothman, J. Introduction to part one. In F. J. Cox, J. L. Erlich, J. Rothman, & J. E. Tropman (Eds.), *Strategies of community organization*. Itasca, Ill.: F. E. Peacock, 1974.

Sarnoff, D. Biofeedback: New uses in counseling. *Personnel and Guidance Journal*, 1982, 60, 357−360.

Sauber, S. R. *Preventive educational intervention for mental health.* Cambridge: Ballinger Publishing Company, 1973.

Shure, M. B., & Spivack, G. Interpersonal problem-solving in young children: A cognitive approach to prevention. *American Journal of Community Psychology*, 1982, 10, 341−356.

Siegel, L. M., Attkisson, C. C., & Carson, L. G. Need identification and program planning in the community context. In C. C. Attkisson, W. A. Hargreaves, M. J. Horowitz, & J. E. Sorensen (eds.), *Evaluation of human service programs.* New York: Academic Press, 1978.

Silberberg, N. E., & Silberberg, M. C. Schoolhouse justice. *Human Behavior*, 1974, 3(12), 38−43.

Simon, S. B., & Clark, J. *More values clarification.* San Diego: Pennant Press, 1975.

Singh, R. K. J. Processes involved in community mental health consultation to help resolve work crises involving interpersonal or psychological issues. In R. K. J. Singh, W. Tarnower, & R. Chen (Eds.), *Community mental health consultation and crisis intervention.* Palo Alto: National Press Books, 1971.

Skovholt, T. M. The client as helper: A means to promote psychological growth. *The Counseling Psychologist.* 1974, 4, 58−64.

Soltz, V. Study group leader's manual. Chicago: Alfred Adler Institute, 1967.

Sonnenstuhl, W. J., & O'Donnell, J. E. EAPs: The why's and how's of planning them. *Personnel Administrator*, 1980, 25, 35−38.

Spoth, R., & Rosenthal, D. Wanted: A developmentally oriented alcohol prevention program. *Personnel & Guidance Journal*, 1980, 59, 212−216.

Sprinthall, N. A. A new model for research in the service of guidance and counseling. *Personnel and Guidance Journal,* 1981, *59,* 487–494.

Steele, R. L. A manpower resource for community mental health centers. *American Journal of Community Psychology.* 1974, 2.

Stensrud, R., & Stensrud, K. Counseling may be hazardous to your health: How we teach people to feel powerless. *Personnel and Guidance Journal,* 1981, *59,* 300–304.

Stern, G. C. *People in context: Measuring person-environment congruence in education and industry.* New York: Wiley, 1970.

Straus, R. G. *Strategic self-hypnosis.* Englewood Cliffs, N.J.: Prentice Hall, 1982.

Taber, R. H. A systems approach to the delivery of mental health services in black ghettos. *American Journal of Orthopsychiatry,* 1970, *40,* 702–709.

Takvorian, D., & Haney, L. S. Strategies for surviving funding assaults. *C/O: Journal of Alternative Human Services,* 1981, (2), 7–14.

Thurman, C. W., Baron, A., & Klein, R. L. Self-help tapes in a telephone counseling service: A 3-year analysis. *Journal of College Student Personnel,* 1979, *20,* 546–550.

T.W.O. Woodlawn's model cities plan: *A demonstration of citizen responsibility.* Northbrook, Ill.: Whitehall Company, 1970.

T.W.O. The Woodlawn Organization/Woodlawn Community Development Corporation: Organization report. Chicago: T.W.O. Files, 1976.

Varenhorst, B. Learning the consequences of life's decisions. In J. Krumboltz & C. Thoresen (Eds.), *Behavioral counseling: Cases and techniques.* New York: Holt, Rinehart and Winston, 1969.

Warrington, D. L., & Method-Walker, Y. Career scope. *Journal of College Student Personnel,* 1981, *22,* 169.

Watson, D. & Tharp, R. *Self-directed behavior: Self-modification for personal adjustment.* Monterey, Cal.: Brooks/Cole, 1972.

Wilcox, B. L. Social support, life stress, and psychological adjustment: A test of the buffering hypothesis. *American Journal of Community Psychology,* 1981, *9,* 371–386.

Winemen, D., & James, A. The advocacy challenge to schools of social work. In B. Denner & R. H. Price (Eds.), *Community mental health: Social action and reaction.* New York: Holt, Rinehart and Winston, 1973.

Wolfensberger, W. *Normalization.* Toronto: National Institute on Mental Retardation, 1972.

Wolfensberger, W., & Zauha, H. *Citizen advocacy and protective services for the impaired and handicapped.* Toronto: National Institute on Mental Retardation, 1973.

Woodward, J. *Industrial organization: Theory and practice.* London: Oxford Press, 1965.

Young, K. M. *The basic steps of planning.* Charlottesville: Community Collaborators, 1978.

AUTHOR INDEX

285

SUBJECT INDEX

289